Andragogy: Contributions to an Emerging Discipline

The author:

Prof. Dr. Jost Reischmann, born in 1943, (www.jost.reischmannfam.de), specialized in andragogy/adult education. He studied Pedagogy, Psychology, and Sociology at the University of Tübingen, Germany, and chaired the Andragogy department at Bamberg University from 1992 until his retirement in 2008. In 1988, he edited the first English-language book on Adult Education in Germany. Dr. Reischmann served as the first president of the International Society for Comparative Adult Education (ISCAE) in 1992.
His contributions to the field were acknowledged with his induction into the International Adult and Continuing Education Hall of Fame in 1999 and receiving the AAACE 'Outstanding Service Award' in 2006. He has presented papers at various international conferences around the world.

Jost Reischmann

Andragogy:
Contributions to an Emerging Discipline

Bibliografische Information der Deutschen Nationalbibliothek: Die Deutsche Nationalbibliothek verzeichnet diese Publikation in der Deutschen Nationalbibliografie; detaillierte bibliografische Daten sind im Internet über dnb.dnb.de abrufbar.

Herstellung und Verlag:
BoD – Books on Demand, Norderstedt

ISBN 978-3-75833-061-2

Content

Preface

For several decades in many countries throughout the world adult education/ andragogy programs exist at universities:

- In 2024 the membership list of ISCAE (International Society for Comparative Adult Education - www. ISCAE.org) displays 358 members in 66 countries, most of them working in universities,
- ICAE (International Council of Adult Education - http://icae.global/) celebrated in 2023 its 50th anniversary with more than 800 NGOs (Non-Governmental Organizations) in more than 75 countries, including many academic institutions and persons,
- and about two third of the members of the International Adult and Continuing Education Hall of Fame (https://halloffame.outreach.ou.edu/) are connected to universities.

This confirms that there is an academic discipline coming into existence in some short decades.

This new discipline - as always in beginnings - still struggles internally for its identity, and outside for its perception and acceptance, sometimes more, sometimes less. In this process we want to contribute to the formation of the emerging academic discipline.

This book presents a collection of "old" articles. articles that were published before. A first that has outside reasons: While publications in my own language German are easy to locate, my English contributions are scattered in many publications and sources throughout the world; this can be confirmed by checking the first-print-places at the beginning of each contribution. This collection therefore makes publications available that were difficult to discover prior to this. A second reason is that topics develop over the years. Bringing them here in a sequence together can document, how a topic developed.

Some of the contributions may sound outdated in the meantime. Others may be not interesting to everybody. But - most important - what is true for all of them: They are exempla of andragogical thinking and arguing. And this may lead deeper into the specifics of Andragogy as distinct discipline.

What does "andragogical thinking and arguing" mean?

At first, this way of thinking is selectively-focused on the idea of learning and education. This is, what makes Andragogy a subdiscipline of Pedagogy. For both the basic focus and paradigm is "learning and education".

In the German language, there exists a term that sheds a specific light on this paradigm: "Bildung". Bildung is a relatively young term in the German language. It was popularized by Martin Luther, when translating the bible into German. When he had to translate the "imago dei"-concept - humans are and have to be image ("Bild") of God -, he used the word "Bildunge". Three elements includes this concept: 1. Humans have to change, not stay what they are, 2. this change has to guide in a certain, a "good" direction, and 3. it should direct to the transformation of the whole person, "from the old Adam to the new Jesus". This concept became later secularized, but the core elements of "Bildung" remained: change, good direction, and transformation.

These elements are basic for all educational thinking. In pedagogy, the education of children is addressed, in Andragogy the learning and education of Adults. The questions are the same: change where to and how, what means "good" direction, transformation why and whereto. However, the answers are different. "Andragogical thinking and arguing" answers these questions focused on the life situations and learning needs of adults.

All contributions in his book deal in various ways with the learning and education of adults ("Bildung Erwachsener"): some more by theoretical discussion, others more by didactical-practical aspects. But in sum, they hopefully illustrate that Andragogy offers a distinctive scholarly approach on many levels.

English is not my native language. Readers will observe this despite the proofreaders I had sometimes, and the correction programs of Word and Grammarly. I hope it will anyway be meaningful reading.

Bringing all these texts together brought back many memories of conferences and other occasions, of various countries, and of course of many dear colleagues. Perhaps meeting these colleagues, exchanging with them, growing by their support and critique, and making friends was the most valuable outcome of all my travel efforts, research, and exchange. They were motivation, fun, and support through the decades I look back in this book. I want to thank all of them.

And I hope that all others can be convinced - if necessary -, that Andragogy is an essential term for an emerging, proud and strong discipline and its members.

Jost Reischmann
Tübingen, Germany, May 2024

1. Autobiographical Note

I was highly surprised when I was invited to contribute to a book with the title "North American Adult Educators". Besides me, there were only two non-North Americans included. The 48 autobiographies from North American colleagues make this volume a grounded "Who is Who" of the American adult education scene. And - as I experienced by writing the required "autobiography" - it turned out that reflecting on my own individual development illustrates as well steps in the development of adult education and andragogy as an academic discipline in general.

This contribution can be read in two different intentions: Older readers can reminisce about their personal journeys and witness the remarkable development of the discipline, while younger readers gain insights into the historical steps and stages that shaped the field. And for all: To be proud of what "we" did and do in a short time, with limited resources, and in manyfold areas in the lives of adults.

1.1 Becoming a Professor in Andragogy - Lived History (2007)[1]

Should I really be a part of this book? I know of at least two arguments against it:

First - I am not an American Adult Educator: I live and work in Germany. However, for more than 25 years I have regularly visited conferences and colleagues at their universities in the USA and have them as guests and friends at my university and home. Phyllis Cunningham commented about me at the annual conference of AAACE (American Association for Adult and Continuing Education) 2002 in St. Louis: "Perhaps Jost is more American than some other professors!" (Still I hesitate - was this a compliment?).

Second I have an identity problem: Am I an adult educator? For a number of years, I clearly would have said: "Yes". Still today I sometimes work in adult education institutions (companies, churches, adult education centers) for some extra money or fun or because I can not say "No." But in my main profession I am and I feel like a professor of Adult Education (officially: "Chair of Andragogy"), educating students aged 20 – 25 in an academic discipline. We teach, learn, and research about the education of adults, but I see my university work not as adult education.

---

[1] First print: Reischmann, Jost (2007): Becoming a professor in andragogy - lived history. In: Keith B. Armstrong, Lee W. Nabb and Anthony P. Czech (ed.): North American Adult Educators: Archive of Quintessential Autobiographies for the 21st Century. Discovery Association Publishing House. Chicago, Il. P. 241-248.

Nevertheless, both anti-arguments also offer opportunities: Sometimes things can be seen clearer from a distance: The international-comparative perspective from the outside provokes to overcome ethnocentrism. Occasionally I had the feeling this provocation was my role in the collegial interchanges. I have to confess: Now and then I enjoy playing this provocation role! Moreover, the professor's perspective has the advantage, that (because I do not have to represent one specific direction of adult education) I have the academic freedom to think beyond the different institutions, traditions, and movements where adult educators in the practical field are sheltered. (Are you aware that I do what I described one sentence above?)

I hope that helps to justify my inclusion in this book.

How I came (not) into adult education

I started fairly early to "work" in adult education. As I could operate a slide projector and a 16mm film projector I was asked in my late teenage years to become the technique guy of our local adult education center (Volkshochschule) - $1 for showing slides, $2 for films. Especially I liked the presenters who brought sides and film ($3). Besides the money being momentous for me, I could listen to lectures without paying. "Beautiful Flowers of the Alps",

End page 241
Start page 242

"Great Philosophers", "The New Movie-Culture", "Traveling to Wheresoever" … that bouquet of enriching and entertaining themes plus a number of language courses represented the majority of public adult education one or two evenings a week in the 1960s in Germany.

Adult education? That was in the 1960s no option for a vocation. In adult education, I met slide-showing or book-selling travelers or humanists with a firm income otherwise. There were the spouses having an earning husband, so they could offer a mixture of social and educational work. There were the school teachers, teaching a foreign language or another school subject to make some extra money and/or to escape for some hours from their child-oriented schoolwork. This all provided no prospect for making a living wage. Adult education was volunteer work, part-time, and no training was available, so it had to be done "by the heart," with conviction and often with pride. Adult education was neither a vocation nor a profession.

This situation lies in many countries not very far back in history. No wonder that this image of adult education - volunteer work with full heart, empty pockets, done with content expertise and teaching intuition, and sometimes with a lot of vulnerable pride - still can be found widely.

Today - only (!) 40 years later - I am chair of andragogy at Bamberg University, Germany. About 100 students study andragogy as their main subject, 150 more as a side subject. This number doubled in the last ten years. They all will work in adult education and make their living as andragogical professionals. This is not an optimistic hope, but a reality, as we know from our own as well as others research about graduates in andragogy/adult education.

Adult Education within one generation - within my life - developed from "volunteer moonlighting" to academic study and profession. No wonder there are tensions and confusion in the field of adult education; they result from the rapid changes that happened in the years between 1970 and 2000 and started a new chapter in the theory and practice of adult education.

Was it a detour?

It was clear from the beginning that I wanted to work in education (at least I knew nothing else). As a teenager, I was in several boy groups and often found myself in leadership-functions, i.e. when at the age of 14 I was taking care of the ten-year-olds in summer camps.

Consequently, after finishing high school I started to study at a teacher training college. I am still thankful that this introduced me systematical and profound way into pedagogical thinking and acting. There I learned - and that still is part of my understanding today - that educational situations have to be rationally planned and designed, that "knowing content" is not enough, but that "designing seminars", "activating methods", or "didactic and methodic" are necessary - these all are contents today in our curriculum at Bamberg university: Andragogues must have the competency to teach didactically as a professional.

There I also learned a more hidden lesson still important to me today: I found there two different groups of professors. One group was the "experienced practitioner," having missions and visions, telling us about their successful years of practical experiences. This group I loved; it was convincing to listen to them, learn their tricks, and follow their un-

End page 242
Start page 243

derstanding of successful education. They knew the answers. There was the other group I liked much less: the young "academic" professors who made us read scientific (= difficult) books. In addition, they made us reflect critically and not to just believe, they made us doubt, compare, and test hypotheses and theories. They knew the questions (and I very much doubted the teaching competencies of these "theoreticians"). In my first years of being a school teacher, I tried to imitate the practitioner-professors and to forget the theory-professors. However, the longer I stayed in education the more often recollections came to me about the theories and books. Today I know that this knowledge of pedagogical theories helped me for a longer period of time, and more than the practical tricks or visions which in the beginning were a survival toolkit, but became either outdated or did not help in complex and difficult situations. I discovered that theory is not theoretical, but a help to understand practice. Some theory-texts of that time I still teach to my students today. "Theories," "history," and "foundations" are of course today's contents of our andragogy curriculum: Andragogues (and I limit this title to academically educated persons) must be able to perceive, describe, analyze, reflect, and criticize andragogical situations, now as well as in twenty years when they will face new institutions, tasks, movements, and problems we don't even know today.

I do not want to be remembered to the following specific experience. Being a young school teacher I was asked to teach a class of adults in the local adult education center. I did exactly what I found later criticized in adult education books: I treated the adults at night the same way I treated children during the day. Please, participants from then, forgive me! What else had I learned?

I taught a couple of years in public schools; then I went to a "real" university (the University of Tuebingen, Germany) where I studied - now 23 years old - pedagogy, psychology, and sociology for another nine semesters.

After graduation (1970) I stepped into academia again as technique-guy: As I could handle punch-cards and do some basic programming I was hired by the university in educational psychology and did my dissertation about the effects of testing in school classes. What remained from this: Academic professionals (= our graduates) must be able to ask questions open-mindedly, research them with methodological rigor, and add new knowledge to themselves and the field. No doubt: Like in other academic studies, research classes, and a research thesis are part of the andragogy curriculum.

Then I was hired by the department of media- and distance education, and still was focused on children and student learning. But - what I did not know at that time - by studying pedagogy I had learned basic lectures for my work in andragogy today.

A whole new world ...

During the 1970s a hurricane-like storm of developments triggered a transformation.

First: The three professors of our chair, headed by Guenther Dohmen, a truly international person and later (1999) in the first group of Germans inducted in the International Adult and Continuing Hall of Fame, team-taught a class about "How Do Adults Learn?" The literature and research at that time in Germany filled one or two bookshelves. However, I had the clear feeling: This is not only a field of application and practice, but it has and deserves a firm and genuine anthropology and theory, going beyond particular convictions and movements. The institutions, the practice, the various "missions and visions" existed,

End page 243
Start page 244

but was an academic (sub-) discipline "above" these fields of practice conceivable? In spite of the scholarly work done since the 1920s in Germany at that juncture, the answer was "No." Nevertheless, the fact that university faculty asked this question and started to include topics dealing with adult education in their curricula (and not only exchanged it at outside institutions or within interest-groups) helped to change perspectives and awareness.

Second: From the international contacts of Guenther Dohmen we learned about a project "Courses by Newspaper" at the University of California – San Diego: Nationwide newspapers published a series of weekly articles for 12 to 16 weeks, covering a specific topic (i.e. "Oceans", "Death and Dying"), additional textbooks were available, and colleges offered courses. I transformed this idea into the German system and for five years was director of "Zeitungskolleg" at the German Institute for Distance Studies (DIFF) (Reischmann1982) [see 4.1 in this book]. In this practical work grew the awareness that general theoretical concepts were blended into the practical project, worthy of being researched and developed: "open learning" including "nontraditional learning," "self-directed learning," and "life-related (meaningful) learning." All together I focused on two questions; one of practical-application, and the other of theoretical-reflection. The practical-application oriented question was, "How can adults be supported in lifelong and - as I called it later - in 'lifewide' learning?" The theoretical-reflection oriented question was, "What sort of 'learning' is that, and how does this experience help us to better understand the learning of adults in their lives?" I currently require my students at Bamberg University to answer these two standard questions in their diploma thesis.

Third: In the mid- and late 1970s a new movement sprang up - the encounter movement. The term "Encounter-Groups" originated from a book title by Carl Rogers, but besides his "person-centered approach" many other concepts added to that movement: Fritz Perls' Gestalt Therapy, Alexander Lowen's Bioenergetic, the T-Group movement and others. Some were more reflection-oriented, some focused more on feelings, others on sensory-awareness and body work. My pilgrimages included Carl Rogers "Center for Studies of the Person" in La Jolla, CA, and the Esalen Institute, Big Sur, CA. "Touch me, feel me, heal me" was a great message. Moreover - as I saw it – all these were oriented toward learning and education. Adults were learning in a powerful and personal way, sometimes painful, sometimes joyful, in learning settings far from school-formats. Here I learned about "Freedom to Learn" (Rogers) and the personal power of meaningful learning. Even more: I learned methods how to support this type of learning: not by teaching, but by counseling. This opened the access to listen carefully to adults on their journey "on becoming a person," and to facilitate and accompany "their" personal learning in a professional way - another professional method andragogues must have at their disposal. Classes

14

and trainings about "Communicative Skills for Andragogues," "Strategies of Counseling," and "Coaching" represent these competencies now in our curriculum.

Fourth: "Schools do not solve educational problems, they produce them!" was the provoking statement of authors like Ivan Illich and Paulo Freire, claiming to "de-school society." "More organized and institutionalized learning, or less?" seemed to me a difficult question for children learning, but for adult education it made sense: Alan Tough had empirically proven that adults spend about two hours every day in learning projects, most of them self-directed, using a wide variety of outside resources. This confirmed: Self-directed adult learning was not a romantic myth. Moreover, for institutionalized learning Malcolm

End page 244
Start page 245

Knowles offered methodic and didactical arrangements for "modern practice of adult education." This taught me the next new lesson: Adult education is only a part of the education of adults. The learning of adults happens not only lifelong, but also *lifewide* [see 3.3 in this book] in a multitude of traditional and nontraditional, formal and informal settings (workplaces, families, churches, market-places, television, "the life" ...). Consequently, internships, classes about "institutions of adult education," research, and workplaces today exceed the traditional institutions and fields of what was perceived to be adult education four decades ago.

Looking back on these hurricanes of adult learning and education ideas in the 1970s and later, the challenges in understanding adult learning my age-group went through, seems to me nearly incredible. In this formative decade of the 1970s the face and understanding of adult learning changed for me as a person as well as for the field as a whole. This may be a common experience my age group can report in Germany as well as in the USA.

In this stream of experiences, my adult education baptism-experience took place: I had to teach a credit course "Educational Psychology" at an adult education center in a little city in the Blackforest. I did everything new: Arranging the chairs in a circle, welcoming the 15 participants, and letting them close their eyes to meditate about the goals for which they came. Then I asked them to hold their neighbor's hands for two minutes to come in contact with the group. After that, they had time to interview one other person in the room and to introduce this person to the group. I felt very innovative. Nevertheless, after all of what I thought were beautiful beginnings the group clearly told me: No gimmicks any longer! You are the professor - teach us! At that critical point, I was able to beg them for trust to try this new way of referring to their own experiences for three sessions - then we would make a decision to go on with the new way or change back to the old way. This course became a very enriching experience for the group and me. It clearly felt totally different from my prior teaching experience. After three sessions it was clear: We went on the new way. I had that flash-like insight: Now I am an adult educator!

However, my activity as an adult educator always remained like in the old tradition a side activity - at public adult education centers, with churches, with companies. In my main profession, I made my living at Tuebingen University and the new "chair of adult and continuing education." There I was an associate professor, until I got a call to Bamberg University, as a full professor and chair. As I described about Tuebingen University in the beginning: Here, at Bamberg, I have three professors working with me, and we have twenty to thirty graduates every year (http://www.reischmannfam.de/andra-album/2008/studierende94-08.htm). For most of my life I had the privilege to work in a University context that allowed me to research, read, analyze, theorize, and I had the pressure to publish or perish, and the opportunity to reflect on the practice I had at various institutions. There was a clear difference between my activities and my identity as "adult educator/trainer" and as "researcher/scholar."

The chance of international exchange and learning

I love to travel. This brought me in the last 30 years about 30 times to the USA and other countries, in the beginning mostly to conferences, in the last years more and more for vacations (Snowbird in Arizona).

End page 245
Start page 246

An important role in starting these international contacts was in the 1980s an active exchange between AAACE and the Deutscher Volkshochschul-Verband DVV. Representatives from AAACE and DVV visited for a couple of weeks the other country in organized tours. In 1982 the German group experienced Texas-hospitality in adult education centres and at the AAACE-conference in San Antonio. I was not prominent enough to be invited into the German travel group, but I travelled on my own and got to know not only American colleagues but to their surprise also German adult education representatives officially visiting there. This made me "visible" not only to the American colleagues but also to the Germans. The "visibility" became very rewarding: At most conferences in the USA I was the only German, so I was individually named, welcomed, and had to stand up and smile around (which never happened to me at German conferences). This visibility opened many doors and allowed me to meet respected colleagues and dear friends. Just to name some: Tom Damon, Alan Knox, John A. Henschke, Roger Axford, Alexander Charters, Malcolm Knowles, Douglas Smith, Trenton Ferro, Huey B. Long, Lorillee Sandmann, Sharan Merriam, Judy Koloski - many who today have been inducted in the International Adult and Continuing Education Hall of Fame. A personal and professional enriching network of "internationals" came into being. Contacts and friendships between institutions and persons from that time until today still exist. The problem I fear today and am uncomfortable about is that the persons being active at that time are now 20 years older and retiring. Consequently, these contacts and networks soon will be outgrown, and no young people are following in the footsteps of these pioneers. It seems time to start again such an organized exchange.

In general, I found adult education in theory as well as in practice not more developed in either Germany or the USA - but different. Main topics of American adult education, like Adult Basic Education, ESL, or GED preparation, are marginal in Germany. Historical, institutional, and even theoretical themes in the USA are different. We do not know much about the other country. When I published the book "Adult Education in West Germany in Case Studies" (Reischmann, 1988), I discovered with surprise that this was indeed the first English-language book about adult education in Germany. Americans seldom show up at German conferences and have a language barrier. So my role on one side became a "bridge-builder," informing about foreign experiences, and my role on the other side was a provoker: Asking confusing questions, offering alternative explanations. Perhaps this was the "exceptional and innovative leadership" mentioned in the AAACE President's Award which I received 1998.

After conferences in Montreal, Quebec (Canada), Ljubljana (Slovenia), Prague (Czechoslovakia), and Berlin (Germany) the network of internationals became more formal in the International Society for Comparative Adult Education (ISCAE). 1992 at the AAACE-conference in Anaheim, CA, Alexander Charters nominated me "president" of this society [see 5.2, 5.3 in this book]. About 140 colleagues working in international and comparative adult education in 34 countries are members today. We organized conferences in Bamberg (1995), Ljubljana (1998), St. Louis (2002), and again Bamberg (2006). The upcoming e-mail and internet - becoming a hobby of mine - (http://www.ISCAE.org) opened immediate access to persons, institutions, and information in many countries. Need information about adult education in Alaska? No problem: Send an e-mail to Gretchen Bersch, University of Alaska at Anchorage. Making a visit to Ljubljana, Slovenia? Just call Ana Krajnc or Zoran Jelenc, who will be glad to present their work. One

End page 246
Start page 247

of my students was recovering from graduation stress by traveling in Australia. I gave her the address of Roger Morris. "Yesterday he invited me to attend his class," she tells me on a postcard.

Some of these international activities led to my induction into the International Adult and Continuing Education Hall of Fame in 1999 (http://www.halloffame.outreach.ou.edu/). "Jost Reischmann has been a dynamic force in the field of adult education, building vital bridges between theory and practice" is written there. However, knowing that some of those who recommended me for this honour had been guests in my house I believe, that a substantial reason for my induction was the good German breakfast that my wife presented to those friends when they visited our home.

Enriching value through international contacts helped reduce some personal blindness and ethnocentrism. A better understanding of adult education in other countries helped me develop a broader and deeper understanding of adult education in my own country. The personal benefits of being a more "international" person include understanding, open-mindedness, tolerance, and humility - and good times with good friends in many places in the world (for example, in a Biergarten during the summer in Bamberg, Germany). Moreover, there is also a global perspective. The UNESCO *Hamburg Declaration on Adult Education* (1997) put this in words: "One of the foremost challenges of our age is ... to construct a culture of peace based on justice and tolerance within which dialogue, mutual recognition, and negotiation will replace violence, in homes and countries, within nations and between countries." That is the reason why I try to include my students in international meetings (i.e. Cincinnati, Phoenix, Prague, St. Louis, Sharm el Sheikh).

Towards a scientific discipline: "Andragogy"

The term "andragogy" in the USA is mostly attached to the specific concept of the American author Malcolm Knowles. In Europe this is different. "Andragogy" became connected to academic and professional institutions, publications and programs, as for example the "Yugoslavian Society for Andragogy", the "Andragoski Center Republike Slovenije", the "Katedra Andragogiky" of Prague University (Czechia). Similarly, Venezuela has the "Instituto Internacional de Andragogia"; Korea publishes the journal "Andragogy Today"[see 2.3 in this book].

An academic discipline with university programs, professors, students, and graduation is a rather young element in the history and division of labor of adult education - I experienced its development firsthand. It exists today in many countries - perhaps not for very long, but it exists. Furthermore, this new element (in most parts of the world) confusingly still labels itself with the old name used for the field of practice. So we are not clear what we talk about when we discuss "the future of adult education," "methods in adult education," "the history of adult education" ... - do we talk about places where adult education is practically carried out, or about universities? Teaching an ESL-class or writing a thesis about ESL-classes - should both be named "working in adult education"?!

It confuses the clarity of thinking and acting when we can not discriminate between the field of organized practice ("adult education") and of academic reflection ("andragogy") because we use the same label for both. We need a separate word for the newly grown field of scholarly work at universities.

That is the reason why I aggressively promote the term "andragogy" to brand the scientific discipline dealing with the lifelong and lifewide education of adults (http://www.andragogy.net).

End page 247
Start page 248

I follow here Dusan Savicevic (Yugoslavia), who provided Knowles with the term "andragogy". He claims "andragogy as a discipline, the subject of which is the study of education and learning of adults in all its forms of expression" (Savicevic 1999, p. 97 – see 2.1). (And by this description, I consider andragogy as a sub-discipline of pedagogy - but that starts another discussion).

This discussion is not a mere matter of definition. I want to influence the coming reality: to challenge 'outside' (demanding a respected discipline in the university context), to confront 'inside' (challenging my colleagues to clarify their understanding and consensus of their function and science), and overall to stand as a self-confident academic identity.

We are already far into the professionalized times with a division of labor. The "romantic times" of adult education are over; those were the times of Grundtvig, Miles Horton, Paulo Freire, Alfred Mannsbridge: Convincing in life-practice and enlightening in theory-writings they set an example to many followers. Nevertheless, now and in the future more and more people will have an academic andragogical education, producing theories, knowledge, research, critical thinking. The inspirational amateurs who played a role in the field decades ago will more and more be replaced by academic specialists and their knowledge – both a loss and a gain.

Summary

When I read what I have written here I am surprised myself. It seems I am a living document about beginnings in adult education (don't call me a fossil!). Of course, the history of adult education dates back for centuries. However, within one or two generations the volume, the scope, the necessity, the finances, the institutions, and the theoretical reflections have grown into new dimensions. It was and is fun to be in the midst of this, together with good friends here and there on various sides of the oceans. I hope a lot of younger people will take over in this field of practice and theory. They are our future.

End page 248

2. Andragogy and Andagogues

In the title and throughout this book a central term is "Andragogy". On several occasions, I tried to explain the meaning and function of this term: Andragogy can be defined as the "discipline, the subject of which is the study of education and learning of adults in all its forms of expression" (Savicevic, 1999, p. 97). The subsequent chapter was published in an encyclopedia. Forthcoming chapters will go deeper into the understanding and helpfulness of using this term.

2.1 Andragogy (2005)[1]

The term andragogy has been used in different times and countries with various connotations. There are three main understandings: (a) andragogy as the scholarly approach to the learning of adults, viewed as the science of understanding and supporting their lifelong and lifewide

End page 58
Start page 59

education; (b) andragogy in the tradition of Malcolm Knowles, which refers to a specific theoretical and practical approach based on a humanistic conception of learners who are self-directed and autonomous, where teachers who work with learners to facilitate their learning are also in a learning mode; this understanding is most common in the United States; and (c) andragogy used in an unclear way, with its meaning changing from "adult education practice" or "desirable values" or "specific teaching methods," to refer to "reflections" or a specific "academic discipline," as well as the "opposite of childish pedagogy." Terms make sense in relation to the object they name. Relating the development of the term to the historical context may explain the differences.

The History of Andragogy

The first person to use the term andragogy, as far as we know, was the German high-school teacher Alexander Kapp in 1833. In a book entitled 'Plato's Educational Ideas' he describes the lifelong necessity to learn. Midway through that book, which begins with a section on early childhood, there is a section on adulthood entitled "Die Andragogik oder Bildung im maennlichen Alter" (Andragogy or Education in the Man's Age); a replica of this book can be found on www.andragogy.net and on page 31 in this book. In 60 pages, Kapp argues that education, self-reflection, and character education are the first values of

---

[1] First print: Reischmann, Jost (2005): Andragogy. In: English, Leona (ed): *International Encyclopedia of Adult Education*. London: Palgrave Macmillan. P. 58-63.

human life. He then refers to vocational education for those in the healing professions, soldiers, educators, orators, rulers, and men as fathers. In a common pedagogical pattern, Kapp includes and combines the education of inner, subjective personality (character) and outer, objective competencies; for Kapp, learning happens not only through teachers, but also through self-reflection and life experience, and is about more than teaching adults.

Kapp does not explain the term andragogik, and it is not clear whether he invented it or whether he borrowed it from somebody else. He does not develop a theory but justifies andragogy as the practical necessity of the education of adults. Yet it was not considered unique, which may be the reason why the term lay fallow: other terms and ideas were available. The idea of adult learning was not unusual in the time around 1833, neither in Europe (Enlightenment movement, reading-societies, workers' education, educational work of churches), nor in America (Franklin Institute in Philadelphia, Lowell Institute in Boston, Lyceum Movement, town libraries, museums, agricultural societies); all had important dates between 1820-40. The existing initiatives had their own terminology, so a new term was not needed.

The Second and Third Invention

In the 1920s, Germany adult education became a field of theorizing, especially among a group of scholars from various disciplines, the so-called "Hohenrodter Bund," who developed in theory and practice the Neue Richtung (new direction) in adult education. Here some authors gave a second birth to the term andragogik, now used to describe sets of explicit reflections related to the why, what-for, and how of teaching adults. Andragogy became a sophisticated, theory-oriented concept, used as an antonym to "demagogy" too difficult to handle, not really shared. So again the term fell into disuse and was forgotten. But a new phenomenon

End page 59
Start page 60

was arising: a scholarly, academic reflection level "above" practical adult education. The scholars came from various disciplines, working in adult education as individuals, not representing university institutes or disciplines. The idea of adult education as a discipline was not yet born.

It is not clear where the third wave of using andragogy originated. In the 1950s, andragogy can suddenly be found in publications in Switzerland (Hanselmann), Yugoslavia (Ogrizovic), the Netherlands (ten Have), and Germany (Pöggeler). Still, the term was known only to insiders and was sometimes more oriented to practice, sometimes more to theory. Perhaps this mirrors the reality of adult education at that time. There was little formal training for adult educators, some very limited theoretical knowledge, no institutionalized continuity of developing such knowledge, and no academic course of study. Adult education was still an unclear mixture of practice, commitment, ideologies, reflections, theories, mostly local institutions, and some academic involvement of individuals. As the situation was unclear, the term could not be any clearer. But the increasing use of the term signaled that a sharp distinction between "doing" and "reflecting" was developing, one that was perhaps in need of a separate term.

Andragogy: A Banner for Identity

The heyday for the term andragogy for the English-speaking adult education world came with Malcolm Knowles, a scholar of adult education in the USA. In his 1989 book, Knowles describes his 1967 encounter with the term. A Yugoslavian adult educator, Dusan Savicevic, participated in a class Knowles was giving at summer session in Boston University. Savicevic explained the German roots of the term to Knowles. Following Kapp's use of the term, andragogy lay fallow until it was once more introduced by a German social scientist Eugen Rosenstock, in 1921, but it did not receive general recognition. The term was resurrected when in "1957 a German teacher, Franz Pöggeler, published a book, *Introduction into Andragogy: Basic Issues in Adult Education,* and this term was then picked up by adult educators in Germany, Austria, the Netherlands and Yugoslavia ..." (Knowles, p. 79).

Knowles published his first article (1968) about his understanding of andragogy with the provocative title "Andragogy, Not Pedagogy." In a short time the term andragogy, now intimately connected to Knowles received general recognition throughout North America and other English-speaking countries "within North America, no view of teaching adults is more widely known, or more enthusiastically embraced, than Knowles' description of andragogy" (Pratt & Associates, 1998, p. 13). Knowles' concept of andragogy "the art and science of helping adults learn ... is built upon two central, defining attributes: First, a conception of learners as self-directed and autonomous and second, a conception of the role of the teacher as facilitator of learning rather than presenter of content" (Pratt & Associates, 1998, p. 12), emphasizing learner choice more than expert control. Both attributes fit into the specific socio-historic thoughts in and after the 1970s, for example the deschooling theory (Illich, 1971), Rogers's person-centered approach, and Freire's conscientization. Perhaps a third attribute added to the attraction of Knowles' concept: constructing andragogy as opposed to pedagogy provided an opportunity

End page 60
Start page 61

for educators to be seen as „good teachers" instead of pedantic ones. This flattered adult educators in a time when most were andragogical amateurs, doing adult education based on their content expertise, experience, and a mission they felt, rather than on specific training or educational competence. To be offered understandable, humanistic values and beliefs, some specific methods and a good-sounding label strengthened a group that felt inferior to comparable professionals. And this was accompanied by a significant growth of the field of practice plus an increased scholarly approach, including the emerging possibility of studying adult education at universities. All these elements document a new period ("art and science") in adult education; it made sense to concentrate them in a new term.

Providing a unifying idea and identity, connected with the term andragogy, to the amorphous group of adult educators was certainly the main contribution that Knowles gave to the field of adult education at that time. Another was that he strengthened the already existing scholarly access to adult education by publishing, theorizing, researching and educating students who themselves through academic research became scholars, and by explicitly defining andragogy as science (Cooper & Henschke, 2003).

Issues with Andragogy

Nevertheless, over the years a critique has developed against Knowles' understanding of andragogy. A first critique argues that Knowles claimed to offer a general concept of adult education, but like all educational theories in history andragogy is but one concept, born into a specific historical context. For example, one of Knowles' basic assumptions is that becoming adult means becoming self-directed, a view that is often rejected because many adults are not self-directed. Critics do not agree that the American prototype of the self-directed lonesome fighter is the ultimate educational goal: in family, church, or civic education, for instance, the "we" is more important than the "self." The andragogy concept of Knowles is, as the Dutch scholar van Gent (1996) observes, not a general-descriptive, but a "specific, prescriptive approach" (p. 116). Another critique is Knowles' conception of pedagogy as a pedantic schoolmasters' practice, not as an academic discipline.

This hostility towards pedagogy has had two negative outcomes. On a strategic level, scholars of adult education could make no alliances with their colleagues from pedagogy; on a content level, knowledge developed in pedagogy over 400 years could not be utilized by those in andragogy (for more critical remarks see Merriam & Caffarella, 1999, p. 273ff, Savicevic, 1999, p. 113ff). Thus, attaching andragogy exclusively to Knowles' specific approach meant that the term was lost to those in pedagogy.

The European Development

In most countries of Europe Knowles' view of andragogy has played at best a marginal role. Its use and development in different countries and languages has been more hidden, dispersed, and uncoordinated, yet steady. Andragogy has nowhere been used to describe one specific concept, but from 1970 on it was connected with the development of coming academic and professional institutions, publications and programs, triggered by a similar growth of adult

End page 61
Start page 62

education in practice and theory in the USA. Andragogy functioned in Europe as a header for (in place of) systematic reflection, parallel to other academic headers like biology, medicine, and physics. Examples of this use of andragogy are the Yugoslavian (scholarly) journal for adult education, named "*Andragogija*" in 1969; the Yugoslavian Society for Andragogy formed in 1993; Slovenia's "Andragoski Center Republike Slovenije" founded with the journal "*Andragoska Spoznanja*"; Prague University's (Czechia) "Katedra Andragogiky"; Bamberg University's (Germany) "Lehrstuhl Andragogik", named in 1995; while the Internet address of the Estonian adult education society is "andra.ee." On this formal level "above" practice and specific approaches, the term andragogy could be used in communist countries as well as in capitalistic ones, relating to all types of theories, for reflection, analysis, and training, in person-oriented programs as well as human resource development.

A similar professional and academic expansion developed worldwide using variations of the concept of andragogy: Venezuela has the "Instituto Internacional de Andragogia"; since 1998 the Adult & Continuing Education Society of Korea has published the journal *Andragogy Today*. This documents the growth of new types of professional institutions, functions, and roles with full-time employed and academically trained professionals. Some of the new professional institutions have used the name andragogy in the same sense as adult education, but sounding more like a science-based discipline, but throughout Europe in general, "adult education," "further education," or "adult pedagogy" are used more than andragogy.

Andragogy: Academic Discipline

An academic discipline of andragogy with university programs, professors, and students, focusing on the education of adults, exists today in many countries. But in the membership-list of the Commission of Professors of Adult Education of the USA (2003) not one university program/institute in the USA uses the name andragogy; in Germany one out of 35, in Eastern Europe 6 out of 26 use the term. Many actors in the field seem not to need the label andragogy. However, other scholars, for example Dusan Savicevic who provided Knowles with the term andragogy, explicitly claim "andragogy as a discipline, the subject of which is the study of education and learning of adults in all its forms of expression" (Savicevic, 1999, p. 97; Henschke 2003· Reischmann 2003). This claim is not a mere definition, but includes the prospective function to influence the future: to challenge the "outside" (demanding a respected discipline in the university context), to confront the "inside" (challenging colleagues to clarify their understanding and consensus of their function, and science), and overall to stand up with a self-confident academic identity. The future will show whether the ongoing differentiation in institutions, functions, and roles will result in a need for further clarification of the term andragogy.

References and Further Reading

Cooper, M. K., & Henschke, J. A. (2003). *An update on andragogy: The international foundation for its research, theory and practice.* Paper presented at the Commission of Professors

End page 62
Start page 63

of Adult Education (CPAE) Conference, Detroit, MI, November 2003.

Henschke, J. A. (2003). *Andragogical concepts.* Retrieved December 1, 2003, from Studies in Andragogy and Adult Education website: http://www.ums!. edu/-henschke

Illich, I. (1971) *De-schooling society.* New York: Harper & Row.

Kapp, A. (1833). *Plato's educational ideas* (originally in German). Minden & Leipzig: Ferdinand Essmann.

Knowles, M. S. (1968). Andragogy, not pedagogy! *Adult Leadership,* 16, 350-352, 386.

Knowles, M. S. (1989). *The making of an adult educator.* San Francisco: Jossey-Bass.

Merriam, S. B., & Caffarella, R. S. (1999). *Learning in adulthood* (2nd ed.). San Francisco: Jossey-Bass.

Pöggelner, F. (1957). *Introduction to Andragogy: Basic Issues in Adult Education* (originally in German). Ratingen: Henn Verlag.

Pratt, D. D., & Associates. (1998). *Five perspectives on teaching in adult and higher education.* Malabar, FL: Krieger.

Reischmann, J. (2003). *Why andragogy?* Bamberg University, Germany. Retrieved January 10, 2004 from andragogy.net website: http://www. Andragogy.net

Savicevic, D. (1999). Understanding andragogy in Europe and America: Comparing and contrasting. In J. Reischmann, M. Bron, & Z. Jelenc (Eds.), *Comparative adult education 1998: The contribution of ISCAE to an emerging field of study* (pp. 97-119). Ljubljana, Slovenia: Slovenian Institute for Adult Education.

van Gent, B. (1996). Andragogy. In A. C. Tuijnman (Ed.), *International encyclopedia of adult education and training* (2nd ed., pp. 114-117). Oxford, UK: Pergamon.

In 2006, a conference titled 'On Becoming an Adult Educator' took place in Bamberg, Germany. It attracted 63 participants from 24 countries, featuring the presentations of 26 papers (available at http://andragogy.net/ conference2006-papers.htm, the quotations in this chapter refer to this Internet-publication). Important to the idea of the "identity" of adult educators is the second half of the text: Drawing inspiration from the personalities described in both the 2006 and 1996 conferences, 'prototypes' of 'Adult Educators' are constructed. What becomes evident is that the term 'Adult Educator' spans various contexts, functions, and connotations. This is a friendly description. However, a more critical question could be raised: Can an identity or a profession effectively encompass such diverse fields and functions? This observation sets the stage for the subsequent contributions, urging the use of the discriminating term 'andragogy' to define the scope of the academic field.

2.2 Prototypes of Adult Educators
Introduction - and Results to a Conference (2006)[1]

This conference in Bamberg, Germany, September 27-30, 2006 was part of an ongoing series of conferences dealing with the history of adult education. These were the preceding conferences:

Standing International Conference on the History of Adult Education

1986	Oxford/Great Britain	
1988	Aachen/Germany	The State and Adult Education
1990	Jerusalem/Israel	Adult Education in Crisis Situations
1992	Strobl/Austria	National Identity and Adult Education
1994	Brdo/Slovenia	Democracy and Adult Education
1996	Jena/Germany	Personality and Biography in the History of Adult Education
1998	Dundee/Scotland	The Rise and Fall of Adult Education Institutions and Social Movements
2000	Pécs/Hungary	Ethics, Ideals, and Ideologies in the History of Adult Education
2002	Leiden/Netherlands	Adult Education and Globalisation: Past and Present
2005	Helsinki/Finland	Lifelong Learning and Migration: Historical and Contemporary Perspectives
2006	Bamberg/Germany	On Becoming an Adult Educator

The focus "On Becoming an Adult Educator – historical, contemporary, institutionalized, individual aspects" opened a wide range of questions:

---

[1] First print: Reischmann, Jost (2006): Introduction - and Results. In: *Papers presented at the 11th Standing International Conference on the History of Adult Education in Bamberg*, Germany, Sept. 27 to Oct. 1, 2006. http://andragogy.net/conference2006-papers.htm. P. 3-6.

One root of this conference theme can be seen in the 1996-history-conference in Jena, Germany, exploring the theme "Personality and Biography in the History of Adult Education", dealing with personalities (internationally well-known or just of regional/local influence), their biography, influence, and legacy. In our conference historical personalities can be researched under the specific focus:

- How did important (historic) personalities/individuals "become adult educators"?
- What was their understanding of "adult education"?
- How did their surrounding "world" then (and perhaps now) perceive their activities?
- Volunteers, "Moonlighters", moral leaders, knowledge-experts, (semi-) professionals - historic examples and developments.
- In which different ways in different times/countries/cultures one became an "Adult Educator"?
- Are there / had there been different types/categories of adult educators?
- How did the role of adult educators develop in institutions?

A second aspect this conference deals with the contemporary situation of adult educators:

- What is the knowledge, are the competencies/attitudes expected from adult educators in different historic and contemporary movements/institutions/traditions?
- What are individual growth- and learning processes adult educators go through?
- Education of Adult Educators: What training schemes are available?
- Certification of adult educators?
  Is an adult educator a teacher? Professional roles of adult educators.
- What can be trained, what is "personality"?

Of course, not all these questions could be answered. But the papers and discussions showed a richness of aspects to "on becoming an Adult Educator".

A grounded summary of the conference certainly needs more time and space to prepare. But at least three observations and results shall be summarized here:

First: The participants came from 24 different countries, including Hong Kong, India, Israel, Nigeria, Russia and the USA. This may document how internationally widespread the interest in the history of Adult Education has grown.

Second: In the historical part a great number of paths and roles into and in the field of adult education were described. Beyond each individual case, the material lets us identify "prototypes" of what was described as being "an Adult Educator".

The following prototypes tentatively could be constructed from the presented papers:

Scholar/Professor: Clearly scholars are new in the "division of labor". Often the description sounds like "growing into that role". The paper of Faber (pp. 250) is an autobiographical reflection a good example of a scholar's "way to andragogy".

The Professional graduated from a University Adult Education Program and works mostly on a higher hierarchy-level in an Institution (not necessarily "adult educational"), but in staff or organizational development, politics, parliament, CEO, armed forces, church, hospital, research, … The historic papers do not contain examples (no wonder - this is a quite new development), but the "contemporary" papers describe this group (Gross pp. 271, Egetenmeyer pp. 337, Hinzen/Przybylska pp. 347).

Vocational: Fully employed/paid, often planning, managing - which implies that institutions exist. Not necessarily for adult education, but also in HRD, cultural institutions, media etc. Often not trained in Adult Education (Karm: "that they often have not had the opportunity to study how to do their job" p. 275, but "grown into the field" (Karm pp. 281, Henning-Loeb pp. 295, Zmeyov pp. 376).

Developer: Grassrooter, facilitator, not teaching, but supporting individuals, groups, and institutions to solve their problems themselves by learning. Could be vocation or volunteer, (selfmade) grassrooters, .dialogers, interactionists, integrators. Not "knowing better", but "supporting learning". Example: Oleson and the Study Circle Movement (Tosse, esp. pp. 58).

Teacher: Could be andragogical trained, or subject matter specialist (often not feeling as "adult educator"). Range from fully paid to (mostly) part-timer to high-spirited volunteer, from trainers in companies to grandmas offering cookie courses. Often descriptions document development from "just doing to learning". (Karm pp. 281, Henning-Loeb pp. 295, qualifying activities Schiebel/Miethe pp. 221, Morris pp. 237).

Organizer: Building and leading an organization. Someone other had the idea – he/she is building and administrating the organization

Humanist, philanthropist: Enabling learning by political or private infrastructure, not teaching in person (Nemeth pp. 161: István Türr, Hungary: "Türr was the founder ... of so-called Folk Education Circles ... in order to start the education of more than 4 million Hungarian illiterate adults.")

"Dedicator": Moral/spiritual leader, romantic, ideology-oriented. Knowing, what learners "really" need: a new nation, a good culture. Adult Education has to fulfill the function the dedicator wants to come true. Isaac pp. 136 describes personalities (Nicolae Iorga, Dimitri Gusti, Romania) that "had in mind the building of pedagogy of culture-specific to Romanian people as well as Romanian ethics." In a somewhat extreme form also political leaders can be seen as "dedicators", for example, "freedom-fighters", as described by Theiss/Bron pp. 203, for Poland.

Orator: Spreads his knowledge/wisdom to everybody who wants (or not), with no training, no institution. Kloubert (p. 147) describes Hryhoriy Skovroda, Ukraine, - "a wandering teacher and searcher for happiness". Classical personalities might be seen in the same category: Socrates, the Hyde Park Speakers; also authors that want to educate can be included here (i.e. Rousseau).

"The Wise" is asked for advice (spiritual, health, practical). No teaching, no institution, but learner activity (Bin-Sallik[1] describes the Australian aborigines Chief David Unaipon).

Of course, these types are overlapping and might be better sorted or differentiated. But it seems worth looking for typical elements, to understand better what the term "adult educator" may mean, such reducing confusion in understanding and discussion. What became clear: "Adult Educator" encompasses many contexts and connotations.

A third result from the contemporary part of the conference might be: Even in this small conference a number of activities to qualify adult educators were described: Morris (pp. 237), Egentenmeyer (pp. 337), Hinzen/Przybylska (pp. 347), Popovic (pp. 362), Zmeyov (pp. 376). It seems, that this important task has received attention and priority (Nuissl pp. 323). It might be interesting to do an evaluation ten years from now to find out what was achieved.

These conferences brought together again international scholars, researchers, and professionals, and gave the chance to meet international colleagues, perhaps old and certainly new friends, offered the exchange between experts, and - last but not least - let experience the 1000-year-old Bamberg, UNESCO world heritage, with its romantic streets, beer-gardens with the unique smoked beer, cathedral and the city-hall in the middle of the river. We - faculty and students of the chair of Andragogy - are proud we could welcome so many international and national experts at our university. Thank you!

Jost Reischmann, Chair of Andragogy, Bamberg University, Germany

---

[1]   in: Friedenthal-Haase, Martha (ed) (1998): *Personality and Biography in the History of Adult Education.* Vol. II. Frankfurt: Lang. Pp. 503 - 515

The preceding article summarized after the list of prototypes: "Adult Educator encompasses many contexts and connotations". The subsequent article, written about 10 years later, takes a more critical stance. Focused on the emerging university-based programs, faculty, and graduates, it warns against the indiscriminate use of the 'everybody-label' adult educator, judging it dangerous for the (new) professional identity.

This article shares parallels with section 2.1. We decided, to keep it unchanged without deleting parallel segments. Each article in this book should remain original and understandable on its own. We hope, that "whole-book-readers" can accept these duplications.

2.3 Andragogy: Because „Adult Education" is not beneficial to the Academic Identity! (2015)[1]

Abstract: In many countries of the world a new educational (sub)discipline dealing with the learning and education of adults came into existence in the last decades. This contribution focuses on this academic discipline and its struggle to find a professional identity in universities and for their graduates. It suggests that "Andragogy" helps to clarify the specifics of the scholarly approach, thus contributing to a professional identity of this group of academics and graduates. International readers are invited, to compare the following arguments coming mainly from the German and European background with the developments in their countries, the similarities and differences.

The growing of a new academic (sub)discipline

In Europe, universities from Finland and Estonia to Serbia, Hungary and Italy, from the Netherlands to the Czech Republic, Slovakia and Romania offer programs dealing with the learning and education of adults. The same is true for Thailand, Korea, Australia, Nigeria and Venezuela and many other countries. In Germany, more than forty, in the United States and Canada more than eighty universities offer programs for students, execute research and theory-development. A wealth of publications, national and international societies, conferences, and cooperation demonstrate that today a new reality in adult education with specific tasks and professionals exists: an academic discipline.

But this new academic field is still under question in many places. It appears that sound academic work and successful graduates are not sufficient enough to build a professional identity in universities and for the graduates. What seems necessary in addition: to work explicitly on the image and identity. As an attempt to contribute to a distinct identity it will be argued that the term "adult education/educator" is "destructive" for the identity, the role and perception of this new discipline and its graduates.

---

[1] First print: Reischmann, Jost (2015): Andragogy: Because „Adult Education" is not beneficial to the academic identity! In: *International Perspectives in Adult Education - IPE 71. Bonn/Germany: DVV-International, p. 87-97.

„Adult Educator" - an everybody label!

When using the term "adult education" most people connect this with the institutions of practical adult education. In the everyday perception "everybody" can be labeled as "adult educator":
- the grandma sharing her knowledge of baking cookies,
- the engineer instructing his staff about a new technology,
- the political or religious missionary preaching at the marketplace or in TV about the true and only life or society,
- the hundred thousand teachers in adult education institutions.

So: "everybody" can be an "adult educator". This also can be confirmed by analyzing historical cases of "key persons", published in two International conferences (Standing Conference on the History of Adult Education 1996, 2006) [see 1.2. in this book]. These cases too confirm the variety of understandings of "adult educator" – from "everybody" to "academic specialist", from "the wise" to "scholar and researcher":

When "everybody" is an "adult educator", then it is difficult to build a specific professional identity of university programs, students and graduates with this label. If persons who graduate after more than five years from a university are labeled "adult educator" similarly to "everybody", this is destructive for the role and perception of the academic discipline and its graduates. In order to differentiate between the field of practice and the academic subject, it is suggested here that for academic programs and their graduates the term "andragogy" and "andragogue" should be used to identify and differentiate this special group and their professional competency.

Andragogik - Andragogy

The first time the term 'Andragogik' was used was with the German high school teacher Alexander Kapp in 1833 (more detailed in Reischmann 2004). In the 1920s in Germany academics started new reflections related to the why, what for and how of the education of adults. There 'Andragogik' found a second birth. A new reality was shining up: a scholarly reflection level 'above' practical adult education. Faber, systemising the academic development of this field, names this "the 'generation of adult educators in passion' ('Erwachsenenbildner aus Leidenschaft'): They came from different fields of the society, they were active in a new sector of life without an academic mandate or an institutional structure" (Faber 2006, 64). The idea of "adult education" as a discipline was not yet born.

In the 1950s andragogy can be found in scholarly publications in Switzerland (Hanselmann), Yugoslavia (Ogrizovic), the Netherlands (ten Have), and Germany (Poeggeler 1974, 17ff). Still only insiders knew the term. But the increasing use of "andragogy" signalled that a new differentiation between 'doing' and 'reflecting' was developing. The background and status of the professors changed. Now we find "'professors in double disciplines'... At universities they were engaged in adult education *within* their main subject. They were, so to say, double interested, as professors of pedagogy or sociology and - as first academic ones - reflecting as individual persons on professors´

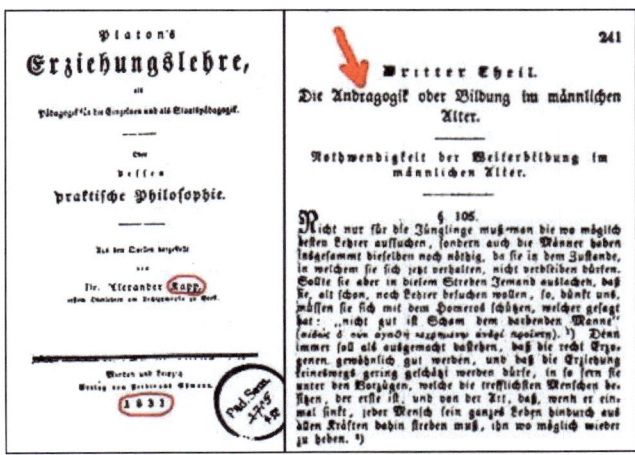

Figure 1: Kapp 1833 first printing of "Andragogik"

positions at universities on questions of adult education" (Faber 2006, 66). And - something that was new too - now students in university programs could study adult education, at least as a side subject.

The American understanding: Andragogy - a banner for identity

The breakthrough of the term 'andragogy' for the English-speaking adult education world came with Malcolm Knowles. He describes:

> "… in 1967 I had an experience that made it all come together. A Yugoslavian adult educator, Dusan Savicevic, participated in a summer session I was conducting at Boston University. At the end of it he came up to me with his eyes sparkling and said, 'Malcolm, you are preaching and practicing andragogy.' I replied, 'Whatagogy?' because I had never heard the term before" (Knowles 1989, 79).

In a short time the term andragogy, now labelled as Knowles' concept, received general recognition; "within North America, no view of teaching adults is more widely known, or more enthusiastically embraced, than Knowles' description of andragogy" (Pratt 1998, 13). Providing a unifying idea to the amorphous group of adult educators connected with the term andragogy - "the art and science of helping adult learners" - as well as the scholarly access, certainly were the main benefits Knowles brought to the field of adult education. The problem: attaching 'andragogy' exclusively to Knowles' specific approach means that the term is lost for general use.

The European development: Andragogy - an academic discipline

The European understanding is broader (Reischmann 2004). Where 'andragogy' is used, it functions as a header for (places of) systematic reflections, parallel to other academic headers like 'biology', 'medicine', 'physics'. It covers the academic discipline, "the subject of which is the study of education and learning of adults in all its forms of expression' (Savicevic 1999, 97).

Andragogy became from 1970 onwards connected with new academic and

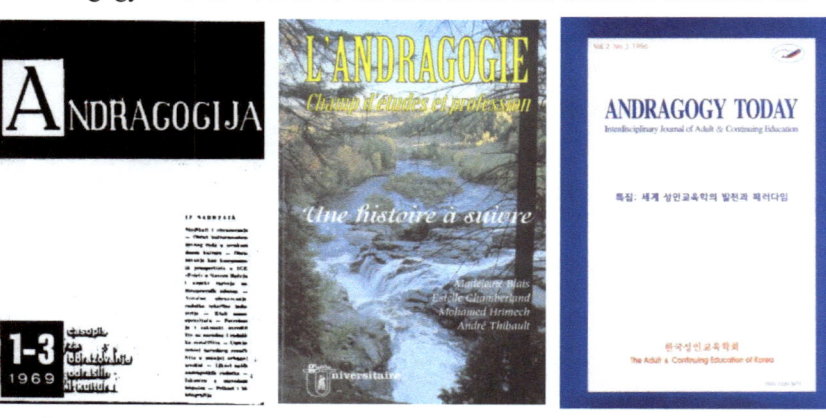

Figure 2: Publications from Yugoslavia, Canada, and Korea, using the term "Andragogy"

professional institutions, publications, and programs. Examples are: The Yugoslavian (scholarly) journal 'Andragogija' 1969 and the 'Yugoslavian Society for Andragogy'; Slovenia's 'Andragoski Center Republike Slovenije' (1993) with the journal 'Andragoska Spoznanja'; Prague University (Czechia) has a 'Katedra Andragogiky'. A similar professional and academic expansion developed worldwide: Venezuela has the 'Instituto Internacional de Andragogia', since 1998 the Adult & Continuing Education Society of Korea publishes the journal 'Andragogy today'.

So now again we find a new reality with new types of professional institutions, functions, and roles, with fulltime employed and academically trained professionals, with " 'explicit andragogy-professors': with this specification I will express that now for the first time we have the academic reality in our science that adult education or andragogy is not an additional subject but - expressis verbis - only the main one" (Faber 2006, 73).

But still: The lack of identity

As described: university programs, research, publications, and institutions give proof that such an academic field exists worldwide. But there are problems threatening the further development and identity of the discipline.

To name four:

1) An old-fashioned approach still can be found - in public und with university colleagues, administrators and other andragogical amateurs: "the knowledge that is utilized in the education of adults is, fundamentally, knowledge from other disciplines, which is applied to the education of adults ... Adult education is an integration of branches of disciplines, rather than a discipline in its own right" (Jarvis 1987, 311). For sure all disciplines (i.e. physics, biology, history ...) utilize knowledge from other disciplines, but that does not mean they are a blunt mixture. This outdated position has critical consequences: academic posts are given to persons that have not studied this field, such leading to a loss of identity and knowledge. A voice from Africa expresses it unmistakably clear: "it is too late in the day to toy with the idea of recruiting persons not trained in adult education into Departments of Adult Education ... about a century after the establishment of the first Department of Adult Education in the world and after 40 years of the establishment of the first Department of Adult Education in Nigeria" (Biao 2005, 13f). It seems that the professors, using the "everybody" term "Adult Education", now reap what they had sown: "Everybody" can take over that university position.

2) Another problem is that adult education sometimes becomes primarily focused on one "fashionable" field of praxis. Carroll Londoner, past chair of the International Adult Education Hall of Fame (www.halloffame.outreach.ou.edu) outlines this problem (private mail Jan. 31, 2014): "The Adult Education programs in the States have shrunk dramatically as the Universities do not seem inclined to support adult education because they do not understand it. They have too quickly identified the broad field of adult education with the notion of 'adult literacy'. That is a sad misunderstanding but nevertheless it exists because in the past there has been such huge amount of federal dollars available to support the US literacy efforts. This is no more and that is for certain. We in the universities have not done a very good job of explaining to our administrators what the broad field is about and why it should be studied academically". Supporting practical fields certainly is praiseworthy, but for surviving in the academic arena it might have been better "explaining to our administrators what the broad field is about and why it should be studied academically"! The discussion about andragogy as a discipline could support that, also to keep the necessary distance 'above practice' and above specific approaches.

3) A third threat for identity came - at least in Germany - with the Bologna-system and its Bachelor-Master-system: Reputable professors report (in Egetenmeyer/Schüssler 2012), that in the changing University programs adult education becomes marginalized and disintegrated (p. 37), loses profile (p. 37), operates under dozens of names (p. 36), has a low reputation (p. 197), has difficulties to identify the core of the discipline (p. 278), and becomes invisible (p. 256) in the mixture of contents.

4) And a fourth thread is the confusing plurality of workplaces reported from the graduates. In the last three decades in many countries the working fields of the graduates far exceeds the traditional understanding of "adult educators" or "teachers of adults". Only a small portion work in the traditional fields of adult education, only a small portion teaches as "adult educator". The disadvantage of this multi-functionality is: the graduates are not perceived (from the outside and even worse: from the inside) as a distinct group of professionals.

A shared identity of the academic field of adult education and its graduates seems further away than before.

Andragogy: A Chance for Identity?

How can the identity (and hopefully reputation) of this new academic field be supported?

1. Elaborating on the specific tasks of "andragogy" (academic) and "adult education" (practical) prevents confusion about the different responsibilities and strengths of each field.
2. When using andragogy in the academic arena, it is necessary to carve out the specifics of this subject, its identity and image. To support this, professors have to
   - explicitly work on and for policy, legitimation and identity of their subject, and make this obvious to the outside world.
   - differentiate the subject against other subjects.
   - take care that in study programs the visibility and identity of the discipline is respected - which also means to exclude persons that have not studied adult education/andragogy from appointments in this subject.
   - supply the students/graduates not only with knowledge and skills, but also with the awareness of their uniqueness and what only they have to offer.
   - stay away from the confusing bunch of different names for the discipline.
3. Andragogy, by opening the perspective to "more" - to "Lifewide Education" (Reischmann 1986, Jackson 2012) [see 3.2 in this book] in all forms and expressions - creates a new identity, not defined by "adult teacher", but by "change specialist". This new understanding makes clear that it is not by chance or mistake that the graduates can be found in companies, churches and culture, in armed forces and adult education centres, in management and media, in tourism, hospitals and many other fields. This plurality of workplaces is confusing only when thinking in the limiting category of "adult educator". Andragogy makes aware that there already exists a unifying, identity-giving function: to support change for individuals, institutions, and society - in various institutions, in various functions.
4. To support a shared identity under the perspective of andragogy, the curricula must prepare for this plurality of workplaces. The competencies of

andragogues in this complex field are highly valued: to professionally teach, to plan and organize learning occasions, to consult and moderate, to evaluate and research – and produce the most successful mix of these ingredients.

5. For building a distinct identity of the graduates ("andragogues") the ingredients are available: first of all, the graduation from a University program. Second of all, the insights that learning and change processes happen in many contexts far beyond schooltyp-learning. Thirdly, the awareness that the graduates have for all these contexts shared competencies, unifying them to a distinct group: *professionals supporting change*.

The label "andragogue" is - as our graduates reported - also helpful on the labour market: it made the employers curious to invite them for interviews. In many cases this led to employment. This seems true even in Brasilia, as I learned in a mail from there: "I prefer being called as 'andragogue', because it … is better for my professional marketing".

This too may confirm: to be perceived as a distinct group they have to avoid the everybody-term "adult educator".

Identity does not come by itself. Professors and graduates have to explicitly work on this identity. It seems this was forgotten in the past. The discussion about andragogy as a unifying label has the potential to direct our attention to this missing identity-development.

Summary

Claiming a separate name for the academic discipline is not meant to devaluate the field and institutions of practice. Many institutions in many countries are a persuasive evidence of valuable work in practical adult education. Often we find convincing examples of cooperation between the practical and academic access to adult learning and education. A self-confident academic identity, however, will in many ways strengthen practical adult education as a powerful concept and key to the twenty-first century.

References

Biao, Idowu (2006): Pedagogical and Andragogical Warfare and the Psycho-Soziology of Andragogizing in Nigeria. Calabar: University of Calabar Press. ISBN979-36245-9-8

Faber, Werner (2006): My Way to Andragogy - Autobiographical Reflections. Paper presented at the 2006-conference on History of Adult Education. http://andragogy.net/conference2006papers/Faber.pdf

Egetenmeyer, Regina and Schüssler, Ingeborg (ed) (2012): Akademische Professionalisierung in der Erwachsenenbildung/Weiterbildung. Hohengehren: Schneider.

Henschke, John (2003): Andragogy Website http://www.umsl.edu/~henschke.

Jackson, Norman. J. (2012): Lifewide Learning: History of an idea. In: Jackson, Norman J. (ed): The Lifewide Learning, Education & Personal Development e-book.: 1-30. http://lifewideeducation.co.uk/sites/default/files/chapter_a1_jackson.pdf

Jarvis, Peter (1987): Towards a discipline of adult education?, in: Jarvis, Peter (ed): Twentieth Century Thinkers in Adult Education. London: Routledge, p. 301-313.

Kapp, Alexander (1833): Platon's Erziehungslehre, als Pädagogik für die Einzelnen und als Staatspädagogik. Minden und Leipzig: Verlag Ferdinand Eßmann.

Knowles, Malcom S. (1989): The Making of an Adult Educator. San Francisco: Jossey-Bass.

Pöggeler, Franz (1974): Erwachsenenbildung. Einführung in die Andragogik (Handbuch der Erwachsenenbildung Bd. 1). Stuttgart u.a.: Kohlhammer.

Pratt, Daniel D., & Associates (1998): Five perspectives on teaching in adult and higher education. Malabar, FL: Krieger.

Reischmann, Jost (1986): Learning „en passant": The Forgotten Dimension. http://www.uni-bamberg.de/fileadmin/andragogik/08/andragogik/ aktuelles/86AAACE-Hollywood.pdf.

Reischmann, Jost (2004): Andragogy. History, Meaning, Context, Function. http://www.andragogy.net. Version Sept. 9, 2004.

Reischmann, Jost (2010): Adult Educators as HRD Trainer, Moderator and Coach. In: Medic, Snezana/Ebner, Regina/Popovic, Katarina (ed): Adult Education: The Response to Global Crisis. Belgrade: Department of Pedagogy and Andragogy, University of Belgrade, Serbia. p. 81-90. http://www.uni-bamberg.de/fileadmin/andragogik/08/andragogik/jr/10-Belgrad2009-2.doc

Savicevic, Dusan (1999): Understanding Andragogy in Europe and America. In: Reischmann, Jost/ Bron jr, Michal/ Jelenc, Zoran. (Hg.): Comparative Adult Education 1998. Ljubljana: Slovenian Institute for Adult Education, p. 97-119. http://www.uni-bamberg.de/fileadmin/andragogik/08/andragogik/iscae /ISCAE-Book1999.pdf.

Standing Conference on the History of Adult Education (6th and 11th), Jena, Germany 1996 (Friedenthal-HaaseMartha ed. 1998: Personality and Biography. Frankfurt et al.: Lang) and Bamberg, Germany 2006 - http://andragogy.net/conference2006-papers.htm

A word alone - Andragogy - does not constitute an academic discipline or a self-convinced identity. Over the decades of the development of Adult Education/Andragogy at universities much more than "a word" was achieved. The following article advances beyond the preceding articles by outlining concrete outcomes and developments that took place in the meantime.

2.4 What are Andragogues good for?
Workplaces, Competencies, Study Contents, Identity (2017) [1]

Abstract: This paper wants to strengthen the identity of Andragogues - to make Andragogues strong and proud. It starts from the observation, that the term "adult educator" labels many different functions, roles, competencies, and educational backgrounds - which leads to an unclear identity. To shape the identity it is suggested to differentiate the various groups of individuals working in this field: the focus is on the graduates of university programs: Andragogues.

Workplaces are described as places where graduates of university programs can be found working successfully. Four competencies are identified needed at these workplaces: teaching, organizing, consulting, and evaluation. These competences have to be included in the education of Andragogues. The question is asked: Is there a "unifying concept" for people working in that field, a shared identity? The answer will be: unifying is the idea, the need, and the function to organize change: for individuals, for organizations, for society. *Andragogues - no matter were they work - are change specialists.* To strengthen the self-understanding, the identity of the professionals, graduated from university programs and educated for this complex task (and to discriminate them from "everybody" doing some sort of adult education), this group should use the name/label "Andragogue". And to feel strong and proud: In a changing world change specialists are bitterly needed.

Introduction

It is strange: data and experience worldwide document that adult education in volume, scope, public, financing, economic and political perception has clearly grown. But in spite of this positive development in many countries the professional academic graduates are missing a feeling of unity or identity, as Kleisz states for Hungary: "The younger and trained generation does not feel the unity of profession" (Kleisz, 2015, p. 22). In spite of the positive development in reality still the critical question remains - from outside but as well from inside the profession: what are Andragogues good for? What is their identity?

Threats for identity

A number of reasons may count for the fragile identity. Just to name some:

1. Everybody is an "Adult Educator"

Who is an Adult Educator? The answer is easy: everybody. In the everyday perception "everybody" can be labeled as "adult educator":

---

[1] First print: Reischmann, Jost (2017): What are Andragogues good for? Workplaces, Competencies, Study Contents, Identity. *Andragoške studije*, ISSN 0354–5415. Institut za pedagogiju i andragogiju; Belgrade. 1, jun 2017, p. 9-24. doi:10.5937/andstud1701009R.

- the grandma sharing her knowledge of baking cookies,
- the engineer instructing his staff about a new technology,
- the political or religious missionary preaching at the marketplace or on TV about the true and only life or society,
- salespersons, police, medicine, media, tourism, priests, ... ("implicit" adult educators),
- the hundred thousand teachers in adult education institutions (community, church, business and industry, museums, music schools, etc.), teaching some hours at night - volunteers, not paid, or trainers, paid (poorly) per hour/day.

A similar confusing picture can be found when looking at conferences (i.e. 6th and 11th Standing Conference on the History of Adult Education, Jena, Germany 1996; Bamberg, Germany 2006) that describe "leading personalities in adult education": from „the Wise", over humanists, organizers to professors a high number of „prototypes" are presented under the label of „Adult Educator". [see 1.2 in this book].

So: Just "everybody" can be an "Adult Educator". But: *an identity of "everybody" is not possible!*

2. No obligatory education

Looking at the academic preparation of teachers in Adult Education also shows no shared background or identity. In a recent study, Martin et al. (2017, p. 115, n= 3961) prove that only about one-third of the teachers in (public) adult education have some sort of educational academic background (it might be telling that a separate category "study in andragogy/adult education" was not even posed!):

- education full subject: 16,3%
- education as a side subject: 7,0%
- not-educational degree: 33,3%
- no academic degree: 33,4%

A slightly more positive picture showed the participants in a recent conference

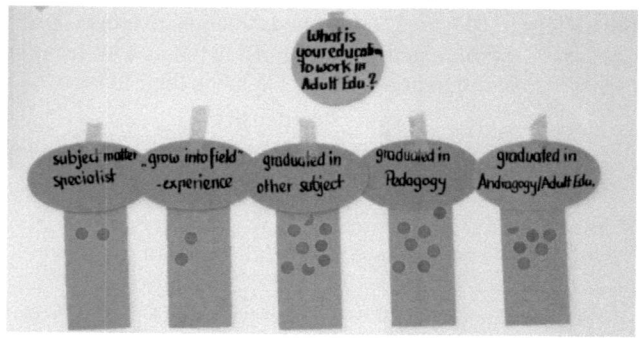

Fig. 1 Educational background of participants of the Conference 2017

(International Scientific Conference on Adult Education: "Developing and understanding Professional Identity of Adult Educators", Rijeka 2017): half of the participants have graduated in pedagogy or andragogy.

Asking for the professionalization of this field these results show that we are still at the beginning. The idea of a shared qualification is still a task to come. While other professions like medicine, law, or engineering have clear and compulsory educational criteria for their identity, an identity for Adult Education cannot be based on a shared education for this field.

3. Plurality of functions and workplaces of Andragogues

But even in the group of graduates of university programs of adult education/andragogy the workplaces give no clear picture that could form identity: starting with the belief that our university program ("Chair of Adult Education") was to educate teachers for adults, our experiences around 1995 were shocking: We asked our students some years after graduation: "What is your workplace now - after finishing your studies?" The shocking answer was: only a small portion (10-30%) was employed in a teaching position at an adult education institution - most of the "adult educators" did not teach! 20-30% of our graduates work as freelanced workers ("training, development, counseling/consultancy"), about 10-20% have a career at colleges/universities (Bender et al., 2008). Other programs at other universities reported similar results. Horror: did we educate our students for unemployment or cab driving?

This "horror" gladly could be disproved by another result of our and others' research: The graduates overwhelmingly let us know that they had no problem finding a well-paid workplace, are happy with their employment, and feel that our program prepared them well for their specific workplaces!

However: by asking for the names of their workplaces we still got a vast and confusing variety of descriptions: teacher, trainer, evaluator, coach, moderator, HRD-employee, manager, administrator, personal or organizational developer. Just to give some examples:

- Antje is working as a freelance worker; she founded the institute for "art-dialogue" (continuing education for art- and cultural managers)
- Sabine (freelance worker) is a communication trainer "clarifying and solving difficult communication situations" for individuals and institutions.
- Yvonne was employed by a local brewery as a manager.
- Helga offers conflict management training in business and industry - and reported how she solved a conflict that had cost five million EUR the year before!

It seems we taught our students competencies useful in many fields of the job market, and in the beginning did not really know what these competences were. We will come back to this problem later.

Even vaster and more confusing was the answer in response to the question of which institutions they work in: in business and industry, adult education centers, health-care, charities, cultural institutions, churches, in armed forces, management and media, in tourism, journalism and many other fields ... This confirms that Andragogues are beneficial in many fields, but the *disadvantage* remains: they are not perceived as experts in one specific workplace or direction - and sometimes they themselves are not clear about that. So the functions, workplaces, and institutions do not offer a unifying identity.

4. Restricted to one field

Threatening an identity is, in addition, the fact, that Andragogues are often seen limited to one segment of the field (which could be social change, or second chance/compensatory education, or community education, or political education, or cultural capital, or human resource development, or 'learning to acquire employability', or minority education - just to name some). Depending on the money-giver or what is in a certain time in fashion one segment is in an oversimplified way claimed to be the total, and the others are either not seen or not valued.

Carroll Londoner, past chair of the International Adult Education Hall of Fame (http://www.halloffame.outreach.ou.edu) outlines this problem for the USA (private mail Jan. 31, 2014): "The adult education programs in the States have shrunk dramatically as the universities do not seem inclined to support adult education because they do not understand it. They have too quickly identified the broad field of adult education with the notion of 'adult literacy' ... We in the universities have not done a very good job of explaining to our administrators what the broad field is about and why it should be studied academically".

It is a mistake to perceive and value just one segment as the only legitimate field for Andragogues. The study of andragogy opens the doors to a growing number of workplaces, in different settings and functions, and with a catalogue of needed competencies. Again: this plurality is an *advantage* of andragogy. At the same time again a *disadvantage*, because it is difficult to perceive that all these different fields belong to a shared identity: andragogy.

5. Manyfold different tasks

We also can refer to statistics that show that Andragogues fulfil a number of different tasks: Martin et. al. (2017, p. 99), asking 5244 individuals in adult education, could prove that people working in adult education institutions fulfill in their daily work a number of different activities: Full-time employees spend 9,9% of their time for management or control, 20% for administration, 6,4% for consulting, 26,6% for teaching, 10,7% for program-planning, 4,9% for acquisition, 5,4% for marketing, 11,2% for assisting participants, 2,3% for staff development.

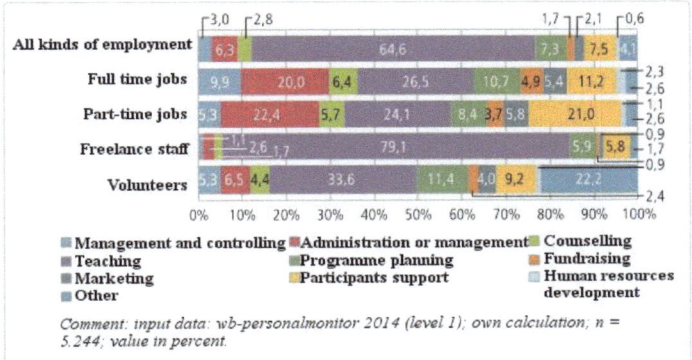

Fig. 2: Activities of fulltime-employees in adult education institutions
From: Martin & others. 2016 p. 99.

Non-representative, but still confirming are the answers we got at a recent conference (International Scientific Conference on Adult Education: "Developing and understanding Professional Identity of Adult Educators", Rijeka 2017): Working in adult education most persons fulfilled a number of activities and competencies.

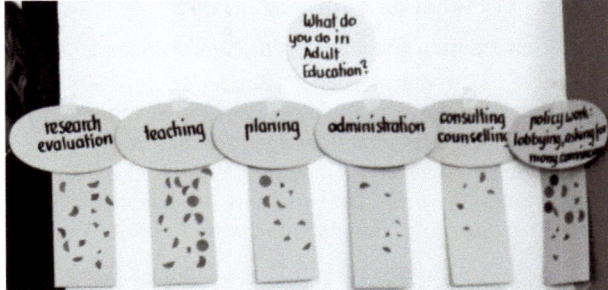

Fig. 3: Activities of Adult Education conference-participants

A simplified perception may perceive this as confusing or "borderless". But this plurality of functions describes the reality and strength of the workplaces in adult education: that is what Andragogues are good for.

Summary

The institutions and workplaces of Andragogues, the education they have, are multifold, and different - far more than the traditional "teacher of adults" in adult education institutes. That means: institutions, workplaces, education, and functions do not constitute an identity.

The unclear borderless term "Adult Educator" makes it difficult to differentiate academically educated graduates from "everybody". That makes the term "Adult Educator" destructive for the perception and identity of our discipline and our graduates (Reischmann, 2015b) [see 2.3 in this book].

As a consequence: To describe and guarantee quality standards, to claim academic theory and research, and especially to grow an own identity and offer a unique and specific "label"[1] in the labour-market, I changed 1996 the name of my chair in Bamberg from "Adult Education" (Erwachsenenbildung) to "Andragogik" (Andragogy). Andragogy is the educational discipline, the subject of which is the study of lifelong and lifewide learning and education of adults (Savicevic, 1999, Reischmann, 2004, Henschke, n.d.). The following will focus on the group "graduates of university programs of adult education/andragogy".

But referring to the described multitude of functions and workplaces it also can be summarized: There exists a unifying idea/concept of all these workplaces: Andragogues teach, organize, manage, inform, mediate, moderate, motivate, and interfere in various ways in tensions, conflicts, friction between:
-   people and people; or people and organizations; or people and things; or organizations and organizations.
This widespread usefulness of Andragogues can be seen as a strength, value - and identity (Reischmann, 2015a).

What do Andragogues do?

What are their (needed/given) competencies?

The reports we received from our graduates (Bender et. al., 2008) parallel to the insights from theory and research, made us analyse, what in the multitude of workplaces andragogues do, and what they need for their daily work. We identified four core competencies, which consequently became a part of our curriculum - in addition to the traditional contents - to enable our students/graduates to act as professionals in the wide field of lifewide education:
-   First, it is expected that an Andragogue is able to teach. We found that teaching was often a starting point for our graduates, but that after a short while they moved up into a supervising, planning, managing position. However, even in this position, it is expected that they can convincingly "teach" and advise others how to teach (i.e. "train the trainer" programs).

---

[1]   It might be helpful to draw an analogy to the identity of other recognized professions like medicine, law, architecture, and engineer. A "Mediziner" (German) = doctor, physician, health professional is not "everybody" doing something for health, but exclusively experts that studied this subject. Even there it took centuries to install this identity: In the corpus of the German language the frequency of the term "Mediziner" was 2 (per million tokens) in 1800 (= "nearly unknown"), 4 in 1900, and increased to 19 in 2000 (Source: DWDS – Verlaufskurve, 2017). May be we will see a similar development with "Andragogue" in the time to come.

- Second, we have to prepare them for planning, organizing, and managing programs and measures. The success of an educational program does not only depend on the quality of teaching (micro-didactics) but also the learning-supportive planning and organizing of the program (macro-didactics): How can learning be started and supported by organizational measures? This includes the challenge of how learning occasions can be identified and supported in workplaces, cultural institutions, hospitals, tourist places, hospitals, political and religious organizations etc.
- Third, they need the ability to consult and counsel (moderator - counselor - consultant - mediator - coach). The manyfold learning challenges in "lifewide education" (Reischmann, 1986; Jackson, 2012) opened the insight into a new role of Andragogues: not presenting/transporting knowledge (teaching), but helping persons or groups to find their way and solve their problems by counselling/consulting strategies - often in a one-to-one-situation.

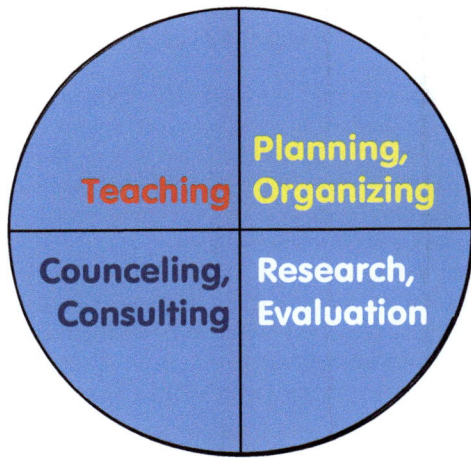

Fig. 4: Core competencies of Andragogy Curriculum Bamberg University

- And finally, they must be able to do evaluation and research. This ability is not only expected from scholars and members of research–organizations but is also needed in the practical work in many positions and organizations for needs-assessment, evaluation and quality control, planning of (political, strategic) programs, and feedback to organizers and boards.

How to learn these competencies?

"Competencies" in our understanding include the capability to perform (practice) and to reflect (theory). Similarly to other professions (medical doctors, lawyers, architects...), it is not enough that Andragogues have knowledge; professionals also have to be able to act in their field. These competencies do not come by themselves. For the ability to perform we developed so-called competency-trainings. They usually last three full days, filled with acting, training, trying, and demonstrating, and are limited to not more than 20 students. These three days are theory-reduced and focus on performance. Of course, these competency-based classes have to be supplemented with the "normal" knowledge- and theory-oriented classes, lectures, and readings. Performance has to be melted in and interwoven with knowing and understanding to lead to competency. These competency-trainings cover:

-   *"Visualising, presentation, moderation"*. Here, students learn to stand in front of a group, design presentation-material, work with an auditory, present learning material, and interact with groups – including conflict situations.
-   In a second module they learn how to *design classes and seminars.*
-   The module *"program-planning"* supplies planning/organizing strategies. An important role for this competency is the *internship* each of our students has to go through.
-   *"Communication competency"* is a module in the competency *"consulting / counseling"*, another module is *"consulting-strategies and -techniques"*.
-   In the competency-training *"coaching"* they learn to support individual trainers and managers to solve practical problems [see 4.2 in this book].

In all these classes students learn an active, acting approach to solving problems of people and institutions in a professional way.

At the end of the final examination, we sometimes ask our students what has been the most important part of their study. The majority names the competency-trainings. This is also true for our alumni, when asked years after graduation. It seems that the preparation to perform successfully and professionally in the practical field adds an important factor to their identity and employability.

Summary

Andragogues are beneficial in manifold positions and institutions - this can be easily proved by monitoring the workplaces they are in and the activities they perform there. The reality of the workplaces of Andragogues shows a wide variety of functions and activities:

-   They have to practically perform and theoretically reflect.
-   They need the competencies to a) professionally teach, b) plan and organize learning, c) consult and moderate, and d) evaluate and research.
-   And they have to produce the most successful mix of these ingredients.

To make Andragogues perceived as professionals they not only need knowledge, but they also need performance skills. This has to be incorporated into the curricula of the University programs (and/or continuing professional education). And to be aware that for complex tasks not only one but all these competencies are needed.

The shared identity: Change Specialist

Using this complex observation of different workplaces, functions, organizations, competencies, and expectations the question is asked: Is there a "unifying concept" for people working in that field? Is a shared identity possible?

The answer for me is: unifying this - sometimes confusing - variety is the idea, the need, and the function to organize change: for individuals, for organizations, for society. Andragogues - no matter where they work in business and industry, cultural organizations, hospitals or the armed forces, tourism or media, political or social institutions - are change specialists.

This world, in which we live, is full of change. And change deserves learning – throughout life, lifewide. Change specialists ask and answer questions such as:
- What effect, impact, transfer is needed? And how can it be reached successfully?
- What is that good for? For the person, institution, etc.?
- What is better: More or less? Or different?
- What do THEY need? And what do they really need?
- How does the other see this?
- Who can (not) do what with whom?
- What already exists that supports/hinders a good development?
- Could that also be seen differently? And how does the other see this?
- Where are we going to? Short-term, long-term?
- What might be understood as the message behind it? What effect will that message have that is good/bad?
- What are the advantages AND the unavoidable disadvantages of the planned action? (Persons, products, institution? Short- / middle- / long term? Who can (not) do what with whom?)
- How do you plan something that later on will be different anyway?

All these questions belong to the toolbox of Andragogues, are the daily business of Andragogues, and take account of the competencies they (should have) learned. That makes them the sought specialists in the labour market. Who else asks and answers these complex questions, and who asks for the consequences from the answers and develops an action plan?

To strengthen the identity of the professionals, who graduated from university programs and were educated for this complex task (and to discriminate them from "everybody" doing some sort of adult education), this group should use the name/label "Andragogue".

Of course, we know: We are only at the beginning of the development of this new academic discipline. In Germany, it is just brief four decades ago that the first graduates in Adult Education left university. Looking at the academic discipline the glass can be seen as half empty or half full: at many universities in many countries programs for Andragogy/Adult Education exist, as well as research, literature, conferences, societies, journals, professors, students/ graduates, and the need from the market to have the described competencies available. For the sake of developing and strengthening the identity of the Andragogues, it may be more helpful to look to the "half-full glass" by valuing what has already been developed. That can make self-convinced and strong, while overcritical asking what is missing makes the profession and the individuals in the profession weak.

A main starting point for further directions may not be to start with the old picture of the teacher but with the idea of the "change specialist". This opens the perspective to many more workplaces, to new tasks, and to a different curriculum. This changed perspective makes us aware of the many places in a changing world where change specialists are bitterly needed. And makes us feel strong and proud to be part of this world-moving development.

Closing summary and challenges

The field of adult learning and education and consequently the working fields of andragogues are nowadays perceived as much wider and diversified than three decades ago, and have reached new horizons. And it is perceived much more important, as UNESCO stated (The Hamburg Declaration On Adult Learning, UNESCO, 1997):

> "Adult education ... is a key to the twenty-first century. ... It is a powerful concept:
> - For fostering ecologically sustainable development;
> - for promoting democracy, justice, gender equity, and scientific, social and economic development, and
> - for building a world in which violent conflict is replaced by dialogue and a culture of peace based on justice.
> - Adult learning can shape identity and give meaning to life." (p. 1)

Andragogues can be the specialists to support these change processes, leading into a future worth living in.

For the academic subject "andragogy" there exist several challenges, problems, and tasks:
- to identify the specifics of the subject and the shared paradigms of andragogy and Andragogues, to discuss what Andragogues are good for, what their specific identity is, to document the results (for the outside and self-perception), and then to convince inside and outside how important this subject is.
- To develop a curriculum including convincing competencies that respect the variety of expectations in the variety of possible workplaces.
- To be self-aware and convince others that is not confusing or "unclear", that Andragogues are beneficial in companies, churches, and culture, in armed forces and adult education centers, in management and media, in tourism, hospitals, and many other fields, but that this documents the value and

richness of this complex subject and profession, and the shared vision of Andragogues as "change specialists".
-   To become aware that the term "adult education/educator" is destructive for the university-based profession. The term "Andragogue" could be a discriminator, a name that supports identity to the graduates and the discipline.
-   And most importantly: to decide strategically where and when to be critical and talk about the half-empty glass, and where it is more viable, more supportive for the academic subject, the students, and the field, to point out that the glass is half full, that good examples of success document the potentials of andragogy and Andragogues.
-   But also: to be aware of the limitations on what can be achieved through adult education. To expect (or promise) to save with some pennies the whole world is a romantic expectation but for sure leads to disappointment, frustration, and a ruined reputation.

This paper focussed on the graduates of university-based programs. But still needed is the whole range of adult educators at all levels and in all fields: the volunteers, the partly paid part-timers, the fully employed subject-matter-specialists, the organizers and administrators and teachers - they are all still needed (analog to medicine, where besides the professionals = studied doctors still nurses, midwives, ambulance-drivers etc. are needed). But it also became clear that for the complex and difficult challenges of a "society in change" in addition to professional experts - Andragogues, scientifically educated at a university are needed to support change and learning successfully to make, as UNESCO expressed it, "Adult learning: a joy, a tool, a right and a shared responsibility" (The Hamburg Declaration On Adult Learning, UNESCO, 1997).

There are many reasons to be proud and strong in this identity!

References

Bender, Walter/ Emmert, Kerstin/ Gröne, Susanne/ Heglmeier, Helga / Jäger, Mathias/ Lerch, Sebastian (Hg.) (2008). Die Bamberger Andragogik. Studium und Berufsperspektiven in Erwachsenenbildung, beruflicher Weiterbildung und Personalentwicklung. Tönning: Der andere Verlag.

DWDS – Verlaufskurve. (n.d.). Retrieved on June 21, 2017, from https://www.dwds.de/r/plot?q=Mediziner&view=1&norm=date%2Bclass&smooth=spline&genres=0&grand=1&slice=10&prune=0&window=3&wbase=0&logavg=0&logscale=0&xrange=1600%3A2016)

Henschke, John (n.d.): Andragogy Website http://www.umsl.edu/~henschke.

Jackson, Norman J. (2012): Lifewide Learning: History of an idea. In: Jackson, Norman J. (ed): The Lifewide Learning, Education & Personal Development e-book. P. 1-30. http://lifewideeducation.co.uk/sites/default/files/chapter_a1_jackson.pdf

Kleisz, Teréz (2015): The state of profession-building in the field of Andragogy in Hungary. In: International Perspectives in Adult Education Vol. 70 (Editor Balázs Németh). DVV International Bonn, Germany. P. 16-25.

Martin, Andreas; Lencer, Stefanie ; Schrader, Josef; Koscheck, Stefan; Ohly, Hana; Dobischat, Rolf; Elias, Arne ; Rosendahl, Anna (2016): Das Personal in der Weiterbildung - Arbeits- und Beschäftigungsbedingungen, Qualifikationen, Einstellungen zu Arbeit und Beruf. Bielefeld: Bertelsmann. Download: www.die-bonn.de/doks/2017-weiterbildner-01.pdf

Reischmann, Jost (1986): Learning „en passant": The Forgotten Dimension. Paper presented at the Conference of the American Association of Adult and Continuing Education. Hollywood/Florida, 23. 10. 1986. ERIC Clearinghouse on Adult, Career, and Vocational Education. Columbus/Ohio 1986. http://www.reischmannfam.de/lit/1986-AAACE-Hollywood.pdf.

Reischmann, Jost (2015a): Profesionalizacija obrazovanja odraslih – neki aspekti. (Professionalization of Adult Education – Some Aspects). In: Andragoške studije. Èasopis za prouèavanje obrazovanja i uèenja odraslih. (Univerzitet u Beogradu, Filozofski fakultet). p. 23-37. http://www.reischmannfam.de/lit/2015-KatarinaBelgrad-a.pdf

Reischmann, Jost (2015b): Andragogy: Because „Adult Education" is not beneficial to the academic identity! In: International Perspectives in Adult Education - IPE 71. Bonn: DVV-International, p. 87-97. http://www.reischmannfam.de/lit/2015-Andragogy-HeribertHinzen.pdf

Savicevic, Dusan (1999): Understanding Andragogy in Europe and America: Comparing and Contrasting. In: Reischmann, Jost/ Bron, Michal/ Jelenc, Zoran (Hg.): Comparative Adult Education 1998: the Contribution of ISCAE to an Emerging Field of Study. Ljubljana, Slovenien: Slovenian Institute for Adult Education. P. 97-119. http://www.iscae.org/ISCAE-Book1999.pdf).

UNESCO (1997): CONFINTEA V: The Hamburg Declaration On Adult Learning. https://unesdoc.unesco.org/ark:/48223/pf0000116114

3. Concepts for Adult Learning: "Learning en passant", "lifewide learning", "compositional learning"

"Concepts" are theoretical constructions that focus our perception on certain clusters of observations. They allow us to find meaning in the interpretation of complex, "chaotic" life situations by selecting an overarching perspective, thereby structuring and understanding these situations. Such concepts, as customary in the hermeneutic tradition, work in both directions: approaching reality with an existent concept (as presented in this chapter) can open our eyes to perceive phenomena, that were previously hidden, and by interpreting complex situations we can discover "concepts" that provide meaning and understanding.

3.1 Learning "en passant": The Forgotten Dimension (1986)[1]

Summary

"Lifelong Learning" often has the connotation of "lifelong schooling": an activity planned and organized by specialists for others. In contrast here "lifelong learning" is understood as the description of a continuous life process, including not only formal and self-directed intentional learning, but also unintentional but nevertheless important and effective learning. By focusing on this type of learning this paper seeks to broaden the understanding of learning and asks about the consequences for the theory and practice of Adult Education.

The Position

Adult Education often regards the adult as incomplete, deficient, lacking something. The consequence is that he has to be educated, trained, treated. "Adult educators in Britain have an unnatural appetite for classes and getting people into groups in their centers" (Cann 1984, p. 47) - this describes the position certainly in many countries. Under this perspective, "lifelong learning" is limited to school-like arrangements and becomes a banner and program how "one human being imposes his will, or knowledge, or skill, upon another" (Kidd 1977, p. 13).

The following considerations of adult learning start from a different point of view: from the observation, that all adults already have a universe of knowledge and strategies and values at their disposal that enables them to live their lives in a complex and changing world. No matter which field we take under consideration - profession, family, leisure, time, political, cultural, social behavior, valuing - we will find wide fields of knowledge, abilities, attitudes that are available and clearly do not come from any form of outside organized education. But where else do this knowledge, these skills, and even wisdom come from?

---

[1] Paper presented at the Conference of the American Association of Adult and Continuing Education, Hollywood, Florida, October 23, 1986. Download: http://www.reischmannfam.de/lit/1986-AAACE-Hollywood.pdf

In the seventies, adult education focused on a new concept that views man as a self-directing organism. This new direction, often shortly described "from teaching to learning", was the basis for "self-directed learning", as proposed for example by Knowles, Rogers, Tough, Freire, Illich, Brookfield. But whether "self-directed learning" was understood as a new method within formal education (sometimes supported by a "facilitator" who stimulates, guides, helps), or as a new dimension of learning that happens outside formal settings - still learning was seen as a deliberate, intentional activity. Tough's definition may be an example: "A learning project ... is ... defined as a series of related episodes, adding up to at least seven hours. In each episode, more than half of the person's total motivation is to gain and retain certain fairly clear knowledge and skill, or to produce some other lasting change in himself" (1979, p. 71).

The self-directed learning movement certainly added significant perspectives to the perception and concept of learning. The learner is no longer seen as incompetent, as a person who missed something and should be treated. But also this type of learning can not explain all of the knowledge and skills people have.

Besides these described types of learning in school-like settings and self-directed learning projects there exists another type of permanent, lifelong, daylong learning. I will tentatively call this "learning en passant"; it includes
a) short learning situations,
b) situations where less than half of the person's total motivation is on learning,
c) contents that are not "clear" in the sense that the learner knows in advance
what and how to use it or whether it will produce lasting changes in himself. The French phrase "en passant" is used in German-speaking and other countries as well; it means literally "by passing by". This phrase nicely pictures what the attention should be drawn on in this paper: By actively passing through life people meet all sorts of learning challenges; these educates and transforms them as a way of "becoming a person" (Rogers). The usually used terms "informal, non-formal, non-traditional learning" - certainly necessary for various discriminations - describe with "in-" and "non-" what is not meant. "En passant" pictures positively, that for this learning people have to be active, and that important learning takes place interrelated to other activities, not only in classes but in the "school of life".

Forgotten, hidden

This type of learning is often forgotten - in theory and practice. So even key def-initions of lifelong learning focus only on the intentional, doable, producible part of learning with the activities of planning, preparing, and aiding. So for example Peterson: "Lifelong learning is a conceptual framework for conceiving, planning, implementing, and coordinating activities designed to facilitate learning by all Americans throughout their lifetimes" (1979, p. 5). Or when Patricia Cross states: "Individuals living in today's world must be prepared to make learning a continuing lifelong activity" (1981, p. ix). Kidd describes in the introductory Chapter ("Learning Throughout Life") of "How Adults Learn" learning in an open, comprehensive way: "the learner opens up himself, he stretches himself, he reaches out, he incorporates new experience, he relates it to his previous experience, he reorganizes this experience, he expresses or unfolds what is latent within him." But in the next sentence, he is back to the intended, aided, produced type of learning: "The critical part of the process of teaching-learning is how the learner is aided to embark on this active, growing, changing, painful, or exhilarating experience we call learning" (1978, p. 14). And also Knowles' description of the learning process of adults ([2]1978) includes general learning perspectives but also finishes, how the andragogic teacher, the Human Resources Developer applies the theories to planned and intended learning. All this is good, necessary, helpful, and often appropriate - but it is no everything: A wide and important field of learning is forgotten!

One reason for overlooking this dimension of learning may be that the mainstream of books about Adult Education is written by people who earn their money by making people learn how to make people learn. For this intention, non-manipulatable learning seems of less significance. Another reason may be that this learning is hidden between other activities, unintentionally, without clear objectives and settings. But nevertheless, it happens continuously in life.

Exploring "lifewide learning"

As a first result, it seems important to point out, that "adult learning" and "lifelong learning" not only include intentional learning; it includes as well unintentional, hidden, small-scale, incidental learning (see Figure 1). To make aware of this wide, "universe", the whole life embracing understanding of the learning of adults I will use the expression "lifewide learning":

A method to identify this learning is to "zoom" down onto complex life situations and by this to discover the learning aspects. For example:

Zoom 1: Flying USA

From the Conference Center in San Antonio I step over to McDonalds. Suddenly I stumble over lines in the pavement. There is a map of the USA on the ground - 80 feet wide. I try to find New York and stand there - looking to San Francisco. I cross the continent and read the names of the states. I "fly" back to San Antonio. Other people start smiling at me. I leave the place - wondering about the distances and the states and towns I crossed by plane.

Zoom 2: Remember the Alamo!

I hear that some colleagues in a conference break walk to the Alamo. I have heard the name but I do not know really what it is. I have nothing better to do. So why not the Alamo? I participate in a guided tour, I drop out when I see in a corner a video presentation of actors playing what happened there. I hurry back to the conference but return the next day to visit across the street a slide show (five projectors, beautiful effects, and sound) about the history of the Alamo. On the last day, I visit the gift shop and buy postcards, souvenirs.

Zoom 3: Conference

Conferences are organized for information. But experienced conferences know that the real valuable output comes not from the big lectures, but from what happens "beside": meeting people, job market, and having a good time. Spread in-between are information, experiences, that will be useful for more efficient behavior in the future (= "learning"): A useful book or problem solutions in other projects are discovered, helpful persons, institutions, telephone numbers are found, short discussions between chips and dips help to clarify specific questions, and - most important - "zero helpers" are identified: Great names without experience, specialists unable to deal with practical problems, books, media, programs not worth the material they are made of. So there is significant information not coming from the educational main-program but happens "en passant" - from sunrise to sunset (and after), highly specific, individualized, and everybody can handle that.

Zoom 4: Pearl Harbour

To be honest: When landing in Honolulu I even did not know that Pearl Harbour is located on the Hawaiian Islands. It was just a name I had heard in some history lessons. So my motivation to visit Pearl Harbour war rather extrinsic: #1 - A tourist has to visit specific landmarks. #2 - People at home looking at my slides would be impressed. #3 - As a well-educated person you must not leave out such historical places. Again I was surprised to zoom easily on learning: I found a museum with pictures, models, descriptions, objects. An impressive 20-minute movie with historical background information overcame the disadvantage of most historical places: that not much of the event is to be seen. A boat then takes us over to the US Arizona memorial. People became quiet and I felt my heart when we stood before the marble wall with more than a thousand names killed her. On the way back I buy in the bookshop a reprint of the Honolulu Star from December 12, 1942, with the headline: "War!"

Zoom 5: Cannery-Street

Two attractive Hostesses wait for us in the entrance hall of Dole Pineapple Factory for the guided tour. Everything is well organized: At first, everybody gets a brochure with pictures and explanations. Then we are guided between two lines on the ground through the factory. Posters give information, in addition to the hostess. And of course, pineapple slices are offered to test.

Zoom 6:Grand - this Canyon

We - eleven of my students of Adult Education and me - came just as tourists: without any learning intention. "Every word and picture ever made about the Grand Canyon is an understatement" - the truth of this word out of a tourist brochure was stamped in our hearts the very first moment at the rim. But walking and looking there we found well-prepared learning opportunities: The museum where we bought the postcards offered models, presented videotapes, and sold information brochures. The rangers gave short explanations and answered questions. And at several places information was available on signposts - "en passant".

It would be interesting to analyze each of the zooms in detail to find out what was learned and how this learning happened. Because of space reasons and because it may be more effective when the reader tries this himself I make a shortcut to general characteristics of this type of learning.

General Characteristics

These zooms illustrate general aspects of "learning en passant":

They make aware, that coping with life situations is always included, life-integrated. They show that this learning is low compulsory and highly individualized: it can happen - or not, and different people learn different things from the same situation. This type of learning cannot be produced in advance; there is nothing like a prepared curriculum; it only can be identified by looking back. Often this learning is holistic; it includes not only knowledge but also reality-handling, emotions, valuing. By being integrated into reasonable activities it is meaningful and useful in itself, which means that it is not only stored for later use. It is successful without much effort (with increasing explicit effort we move over by definition to self-directed or formal learning). It uses a wide variety of support (people, media, objects, institutions), educationally prepared as well as natural. Often it uses and continues and reactivates and builds on previous learning. The level of threat, stress, and frustration is mostly low, or even a feeling of success, interest, or thrill can be observed. This learning teaches answers as well as it opens questions when incorporating it into the set of experiences the person already has. All these situations can be used as a basis for further learning. And they can be a starting point for intentional learning.

Typology

The zooms also illustrate different types of unintentional learning:

Special activity learning (planned, but learning not main purpose):
Sometimes learning en passant can happen parallel or in addition to other planned and intended activities (visiting a museum, taking a tourist trip, participating in a cultural, political, social activity). These activities are more or less planned, intended, organized. Anyhow, by these activities, new information is found - more or less inevitable. The primary motivation is not to gain knowledge, but perhaps curiosity, or entertainment. In these situations, it is not clear in advance that something will be learned or what will be learned. So often the main reason is perceived, but the learning segment remains hidden.

Single event learning (happening):
Sometimes learning is initiated by a clearly describable event (i.e. zoom 1, or car accident). By an outside event, not planned and not expected, something happens that makes old experiences obsolete and brings new perspectives into deliberation. These change-triggering situations can be accompanied with shock

as well as pleasure, the changes can be minimal to dramatic, the coping time can be seconds to years. But the triggering situation will, later on, be clearly identifiable.

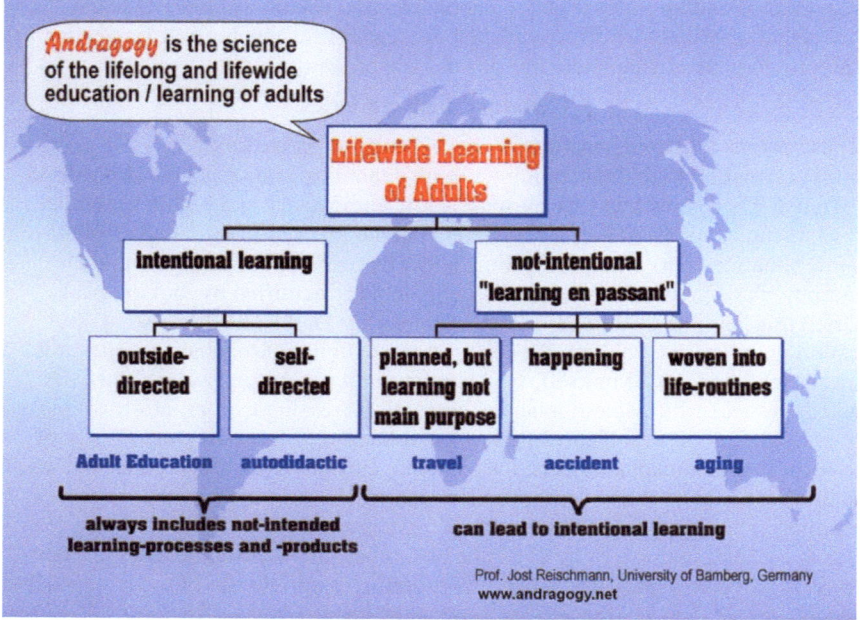

Figure 1: Fields of Lifewide Learning

Mosaic stone Learning (woven into life-routines):

All long-term competencies in the professions, family, and other fields are composed of numberless learning events. Reading books, magazines, newspapers, watching TV, talking to colleagues, observing others, and exchanging with whomsoever, form a universe of small-scale learning experiences up to the gestalt and character and competency a person has available, represents, identifies with. Here we face the result of the wholeness of lifelong learning. The picture of a mosaic is appropriate in the sense that an endless series of learning has formed up the whole image. It makes clear, that these stones do not swing around in random chaos but are incorporated and organized into a gestalt. This picture is not appropriate in the sense of a fix-pre-planned or finishable task; on each stage it is all well finished as open for growth and change.

Consequences for Adult Education

The consequence definitely is not to leave out intentional learning in adult education: there is no doubt that learning "en passant" never would be sufficient to fulfill all learning needs. On the other side, we should not overstress the necessity of intentional learning of adults in our society: A great portion of our adult population never uses formal courses, and also the descriptions of self-directed learning projects often sound nearer to "learning en passant" than to deliberate learning efforts. And even if professional adult educators do not like that truth: There are no clear indicators that prove that those persons using adult education live a life that is more round, satisfying, and fulfilling than those who do not.

1. Here I see the first consequence for adult education: to face the reality, that all people learn lifelong - with or without educators and programs.
2. This consequence includes another: We have to widen our concept of learning. Learning is not only an activity related to specific educational enterprises but is a life strategy (such as eating and breathing) that enables men to survive as individuals as well as a species.
3. In consequence "lifelong learning" should not be used as an activist banner for getting people into classes. It should be used to describe the all-encompassing process of learning, not to justify a program.
   All professions tend to limit their field to phenomena they can manipulate, and by this mechanism they leave out the "full life". This is helpful for the professionals - it makes them important, necessary, admired. But by this, they make their clients dependent on them and spoil their natural ability to cope with their lives themselves. This sort of professionalism is not helpful for the clients.
4. So professionals in adult education should be aware of this unintended learning and decide thoroughly, what in a given situation would be the best for a learner: to do something, or perhaps to do nothing, or whatever in-between.
5. That also prevents the "guru"-role, to play the big magician, who is expected to make elephants fly - which leads directly to hybrids and burnout. To accept that learning is their business, and knowing that basically they can cope with that business clearly separates the responsibilities and helps to avoid the helper-syndrome.
6. To study unintentional, "en passant"-learning (in a simple introspective way like in the zooms, or in a highly elaborate way like in biographic research) seems to be a great help to move students into the field of adult education. It offers a fresh approach to the field that is not deformed or perforated by our school learning experiences. This approach raises the sensibility for and perception of learning and offers a wider range of understanding and interventions.

And here I am at the connection to intentional learning and learning/teaching. As here there is not the space to deal with that in-depth I will focus only on one general aspect: Reflecting on this wide concept of learning helps adult educators also in formal settings to leave away the professional blinders that again and again focus our attention on the teaching activity, by which even "self-directed learning" can be misused as a tricky way to impose our will, or knowledge, or skill, upon others.

When we observe thoroughly, with open eyes, and hearts, the learning of our learners, this will lead us to a really grown-up, "adult" education. This is nothing else but a consequent going into the direction we encounter in the development of adult education in the past two decades - "from teaching to learning".

References:

Cann, Roger J.(1984). Incidental learning. *Adult Education*, 57(3), 47-49.

Cross, Patricia (1981). *Adults as Learners*. San Francisco, CA: Jossey-Bass.

Freire, Paulo ([2]1972). *Pädagogik der Unterdrückten*. Stuttgart: Kreuz Verlag.

Illich, Ivan (1973*). Entschulung der Gesellschaft. Entwurf eines demokratischen Bildungssystems*. Reinbek: Rowohlt.

Kidd, Roby (1977). *How Adults Learn*. Englewood Cliffs, NJ: Prentice-Hall.

Knowles, Malcolm S.(1978). *The Adult Learner* (2nd ed). Houston, TX: Gulf.

Knowles, Malcolm S. (1975). *Self-Directed Learning. A Guide for Learners and Teachers*. Chicago: Follet.

Peterson, Richard E. & Ass (1979). *Lifelong Learning in America*. San Francisco: Jossey-Bass.

Rogers, Carl R. (1969). *Freedom to Learn*. Columbus/Ohio: Charles E. Merill Publishing Co.

Tough, Allen ([2]1979). *The Adult's Learning Projects. A fresh approach to theory and practice in adult learning*. Ontario: Ontario Institute for Studies in Education.

Comment 2004:

In the meantime critics came up, criticizing that the "boxes" (Fig.1), side by side, give a wrong, separating impression. I fully agree: In the reality of adults lifewide learning the combinations and overlapping are most important to perceive and to work with; it seems that the bottom lines of figure 1, where I thought to give an idea about the overlapping and combinations, do not clearly enough point that out. So in addition to "learning en passant", I use today the phrase "compositional learning" to make aware that learners themselves compose many sources together when going through a learning experience: Reading books, talking to friends, watching television, exchanging with experts in hardware shops or pharmacies, starting trial and error, participating in the local adult education offerings, google, talk to their children …

More details in: Reischmann, Jost (2004): Vom „Lernen en passant" zum „kompositionellen Lernen". Untersuchung entgrenzter Lernformen. In: *Grundlagen der Weiterbildung - Zeitschrift*. 15. Jg., H. 2, S. 92-95.

Appendix 2012: Interestingly in 2012 these ideas and the term were used and developed by:

Jackson, Norman J. (2012): Lifewide Learning: History of an idea. In: Jackson, Norman J. (ed): The Lifewide Learning, Education & Personal Development e-book. P. 1-30. *http://www.lifewideebook.co.uk/conceptual.html*, http://www.lifewideeducation.com/uploads/1/0/8/4/10842717/chapter_15.pdf

The idea and concept of lifelong and lifewide learning, initially introduced in 1986 (see 3.1 in this book), turned out to stay a leading paradigm in my professional development. Therefore, the following contribution partly repeats what I had published already in the 1986-paper. Now, however, it extends further; grounded in the observation of a generation of graduates, it has experienced evidence beyond theoretical reflections: It examines the practical value of these concepts - along the new concept of "compositional learning" - for the training and the workplaces of andragogues. Furthermore, it claims a new understanding of the identity of andragogy and andragogues.

3.2 Lifewide Learning - Challenges for Andragogy (2017)[1]

1. Societies in change

Companies are more and more aware that to keep and develop a competent and engaged workforce and to avoid de-qualification and conflicts specialists are needed. Institutions not only need these specialists for their own workforce but as well for high-quality customer-relations. *Democratic politics* discover how important it is to include citizens into decisions and to develop peaceful and respectful citizenship. *Cultural, religious, or social groups* recognize the vital need to deal sensitively with their target-groups. A "society in change" needs experts and professionals, to support change and learning in manifold ways. Andragogy and Andragogues could be a helpful part of these lifelong and lifewide change processes.

1.1 Lifelong learning

Formal adult education has become the first answer to the learning needs of adults in general as well as in workplace learning. The concept of "lifelong learning" (in Europe first discussed with the French phrase "education permanente") described in the beginning (and often nowadays again) the idea, that adults should attend throughout lifetime formal educational programs.

The positive aspect of this concept was the new awareness that adults are able to learn even at a higher age - self-evident for most of us today. For Hungary Fodor states: "By 2007, there were about three times as many people enrolled in adult education as in 1995" (Fodor 2015, p. 79). In Germany, 51% of the adults participated in 2014 in adult education (AES 2014, p. 4). It still can be puzzling that within one generation the perception of adulthood overcame the old saying "You can not teach an old dog new tricks", in German "Was Hänschen nicht lernt, lernt Hans nimmermehr" (What Jacky has not learned,

---

[1] First print: Reischmann, Jost (2017): Lifewide Learning - Challenges for Andragogy. In: *Journal of Adult Learning, Knowledge and Innovation* (Budapest) 1(1), p. 43-50 (2017). DOI: 10.1556/2059.01.2017.2

Jack will never learn). Also positive was: Money became available to offer and organize adult education, through governments, companies, and other sources.

The negative aspect was: Learning in this understanding depended - because limited to formal educational offers - from teaching and institutions[1]. This was criticized pretty early: Robby Kidd, Canadian scholar of adult education, warned already 1977 that limiting lifelong learning to school-like arrangements makes it a program how "one human being imposes his will, or knowledge, or skill, upon another" (Kidd 1977, p. 13). And Cann (Great Britain) argued in 1984: "Adult educators in Britain have an unnatural appetite for classes and getting people into groups in their centers" (Cann 1984, p. 47). Adult Education in this perspective regards the adult as incomplete, deficient, or lacking something. The consequence is that he has to be educated, trained, treated.

1.2 What is "lifewide learning"?

In contrast to this view the concept of "lifewide learning" refers to the fact, that adults learn throughout life, every minute, through a composition of learning sources, situations, and occasions, ranging from outside planned circumstances to things happening in life, teaching us wanted or unwanted lessons. This learning shows clear results: Adults have knowledge and strategies and values at their disposal that enable them to live their lives - sometimes better, sometimes worse - in a complex and changing world. By actively passing through life humans meet all sorts of learning challenges; these educates and transforms them, forming their unique personality and identity. Most of this learning results not from outside organized, formal education: No matter which field we take under consideration - profession, family, leisure, time, political, cultural, social behavior, valuing - we find wide fields of knowledge, abilities, attitudes, valuing adults have available and clearly do not come from any form of outside organized, formal education.

Understanding adult learning in this wider sense covers the entire range of formal, non-formal, and informal learning activities – both general and vocational – undertaken by adults after leaving initial education and training.

---

[1] In contrast to the rich and complex understanding politics and economy narrowed "lifelong learning" often even more down to market- and company-centred formal continuous retraining of the workforce. Hake (2008) analysed a UNESCO-study "Making Lifelong Learning a Reality: Emerging Patterns in Europe and Asia" (2002), including case studies from Australia, China, France, Japan, South Korea, Malaysia, Norway, Sweden, Thailand, and the United Kingdom. He found overwhelming statements that paralleled lifelong learning with employment-related activities; this "lead to the conclusion that the prevailing policy narratives in a range of Asian and European countries constitute a dominant discourse of 'learning to acquire employability', or what has been referred to as the 'learning for earning' narrative" (p. 176). Of course learning in and for workplaces and better productivity is important (and the largest sector of adult learning), but other fields of adult learning should be valued as well.

This broad understanding of "lifewide learning" of adults can be structured in a scheme that includes two types of intentional learning (outside-directed by institutions and self-directed/autodidactic), as well as three types of partly intentional and unintentional learning that occurs simultaneously with activities not primarily aimed at learning. The terms usually used for this part are "informal, non-formal, non-traditional"; describing pretty helpless with "in-" and "non-" what is not meant. UNESCO (1997) even more vaguely used the term "otherwise" by understanding adult education as the "entire body of ongoing learning processes, formal or *otherwise*, whereby people … develop their abilities, enrich their knowledge, and improve their technical or professional qualifications or turn them in a new direction to meet their own needs and those of their society'. To describe these unintentional learning situations I use the term "learning en passant" (= "by passing by"). This describes positively, that for these here-and-now learning challenges, people have to be active, and that important learning takes place connected to other activities in the "school of life", not only in intended learning/teaching situations.

I discriminate three different types of "learning en passant": [see graphic on page 54]

- Learning en passant can happen *parallel to other planned and intended activities* (visiting a museum, taking a tourist trip, participating in a cultural, political, or social activity). The primary motivation is not to gain knowledge, but perhaps entertainment, doing business, or curiosity. Parallel to these activities new information and insight are found. In these situations, it is not clear in advance that something will be learned or what will be learned. The main activity is perceived, but the learning segment remains hidden.
- *Single event learning (= "happening"):* Sometimes learning is initiated by an explicit life situation that forces us to learn (i.g. an accident, death of a relative, falling in love, or getting a traffic-ticket). An outside event happens, not planned and not expected, making old experiences obsolete and bringing new perspectives into deliberation. These change-triggering situations can be accompanied by shock as well as by pleasure, the changes can be minimal to dramatic, the coping time can be seconds to years. The level of threat, stress, and frustration might be low, even a feeling of success, interest, and thrill can be observed. But it also might be highly painful, and people may wish they never had to learn that lesson. But the triggering situation will later on be clearly remembered.
- *Mosaicstone learning-outcomes, woven into life-routines* resulting from various unidentifiable life-events: We observe that a person knows or is able to do something or behaves in a certain way (e.g. aging, behaving as parents, leading a group), but we can not identify the situation when it was learned.

Long-term complex competencies in profession, family, and other fields are composed of numberless learning events, while the learning events leading to this remain often not identifiable. Reading books, magazines, newspapers, watching TV, talking to colleagues, observing others, and exchanging with whomsoever forms a universe of small-scale learning experiences up to the gestalt, character, and competencies a person finally represents. The picture of a mosaic is appropriate in the sense that an endless series of learning has formed the whole image. These mosaicstones do not swing around in random chaos but are incorporated and organized into a gestalt.

"Learning en passant" in its different shapes makes us aware that in coping with life-situations learning is always included, life-integrated. Some general aspects of this learning are:

- "Learning en passant" is low compulsory and highly individualized.
- Different people learn different things from the same situation; there is nothing like a prepared curriculum.
- Often this learning includes not only knowledge but also reality-handling, emotions, valuing, perspective transformation (holistic).
- By being integrated into life-near activities it is meaningful and useful, it is not only stored for "later" use.
- It can be successful without much effort (with increasing explicit effort we move by definition over to self-directed or formal learning).
- It uses a wide variety of support (people, media, objects, institutions), educationally prepared as well as natural.
- Often it uses and continues and re-activates and builds on previous learning, and can be a starting point for intentional learning.
- This learning teaches answers as well as opens questions when incorporating it into the set of experiences the person has already had.
- These changes can be open and immediate; they can also be hidden and become visible much later.
- This learning encompasses the whole person, develops the person to his individual "form", and leads to a unique "composition".
- In this way, each individual forms himself based on his ongoing life in each minute.

This forming is not only important for private enrichment but also for workplaces and staff development in companies. In two directions: 1. New knowledge and working techniques are to a high degree learned (or not) in the daily work through supervisors, colleagues, handbooks, trial-and-error, etc. 2. Perhaps even more important: Attitudes like responsibility, initiative, identification with the company, "company-culture" grow through daily "learning en passant". But a warning: This daily "learning en passant" can not only grow into a productive direction, it can as well lead to an expensive and profit-draining "I-do-not-care-about-the-company"-attitude. Andragogues (see chapter 2 and 3) can engage here in an essential way.

1.2.1 "compositional learning"

The disadvantage of a graphical structure as above [p. 54] is that it seems to suggest that the different "boxes" are separated and independent. But that is not the reality: Learners compose many sources during a learning experience: Intentional learning by participating in the local adult education institution or self-directed learning, as well as combinations with different forms of learning en passant - trial and error, some help of a friend, reading a book/journal, watching television, exchanging with experts in hardware shops or pharmacies, "google-ing", or talking to their children - the list is endless. Adults compose their knowledge, valuing, and personality through many different sources and connecting, combining and integrating them in ways that are meaningful to them; this may be characterized by the term "compositional learning". The different "boxes" in the above structural scheme of adult learning and education open a deeper understanding of learning in adulthood; but even important are the interactions between the "boxes" - how they are "composed".

One of the main differences between traditional children's school learning and the learning of adults is that adult learning is mostly related to direct and "immediate" use in concrete situations within the context of their life. These life situations do not start or end within an organized learning program in an institution but have many more motivators, supporters, testers, threads, reinforcement, control, informators, criticisers, training situations, correctors that are scattered through different life situations. They together compose the individual learning biography.

1.2.2 Warning

But there has also to be a warning: Certainly, it sounds like a romantic idea that all adults are lifelong and lifewide compositional learners. But this learning has also dangers, limits, and weaknesses.

For example: This learning happens - or not - by chance, by luck, or by contingency; it is not a reliable learning. The results are greatly individualized without standards and comparability in a group. Scope, content, dimension, and quality are highly dependent on the individual learner. No help is available if learning problems come up, if a learner goes in the wrong direction, if he/she misunderstands things and/or learns false things. In all these cases nobody helps with feedback and advice.

Even worse: There is not only the danger of "not learning" or learning false things, but also negative, evil things are learned en passant: political fanaticism, sexism and discrimination, religious fundamentalism, political correctness, hopelessness and resignation, that lying and stealing are acceptable. Tóth describes this in dramatic words: "Citizens have learned... informally ...

behaviour modes, which ... mean hiding, adjustment, lip-service, withdrawal from public life, and the maxims of faked conformity. What is characteristic is distrust, the absence of interest, apathy and retreat into the private sphere" (Tóth 2015, p. 41)! For companies and society, these negative learning results have dramatic consequences!

The composition a person makes out of the en-passant-experiences can not only support but also hinder a good development. Like in music composition, there are virtuoso as well as foul results.

1.3 Summary

The theory of lifewide learning makes us aware, that intentional learning in adult education institutions or self-directed learning is only a segment of the learning and education of adults. Learning of adults happens in every moment of life, intentional and en passant, not only lifelong, but also *lifewide* in a multitude of traditional and nontraditional, formal and informal settings (workplaces, leisure-time, families, churches, market-places, television, „the life" ...). This composition of learning experiences can enrich a person and lead to a helpful basis for further knowledge, abilities, and values, but can also lead to limiting and dangerous outcomes. The concept of lifewide learning allows one to perceive and use manifold learning sources and opportunities. It also helps to understand how blocking or negative learning results were learned en passant, and how they might be reduced, avoided, or healed. A British initiative is an example of how lifewide learning can be developed and supported (http://lifewideeducation.co.uk/home).

2. Andragogy and the practical value of the concept of "lifewide learning"

As is the case often in pedagogical innovations this new theory developed in interaction with observations in the practical field. Not a linear deduction leads from theory to praxis, but a circular relationship enriches both theory and praxis: We observe something, we start reflecting on the observation, these reflections lead to new observations, and this again to new reflections etc. This circular relationship will be illustrated in the following when reporting on practical experiences in our Andragogy program at Bamberg University, Germany (http://www.reischmannfam.de/andra-album/Startseite.htm).

2.1 Andragogy vs. Adult Education

Andragogy is the educational discipline, the subject of which is the study of lifelong and lifewide adult learning and education; it includes "education and learning of adults in all its forms of expression" (Savicevic 1999, p. 97) (more details see Reischmann 2004: Andragogy. History, Meaning, Context, Function. http://www.andragogy.net).

In many countries, this term is not or very limited in use (for example Germany and the USA). But using "adult education" for two different things - the field of academic theory/research and the field of praxis - starts confusion, misunderstandings, and irritation. "Adult Educator" is a very unclear term. It includes a wide variety of species: the grandma sharing her knowledge of baking cookies, the engineer instructing his staff about new technology, the political or religious missionary preaching at the marketplace (today: on television) about the true and only life or society – just "everybody" can be an "Adult Educator". The case studies presented at two Conferences on the History of Adult Education (6th and 11th Standing Conference, Jena, Germany 1996 and Bamberg, Germany 2006) illustrate that variety of understandings - from scholar to "the wise", from academic specialist to "everybody" [see 2.2 in his book].

This unclear borderless term "Adult Educator" makes it difficult to discriminate professional academic educated staff - graduates of university-programs – from "everybody". The everybody-term "Adult Educator" is destructive for the specific role and perception of the academic discipline and its graduates. No wonder that professional academic graduates are missing a feeling of unity or identity in many countries - as Kleisz states for Hungary: "The younger and trained generation does not feel the unity of profession" (Kleisz 2015, p. 22).

So as a first step it is suggested: Scholars in this academic field should feel challenged to explicitly clarify and grow an own, proud, and strong identity. The terms Andragogy and Andragogue should be used to describe and guarantee quality standards, to claim academic theory and research, and especially offer a unique and specific "label" on the labour-market[1].

The terms "adult education, continuing education" of course still make sense and will be used. But now they are connected more precisely and following the everyday-understanding of the fields of practice - in contrast to the academic field.

But a discriminating label alone is not enough. More is needed to build an identity.

2.2 What does "lifewide learning" mean to Andragogy?

At first, it seemed that the theory of "lifewide learning" did not have much practical value. If learning happens unplanned in time, content, sequence, and extent, how could schoolmasters make a practical value out of it? Even worse:

---

[1] Our graduates reported that the specific label "Andragoge" indeed was helpful on the labour-market for employment: It made the employers curious to invite them for interviews, and gave the chance to describe what they had to offer. In many cases, this led to employment.

This opening of the perspective had the danger that the concept of Andragogy became even more confused and borderless.

The opposite turned out to be true: Through this new theory, but as well through the experiences of our graduates (Reischmann 2010) a *first mistake* became evident: Andragogues are not (only) teachers for adults!

Starting from the belief that our task was to educate teachers for adults, the experiences of our program around 1995 were shocking: We asked our students some years after graduation: "What is your workplace now after graduation?" The shocking answer was: Only a small portion (10-30%) was employed in a teaching position at an adult education institution - most of the "adult educators" did not teach! About 30% work in industry, business, and organization in the field of staff development, 20-30% of our graduates work as freelanced workers ("Training, development, counseling/consultancy"), about 10-20% have a career at colleges/universities (Bender et al. 2008), the rest reported workplaces in manifold institutions and functions. Other programs at other universities reported similar results. Horror: Did we educate our students for unemployment or cab-driving?

This "horror" gladly could be disproved by another result of our and other's research: The graduates overwhelmingly reported they had no problem finding a well-paid workplace, are happy with their employment, and feel that the study of Andragogy prepared them well for their specific workplaces!

It seems that for andragogues the perception of the lifewide (positive or negative) learning processes and results opened a new approach of the new discipline of Andragogy and to the whole world of learning of individuals and of institutions. Vice versa: Many institutions start to have an idea that they need specialists for complex change processes - especially when they experienced professional work by an andragogue. School-like activities ("teaching") now are only one segment of the field.

The mistake of thinking that andragogues are solely teachers for adults is widespread in amateurs making a judgment about this academic discipline: politicians, university-presidents, presidents of Chambers of Commerce and Industry (see Kleisz 2015, p. 19!), not knowing that in their institutions already a considerable number of andragogues do valuable work. Typical: "The lifelong learning strategy of Hungary for future years only consider 'teachers' as the reliable key personnel in this area" (Kleisz 2015, p. 21). "Adult educators" (teaching often just by intuition, sometimes with some educational training) may be teachers, but andragogues are much more.

The more the role of andragogues developed away from "schoolmaster" to "learning helper, facilitator, moderator, mediator, conflict solver, consultant, social engineer, change agent" the more it was perceived that these newly discovered theoretical concepts of adult learning and education offered new chances for practical activities of andragogues - in manifold settings, institutions, and well-paid workplaces.

2.3 Workplaces of Andragogy-graduates

The roles and positions our graduates took over after finishing their studies puzzled us. As described the majority of our graduates were not teaching in adult education institutions: They work in business and industry, politics and churches, hospitals, museums, charities, tourism, cultural institutions, and media, as freelance workers in their own "training and consulting businesses"[1], they moderate and coach, manage and solve problems, help to identify and solve conflicts and problems, help to find visions and directions - and sometimes do some teaching.

When asking for the name of their profession we still got a vast and confusing variety of descriptions: Teacher, trainer, evaluator, coach, moderator, HRD-employee, personal or organizational developer, employee or head of learning-institution, manager, administrator, journalist, and many others. In all these cases our graduates told us: "But I am also doing ..." - it seems most of these workplaces require a variety of competencies (more in chapter 3) to react as flexible as needed.

This leads to a *second mistake* when discussing Andragogy: the bureaucratic thinking that Andragogues are limited to one segment of the field (which could be social change, or second chance/compensatory education, or community education, or political education, or cultural capital, or human resource development, or 'learning to acquire employability', or minority education - just to name some). Depending on the money-giver and power position one segment is in an oversimplified way claimed to be the total, and the others are either not seen or not valued.

Carroll Londoner, past chair of the International Adult Education Hall of Fame[2] outlines this problem for the USA (private mail Jan. 31, 2014): "The Adult Education programs in the States have shrunk dramatically as the Universities do not seem inclined to support adult education because they do not understand it. They have too quickly identified the broad field of adult education with the notion of 'adult literacy' ... We in the universities have not done a very good job of explaining to our administrators what the broad field is about and why it should be studied academically".

It is a mistake to perceive and value just one segment as the only legitimate field for andragogues. So a next insight has to be: The study of Andragogy

---

[1] These freelanced andragogues could make available training, development, and
      consulting to small and midsize companies or institutions that could not hire full-timers.

[2] http://www.halloffame.outreach.ou.edu

opens the doors to a growing number of workplaces, in different institutions, in different functions.

2.4 Summary

It is not a weakness, that Andragogues can be found in a wide variety of settings; it is a *strength of Andragogy* that the graduates of our programs work successfully in the complexity of lifewide adult learning. For those whose thinking is limited to clear-cut images, this complexity seems chaos, while - when being able to complex thinking - this, in reality, is richness, flexibility, and future. When "potential users are still confused as to what to expect from these professions", when "Deficits in a clear-cut image of these professions do not help actors in the professions to identify with them" (Kleisz 2015, p. 21), then it is an important task of the professors of Andragogy to point out that the complexity of the andragogical field demands complex, not "clear-cut" answers. Andragogy (like many other professions) relates to a world, where professional acting can not be allocated to clear-cut work-places - not today, even less in ten years from now. Expecting a clear-cut correlation (= studied subject A, entering workplace A' for the rest of life) is a *third mistake* of those not understanding the reality of workplaces today: that functions, tasks, positions, challenges, and needs change in short years. The task of Universities is to prepare for the future. That makes Andragogy so valuable, but also challenges traditional expectations.

And for those who need a clear-cut image: There exists a unifying idea/ concept of all these andragogical workplaces: They organize, manage, inform, mediate, moderate, motivate, and interfere in tensions, conflicts, friction between
- people and people or
- people and organizations or
- people and things.

The concept of "lifewide learning", "learning en passant", "compositional learning" opened the perception for far more learning situations that could be worked on with andragogical interventions than just "teaching-learning". Perhaps the term "change agent", sometimes used in the USA, describes best the competence our graduates offer.

3. Competencies of Andragogues

It is easy to claim that andragogues are professional "change agents" in the broad field of lifewide learning. But what are the competencies needed for this role, and how can students be trained for these tasks?

"Competencies" in our understanding includes both
- the ability to perform and
- to reflect why and for what reason something is done.

Like in other professional fields (e.g. medicine or architecture), it is not enough that students gain theoretical knowledge, they also must learn to perform to a basic extent in the field ("Reflexionskompetenz und Handlungskompetenz").

The described experiences, the feedback we received from our graduates[1], and many exchanges in International conferences and meetings let us define four competencies andragogues are expected to master:

- First, it is expected that an andragogue is able to teach.
- Second, they must be able to plan and organize programs and measures.
- Third, they need the ability to consult and counsel.
- And finally, they must be able to do evaluation and research.

Certainly, there are many ways how these competencies can be learned. We decided to develop for our students a series of "Competency-classes" (Kompetenzseminare) to train them to perform in these four fields. These competency-based classes usually last three full days, filled with acting, training, trying, and demonstrating; with not more than 20 participants. The three days are theory-reduced and focus on performance. Of course, these competency-based classes only make sense in combination with the "normal" knowledge- and theory-oriented classes, lectures, and readings. Performance has to be melted in and interwoven with knowing and understanding to lead to competency.

3a. Trainer/Teacher

The first expectation of "adult educators" is that they teach – in adult education institutions or in companies and businesses (HRD – Human Resource Development). We found that teaching often was a starting point for our graduates, but that after a short while they moved up into a supervising position. However, even in this position it is expected that they can convincingly "teach" and advice others how to teach ("Train the Trainer").

Fig. 1: Competences for andragogy-students

---

[1]   An important source of information about the workplaces and functions of our graduates was an annual alumni-meeting. Graduates and students were invited for reporting, exchange and presentations.

A first module in this competency is *"Visualising, Presentation, Moderation"*. Here, students learn to stand in front of a group, design presentation-material, work with an auditory, present learning material, and interact with groups. In a second module, they learn how to *design classes and seminars*. A third module develops *communication-skills*. These competencies are supplemented by a traditional lecture and seminar in "didactics".

3b. Planning /Organizing

The success of an educational program does not only derive from the quality of teaching (micro-didactics), but also from the learning-supportive planning and organizing of the program (macro-didactics). The module *"program-planning"* supplies planning/organizing strategies under the perspective: How can learning be started and supported by organizational measures? This does not only relate to school-like settings but includes under the aspect of "lifewide learning" the challenge of how learning occasions can be identified and supported in workplaces, cultural institutions, hospitals, tourist places etc.. An important role for this competency plays the *internship* each of our students has to go through.

3c. Moderator - Counsellor - Consultant - Mediator – Coach

A shared observation in adult education programs is: After the teaching sessions, teachers and learners often meet for a coffee or a beer. And then the "real" questions come up … This observation opened the insight into a new role

Fig. 2: Group training in moderation techniques

of andragogues: not presenting/transporting knowledge (teaching), but helping persons or groups to find their way.

"*Communication skills*" is a module in this competency – and overlaps with the teaching/training-competency. This overlapping of modules and traditional seminars is important: It allows repetitions and insight in interrelations. The competency class "*moderation-techniques*" too overlaps with the teaching module. In the competency seminar "*consulting-strategies and -techniques*", our students learn a "new language", and in all these classes they learn a new approach and understanding to the problems of people and institutions.

"*Coaching*" [see 4.2 in this book] is a competency class addressing the widespread problem that most teachers in adult and continuing education are subject matter specialists teaching with limited educational/andragogical ability. This restricts the effect of instruction (knowledge, transfer, application) and gives away the chance to develop company culture

Fig. 3: Communication-Training

and "soft skills". We developed a concept in which the subject matter specialist is supported before, during and after the course by an andragogue. This competency-training builds on the prior training in seminar-design and communication-skills.

3d. Research, Evaluation

The ability to do research is not only expected from scholars and members of research–organizations, but also in the practical work in adult and continuing education for needs-assessment, evaluation, and quality control, planning of programs and feedback to organizers and boards.

Research classes are always included in the normal curriculum of social science students, mostly in the beginning semesters. What we changed: We added one class about *quantitative and one about qualitative research* in the final semesters of the study - the time when students have to prepare their thesis. This relates research work to a "real" research question, to a practical application and performance. To support this competence, we offer a *research colloquium* where students present and discuss their research work and *individual consulting*.

3e. Summary

One clear observation in the last three decades is that the working-fields of andragogues have become diversified and reached new horizons. Change experts are needed who can practically perform and theoretically reflect, have the competencies to professionally teach, plan and organize learning, consult and moderate, evaluate and research – and produce the most successful mix of these ingredients. This has to be considered in the curriculum of andragogical degrees.

4. Perspective for theory and practice

Adult Learning and Education is nowadays perceived much wider and much more important than 20 years ago: for economic prosperity, for the environment, for social expenditures, for enriching personal life, for peaceful and respectful citizenship. UNESCO stated in the Hamburg-Declaration 1997 (paragraph 2): "Adult education becomes more than a right; it is a key to the twenty-first century. It is both a consequence of active citizenship and a condition for full participation in society. It is a powerful concept for fostering ecologically sustainable development, for promoting democracy, justice, gender equity, and scientific, social and economic development, and for building a world in which violent conflict is replaced by dialogue and a culture of peace based on justice. Adult learning can shape identity and give meaning to life."

Adult Educators are needed on all levers and in all fields: the volunteers, the partly paid part-timers, the fully employed subject-matter-specialists, the organizers and administrators and teachers. But it also became clear that for the multifold and complex challenges of a "society in change" professional experts are needed to support change and learning successfully: Andragogues.

This new and widened learning-perspective has consequences for the theory and practice of Andragogy:
- Andragogy as the academic discipline dealing with the lifelong and lifewide learning and education of adults has to perceive, research, and support the multifold learning situations in the life of adults and develop theories that

give a deeper insight into the challenge of change processes in the life of adults. In addition, students have to be supplied with competencies that allow them to perform as professionals in the practical field.

- Institutions and professionals have for their practical work now a much wider pallet of competencies and interaction to identify, use, and support learning processes in change situations. But much more has to be done to learn about this pallet, to develop more strategies, to exchange what has been developed, and to collect experience of what composition of activities are most successful in which situations.

Andragogues - as described - are more than teachers. And their work-perspective is much wider than educational institutions: everywhere where change happens. Under this perspective, the number of different fields where andragogues work is not confusing. *The identity of andragogues is not defined by specific institutions or one single function; it is defined by complex understanding and performing of "supporting change". This understanding of Andragogy and "lifewide learning" and the resulting tasks can contribute to a unifying identity of professional andragogues.*

The future will confirm how important this work is to make "adult learning: a joy, a tool, a right and a shared responsibility" (UNESCO 1997).

Bibliography

6th (1996) and 11th (2006) Standing Conference on the History of Adult Education: Friedenthal-Haase, Martha (ed.) (1998): Personality and Biography in the History of Adult Education. Vol. I and II. Jena, Germany: Peter Lang Publ. Reischmann, Jost (ed.) (2006): "On Becoming an Adult Educator - historical and contemporary aspects". Bamberg, Germany: Bamberg-Univ. http://conference2006.andragogy.net/

AES (Adult Education Survey) (2014): Weiterbildungsverhalten in Deutschland 2014. Bundesministerium für Bildung und Forschung (BMBF) Bonn, Germany (ed). https://www.bmbf.de/pub/Weiterbildungsverhalten_in_Deutschland_2014.pdf.

Bender, Walter/ Emmert, Kerstin/ Gröne, Susanne/ Heglmeier, Helga / Jäger, Mathias/ Lerch, Sebastian (ed.) (2008): Die Bamberger Andragogik. Studium und Berufsperspektiven in Erwachsenenbildung, beruflicher Weiterbildung und Personalentwicklung. Tönning: Der andere Verlag.

Cann, Roger J. (1984): Incidental learning. In: Adult Education 57. Jg., H. 1, p. 47-49.

Fodor, Imréné (2015): Facts and trends in adult education and training in Hungary. In: International Perspectives in Adult Education Vol. 70 (Editor Balázs Németh). DVV International Bonn, Germany. P. 74-83.

Hake, Barry (2008): Comparative Policy Analysis and Lifelong Learning Narratives: The „Employability Agenda" from a Life-Course Perspective. In: Reischmann, Jost & Bron Jr, Michal (eds.): Comparative Adult Education 2008. Experiences and Examples. Peter Lang Publisher, Frankfurt, New York p. 167-178.

Jackson, Norman J. (2012): Lifewide Learning: History of an idea. In: Jackson, Norman J. (ed): The Lifewide Learning, Education & Personal Development e-book. P. 1-30. http://lifewideeducation.co.uk/home, http://lifewideeducation.co.uk/sites/default/files/chapter_a1_jackson.pdf

Kapp, Alexander (1833): Platon's Erziehungslehre, als Pädagogik für die Einzelnen und als Staatspädagogik. Leipzig.

Kidd, James Robin: How Adults Learn. New York: Association Press [5]1977.

Kleisz, Teréz (2015): The state of profession-building in the field of Andragogy in Hungary. In: International Perspectives in Adult Education Vol. 70 (Editor Balázs Németh). DVV International Bonn, Germany. P. 16-25.

Reischmann, Jost (2004): Andragogy. History, Meaning, Context, Function. http://www.andragogy.net.

Reischmann, Jost (2010): Adult Educators as HRD Trainer, Moderator and Coach. Experiences of a Chair for Andragogy in Bamberg. In: Medic, Snezana/Ebner, Regina/Popovic, Katarina (ed): Adult Education: The Response to Global Crisis. Strengths and Challenges of the Profession. Belgrade: Department of Pedagogy and Andragogy, University of Belgrade, Serbia. P. 81-90.

Savicevic, Dusan (1999): Understanding Andragogy in Europe and America: Comparing and Contrasting. In: Reischmann, Jost/ Bron, Michal/ Jelenc, Zoran (eds): Comparative Adult Education 1998: the Contribution of ISCAE to an Emerging Field of Study. Ljubljana, Slovenia: Slovenian Institute for Adult Education, p. 97-119. http://www.uni-bamberg.de/fileadmin/andragogik/08/andragogik/iscae /ISCAE-Book1999.pdf.

Tóth, János Szigeti (2015): Democratic citizenship learning - the Hungarian perspective and its international relevance. In: International Perspectives in Adult Education Vol. 70 (Editor Balázs Németh). DVV International Bonn, Germany. P. 35-41.

UNESCO (1997): CONFINTEA V: The Hamburg Declaration On Adult Learning. http://www.unesco.org/education/uie/confintea/declaeng.htm

Periodically, new concepts emerge in andragogy, with some gaining high prominence. The following paper serves as an example of concept clarification, and critically asking for borders and limitations of a particular concept.

3.3 The American Discussion on Self-Directed Learning: A Test and a Warning[1]

Result One: The Structure of the Discussion on SDL

Since the beginning of the 1970s, the concept of "self-directed learning" has been an identity-forming concept for the adult education debate in the USA. Jack Mezirow, who works at Columbia University in New York, assesses this: "No concept is more central to what adult education is all about than self-directed learning ... Self-directed learning is the goal of andragogy, the prevailing philosophy of adult education" (1985, p. 17). And the Australian Philip Candy in 1991: "Self-direction is such an attractive concept and seems to capture the current zeitgeist so well" (p. xvii). Presented with weighty and enthusiastic arguments by the "opinion leaders", conceptually shaped in various streams of discussion, described in a variety of didactic forms, empirically examined many times, and invoked in a flood of publications, this concept is part of the self-image of an entire generation of theorists and practitioners.

The first step in this paper is to identify key publications to describe the development and the various aspects of the concept and to test it in discussion.

1. The Discovery: Allen Tough's Adults Learning Projects 1971

"Adults really can learn themselves!" is still today my student's eye-glancing reaction to the research of Allen Tough. His work was a real eye-opener: Based on empirical research he showed that adults spend a tremendous amount of their life for learning. But this "learning" was different - and this was the central new aspect - from what was (is?) traditionally perceived as learning: He added learning "how to remodel your house", "how to bake bread", or "how to deal with an illness" to our understanding of learning, and the metaphor of the iceberg: „For many years we paid attention only to the visible portion of the iceberg, focusing our attention on professionally guided learning. ... The massive bulk of the iceberg that is less visible, turns out to be 80% off the adult's learning efforts" (Tough 1979, p. 173).

New is, not to ask: How shall we organize teaching? But: What competence does a person have? And how was it gained?

Eye-sparkling in this type of learning was, that it seemed always successful. Not perceived was, that this was a methodological artifact: Non-successful

---

[1]　Paper presented at International Self-Directed Learning Symposium, Feb. 19-22, 1998, Orlando, Fl. This annual conference exists still in 2024 (www.sdlglobal.com/symposium)

learning was not reported. The result was an overwhelming optimism, fitting into the American dream: there are no limits - you can do what you want.

2. Back to (a bit different) School: Malcolm Knowles 1975

A different concept and understanding can be concentrated around Malcolm Knowles' Self-directed Learning: A Guide for Learners and Teachers. This concept went back to the traditional visible portion of the iceberg by asking: How shall we organize learning (note the shift from "teaching" to "learning")? But he answered differently: Not teaching, but arranging learning opportunities for self-directed learning was the "new" answer

A new concept? "Discovery learning" in the 60th or Dewey's project method in the 1910th had many similarities in method, concept, and reason, but nobody referred to it. It seems typical for that discussion, that roots, parallels, or similarities in history were neglected - up until now!

In Knowles's little book also the set of arguments can be found bundled which are repeated in that discussion:
- the world is changing
- knowledge is continuously losing its value
- maturing, becoming an adult, means self-direction
- learning happens lifelong
- the whole community is a learning resource.

These arguments were continuously repeated in the following discussion but seldom questioned.

Does Knowles talk about the same learning as Tough? For sure not. But both concepts appear often intermingled. This - dangerously - opens the chance of a "concept swing": When SDL type Tough misses arguments, it is possible to swing to SDL type Knowles and vice versa.

3. The Instrument: Guglielmino 1977

Relatively early on, empirical research was also carried out in the discussion about self-directed learning - this is one of the strengths of American educational science. In 1977, Guglielmino constructed the "Self-Directed Learning Readiness Scale (SDLRS)" to capture these person-related variables. This scale has become the standard instrument for determining self-learning maturity in many studies. In the 1998 anthology in the publication series on self-directed learning, Huey B. Long evaluates: "the SDLRS is the scale most often used in the study of self-directed learning", and dedicates this volume to Lucy Guglielmino and her "significant contributions to the study and theory of self-directed learning" (1998, p. xi). The SDLRS consists of 58 Likert-scaled items and claims to represent the construct of "Self-Directed Learning Readiness" with the following eight factors: openness to learning opportunities, self-confidence as a successful learner, initiative, and independence in learning, conscious acceptance of learning responsibility, "love of learning", creativity, future orientation, and learning/problem-solving skills. By this, the measuring scale defines what the maturity for self-control is. And the scale assumes and yields that some people are more mature for self-direction than others.

4. The Warning: Brookfield 1985

When an educational principle is fashionable for a while, somebody comes up and criticizes it. Brookfield did this in 1985 by warning that there could be an "academic orthodoxy in adult education ... this new orthodoxy asserted that all adults were natural, self-directed learners and that the task of the adult educator was simply to release the boundless, peerless capacity for self-directed learning that was innate but dormant in all adults" (Brookfield 1985, p. 2). He now can refer to empirical research which questions basic assumptions of the concept of Self-directed Learning.

But that means for him that it is necessary to optimize the orthodoxy, not to replace it.

5. Research-Summaries: Long & Ass. 1989 ..., Caffarella/O'Donnell 1990

The next step in the development of an andragogical mainstream is the collection, documentation, and summarizing of the many isolated research projects. Hue B. Long did this over the years at the University of Oklahoma. It is not necessary at this conference to go into details, because the experts are here. The tradition of the conference we attend right now documents a specific step in the development of a mighty concept.

Also here a critique might be very quietly formulated: When a circle of experts and believers meets, how likely is it that out of this circle a basic critique can come?

5. The Systematic Diligence: Candy 1991

Again a foreigner - Philip Candy from Australia - offered essential critical perspectives in his incredible literature-consolidated "definitive scholarly treatment of the topic", as Brookfield values the book in the foreword. On 567 pages, including eighty pages of bibliography, he diligently summarizes the literature that is actually considered unmanageable: First, he asks about the different meanings that are attached to the term self-directed learning, about the framework conditions in which this concept was able to achieve such prominence, and warns against uncritical defense. He then presents different approaches to research. Theoretically, he underpins a constructivist approach and constructs the interaction between person and situation from the perspective of self-direction. It then compiles and examines pathways and contexts in which learners' ability to learn independently. He offers clarifications, behind which the further discussion should not fall back, i.e. the concept-"fuzziness" (p. 97) by discriminating four different concepts, the identification of the historic and cultural context (and limitation) self-directed learning was born and raised, or the one-sidedness of research (Does self-directed learning really lead to autonomy?).

This book was praised in the US through AAACE and the Houle-award. It seems it has the fate of a classical text: often cited, but perhaps too definitive and differentiated to really be utilized seriously.

6. Going on: Hiemstra/Brockett 1994

"Overcoming Resistance to Self-Direction in Adult Learning" is the programmatic title of the 1994-book in the reputable new-directions-series of Jossey-Bass. The authors understand self-directed learning as an interaction between "both the external characteristics of an instructional process and the internal characteristics of the learner, where the individual assumes primary responsibility for a learning experience" (p. 1). And they state, that "confusion" and "„misunderstandings" made their work necessary.

Interesting seems, that Brockett explicitly declares it a "myth" to claim that "self-directed learning is always the best approach for adults" (p. 9f). But despite this, the "myth" remains at the end of the book: "the examples contained in this volume can provide a sense of optimism and demonstrate that self-direction is possible in virtually any teaching-learning setting" (p. 89). And that seems typical for the current discussion: Let us call it a myth, and then show in projects and arguments, that it is not a myth.

7. Summary: No Doubts on Self-directed Learning!

Of course, the diversity of the American discussion cannot be traced in this briefness. Nevertheless, similarities can be identified:
- Self-directed learning has been considered good and desirable for about 25 years.
- Self-directed learning is considered a paradigm that is part of the identity of adult education.
- A flood of publications, including a broad research literature and own conferences, deals with this topic, everyone who wants to be "in" in the scene has written about it.
- In a large number of practical projects, implementation strategies of this principle were tested and investigated.
- Despite critical voices, research remains largely oriented toward verification. Difficulties or failures are seen as to be overcome and not as systematically conditioned, from the analysis of which (instead of overcoming) something could be learned. Result takes precedence over knowledge.

Overlooking the three decades of discussion on self-directed learning in these six very rough steps we see that this concept still is undoubted, perhaps sometimes a little bit criticized. But the basic message is: Self-directed Learning is good learning; this concept should be star to steer adult education by.

Result Two: Warning

Three critical observations:

1. Critical questions to be asked:

Going through the concepts and arguments of the self-directed learning debate, questions can be found that were asked but seldomly answered or reflected. To name just three:

- Why are we so eager to document successful learning projects (in the Tough-style), but are not interested in the disasters of this learning - i.e. school-dropouts, not learning the language of neighbors or a visited country, computer-helplessness?
- What does that mean: Knowledge looses its value? The ten commitments, two times two, a human way of living, Thorndike's „law off effect"?
- Is "self-directedness", "autonomy" the ultimate, one and only goal of adult education? And if you agree that not - and we take that seriously: What does that mean for our educational concepts?

2. Traps not to surmount:

a) A person reading a newspaper, or scholars exchanging on a conference: is that self-directed learning or not? The answer shows us an inevitable trap: It is not answerable. The answer always must be yes and no, because all learning always comprises parts from outside and parts of self-direction. So when labeling something "self-directed learning" it is always possible to point out elements that are outside-directed.

b) Arranging self-directed learning opportunities? It needs a lot of goodwill and commitment (= blindness) to accept this logical inconsistency. Can intentional outside-arrangements make self-direction? We know from experience and research that didactic arrangements are helpful for self-directed learning. But on a logical level: When self-directed learning is "good" learning, how can the "bad" outside-organized learning-opportunity lead to "good"?

c) And can theories on self-directed learning answer the problem, that we sometimes have good reasons not to aim education to autonomy and selfdirectedness, but to sociability, relaying, "homology" (Boucouvalas 1988)? How do we come out from that trap?

3. One-sidedness of verification-research:

Hundreds of studies were executed about self-directed learning, as Garrison points out: "Self-directed learning is one of the few areas of research in adult education with an extensive research-based body of knowledge" (1989 in Candy, 1991, p. 98). But the trend is mostly the same: "Let us show that even in field X self-directed learning can successfully be implemented!" The results showed always some - never total - success. This part of non-success was called "misunderstanding", confusion", "not-yet-success"- implicitly expressing the hope that "if we could do it perfectly the results would be perfect". Research looked for verification of old prejudices, not for falsification (Popper!) which would open new understanding (= learning). How can we come out of the trap of transforming to new knowledge instead of confirming our old understanding?

Warning: SDL - a „missionary" theory

Erich Weniger, a traditional German scholar, offered in 1929 the discrimination of three levels of educational theories:

- On a first level we find the "theories" everybody has about education, naive, implicit, small-scale, inconsistent, ex-post.
- On a second level he places the theories of institutions and movements. These theories are mostly well developed, , documented, discussed, researched, published. They show what is behind a movement or an institution are inspiring, convincing, enthusiastic - a banner to follow.
- On a third (scholarly) level we find "theories about theories", reflecting, comparing, explaining.

Self-directed learning as a theory can be found on level two: a theory of a movement: Well-developed, inspiring, convincing, enthusiastic, but also bound by its own limits. To label it negatively: they rely on believe-systems and are "missionary-style": Theories of this type separate themselves from other theories, praise their own paradigms, and try to convince themselves and others, that their movement or institution is more valuable than others. That makes theories on level two so attractive - and blind. Everything has to fit into that system, and if it does not, it is neglected. The price is exclusiveness, rigidity with limited change, and practical and logical inconsistency. Warnings including similar arguments were offered by various authors (i.e. Brookfield, Candy, Hiemstra/Brockett); elements of this general description could be identified in our critical remarks.

A Scholarly Solution

"Theories about theories" are mostly not very inspiring and never enthusiastic. They track history, compare, consider. They make no decisions about right or wrong but search for strategies to find out what is more or less appropriate for different situations. They try to identify the limits and weaknesses of theories, not to criticize the theory but to identify where they are helpful or where other theories are more appropriate.

A helpful tool for the necessary distance "theories about theories" need is the "antinomic" access: educational ideas, institutions, concepts are compared with their opposite counterparts. So self-directed learning is compared with outside-directed learning, but not as good vs. bad, but under the perspective that on both sides are as well helpful as limiting aspects. Under this perspective, we ask: What is the historic and cultural context of self-directed and outside-directed learning? What are the open and hidden arguments for each of them, and what are they based on? What is the strength/weakness of one and the other? In which situation, target-group, for which content which effects and side-effects can be expected? ....

Here we are beyond the believe-system. Arguments have to be found why in situation X theory A is more helpful, and why theory B is more appropriate to situation Y. If we apply this model to the traps pointed out above these traps disappear and become solvable.

So what is suggested here: First to take our subjective observations and research results seriously when they show strengths as well as weaknesses in the application of SDL, and not only look fascinated on one part of the results but are blind to other parts. Similarly, we should take seriously that outside-direction is a legitimate and helpful part of the composition of institutionalized and informal learning. However, admitting that it is a myth that self-directed learning is the best approach is not enough: In consequence, this means that other concepts can be as legitimate and effective and wanted. We have to accept the possibility that not by optimizing self-directed learning we gain a better understanding or proceeding of adult learning, but by using an opposite concept. This transforms the discussion on self-directed learning from a „missionary" concept to a professional, scholarly approach.

No doubt: The discovery, development, research, and discussion of self-directed learning have showered us in the last three decades with knowledge, concepts, methods, learning-opportunities, institutions, and enthusiasm not known before in adult education. This value has to be preserved.

And it has to be accepted, that other concepts have their theoretical and practical value too.

This is based on the characteristic of our field: Education works always in complex situations. Because of that we usually can identify in the reality of adult education (like in most life situations) a whole bundle of concepts in action at the same time. The most appropriate picture of educational reality we do not get by limiting us to one concept and blinding us from all others merged into the complexity of the same situation. While other sciences can work with the reduction of complexity to better understand and handle their subject, the reduction of complexity in education soon leads to artificial situations. As a professional field, we have to handle complexity, not simplicity.

My warning is: One leading concept is reductive and leads to artificial situations and results. My suggestion is: To optimize theory and practice in adult education we sometimes have to optimize self-directed learning, and sometimes we have to overcome self-directed learning and use other concepts, which are more appropriate.

80

References

Boucouvalas, Marcie (1988): An Analysis and Critique of the Concept of Self in Self-directed Learning: Towards a More Robust Construct for Research and Practice. In Zukas, Miriam (ed): Papers from the Transatlantic Dialogue. University of Leeds, SCUTREA, S. 56 - 61.

Brookfield, Stephen (1982): Independent Adult Learning. University of Nottingham: Department of Adult Education.

Brookfield, Stephen (1985) (ed): Self-Directed Learning: From Theory to Practice. Reihe New Directions for Continuing Education, no. 25. San Francisco: Jossey-Bass.

Candy, Philip C. (1991): Self-Direction for Lifelong Learning. A Comprehensive Guide to Theory and Practice. San Francisco: Jossey-Bass.

Caffarella, Rosemary S./O'Donnell, J. M. (1990): Self-Directed Learning. Adults: Psychological and Educational Perspectives, no. 1. Nottingham, England: Department of Adult Education, University of Nottingham, 1990.

Dohmen, Günther (1996): Das lebenslange Lernen. Leitlinien einer modernen Bildungspolitik. Bonn: BWFT.

Guglielmino, Lucy M. (1977): "Development of the Self-Directed Learning Readiness Scale," Doctoral Dissertation. Athens, Georgia: University of Georgia.).

Hiemstra, Roger/Brockett, Ralph G. (1994): Overcoming Resistance to Self-Direction in Adult Learning. Reihe New Directions for Continuing Education, no. 64. San Francisco: Jossey-Bass.

Knowles, Malcolm S. (1975): Self-Directed Learning. A Guide for Learners and Teachers. Chicago: Follet.

Litt, Theodor (1927): Führen oder Wachsenlassen. Eine Erörterung des pädagogischen Grundproblems. 12. Edition 1965. Stuttgart: Klett.

Long, Huey B., and Ass.: Jeweils Norman: Oklahoma Research Center for Continuing Professional and Higher Education, University of Oklahoma:
* (1989): Self-Directed Learning: Emerging Theory and Practice.
* (1990): Advances in Research and Practice in Self-Directed Learning.
* and Redding, T. R. (1991): Self-Directed Learning Dissertation Abstracts 1966-1991.
* and Confessore, G. J (1992): Abstracts of Literature in Self-Directed Learning 1966-1982.
* and Confessore, G. J. (1993): Abstracts of Literature in Self-Directed Learning 1983-1991.

Long, Huey B., and Ass. (1998): Developing paradigms for self-directed learning Public Managers Center, College of Education, University of Oklahoma.

Mezirow, Jack (1985): A Critical Theory of Self-Directed Learning. In: Brookfield, Stephen (ed): Self-Directed Learning, S. 17- 30.

Nolan, Robert E. (1981): Dependency versus Autonomy in Adult Second Language Learning: Proceedings of 22nd annual Adult Education Research Conference. Northern Illinois University, De Kalb, S. 140 - 145.

Penland, P. R. (1977): Self-Planned Learning in America. Pittsburgh: University of Pittsburg.

Rogers, Carl (1974): Lernen in Freiheit. München: Kösel.

Tough, Allen (²1979): The Adult's Learning Projects. Toronto: The Ontario Institute for Studies in Education.

Weniger, Erich (1929): Theorie und Praxis in der Erziehung. In: Ders.: Die Eigenständigkeit der Erziehung in Theorie und Praxis. Beltz: Weinheim ³1964, p. 7-22.

The following contribution features a keynote delivered to the Annual Conference of AAACE (American Association of Adult and Continuing Education), Milwaukee Nov. 7, 2006, and was not printed until now. It is anticipated to have the potential to illuminate conflicts among distinct groups within the field of adult/continuing education, each claiming to 'own' the 'real and true adult education'.

For the start of the presentation and to introduce the overarching theme I offered to the participants the following "statement-sheet":

There are a series of reasons, convictions, and arguments to engage in adult/continuing education. Read the following statements and
mark in each line the (one) statement you personally prefer most!

Adult Education respects the body and the soul	Adult Education must empower for action	Adult Education should invite into the cultural life	Adult and Continuing Education improves society and economy
Adult Education needs a spiritual dimension	Adult Education always has a political dimension	Adult Education must support all dimensions of a person's development (self-actualization)	Adult Education must enable participants to solve practical problems
The goal of Adult Education is a fair and human order of the world	The goal of Adult Education is a better society	The goal of Adult Education is the "enlightened person".	The goal of Adult Education is better performance
Adult Education trusts on understanding, caring, and help	Adult Education has to lead to emancipation from old restraints	Adult Education has to respect the value of each individual	It is important to train Adult Educators to use successful methods
Adult Education means serving	Adult Educators need a vision, of how society should be	The arts play a major role in becoming a person	To reach a goal it is important to define clear objectives
Thinking of an adult educator I like the image of			
Shepherd	Leader	Educator	Trainer

If participants predominantly marked one column, this could assist them in identifying which of the roots 1-4 (from left to right) in the following text they primarily align with. Distinguishing these roots can aid in recognizing the roots of presenters/authors, and therefore to foresee argument and actions, strengths and limitations. This facilitates a (better) understanding and respect for where others ground their understanding of adult education.

3.4 The four roots of adult education "Why will we never understand each other?" (2006)

Often in the many years I participated in the conferences of the American Association for Adult and Continuing Education (AAACE) I heard in different presentations the sentences: "Real Adult Education is/does/means ...", or: "True adult education is/does/means". And (not) surprisingly, these claiming sentences had quite different answers, for example:

- The goal of Adult Education is a fair and human order of the world.
- Adult Education must empower for action!
- Adult Education must support all dimensions of a person's development.
- Adult Education must enable participants to solve practical problems.

So, the question came up: Who decides what the "real" adult education is? Who "owns" adult education? Moreover, no wonder with these diverging demands: Why do we often not understand each other in discussing adult education?

The thesis of this paper is: Adult Education has not one root, but four basic, independent, genuine ideas that lead to adult education. Four traditions, cultures formed their own institutions, theories, and goals. And as each of them is based on its own complex, value-based understanding, each one of these roots believes it is the only "real", "true" adult education - and the others are wrong, or at least second-class. As long as we are bound into such an excluding understanding, we think: We own adult education - and will never understand the others.

What is it good for to know and identify these roots, what is the goal of this paper? When we identify our own thinking-and-acting-regulating root, we are not blindly dependent on implicit conviction but know and understand the strengths *and* weaknesses of our position better. Perceiving, understanding, and respecting the other genuine roots of adult (and continuing) education might hopefully humble us and may help us to understand and respect (better) where others ground their understanding of adult education in.

1. The religious/spiritual root

There is an order in the word: After sunrise comes sunset, and after sunset comes sunrise. We can rely on this. And we must learn and live in that order, which is not manmade.

The oldest root of adult education and lifelong learning is the religious root. All societies since the Flintstones know that to serve the spirits, the gods, god, the ancients, you must "become better" lifelong, you have to learn and change lifelong into the direction and order expected by the spirits, the divine order. Mohamed says in the Koran that we must learn from cradle to grave, this is as well true in Jewish tradition, and as we know in the Christian tradition, we are lifelong sinners (some more, some less - adult educators are of course mostly on one of these sides). Being lifelong sinners means that we also must be lifelong learners to prepare in this world for the next world.

I am not just talking about religious instruction, about "catechesis". Several well-known names give proof that learning in this world and for this world is the other side of the coin "learning for the other world". Bishop Jan Amos Comenius, living in the 17th century, in his "Didactica Magna" and especially in his book "Pampaedia" describes, that "the whole life is a school, from cradle to grave". Learning and changing means preparing our inside and our outside under the perspective and in trusting a divine order. The goal is to develop all the abilities the Lord placed in the human: Intellectualia, sensualia, spiritualia - socialia. Bishop Grundtvig in Denmark, end of the 19th century, started with this background idea of what later became known as the 'Folkehøjskole': He invited peasants to stay during the winter in his house, learning about agriculture, philosophy, arts - and moral and values. When I read Malcolm Knowles (with his background in the YMCA) I find many patterns that include this religious thinking: his deep trust in the self-directed learner, his serving the learner, his arguing for the necessity of learning for a human world. In Germany, the Catholic and Lutheran Church have nationwide organizations offering adult education: MS-Word, literature, guitar-courses, and especially all types of family education - all content without relationship to church-related knowledge (?). We researched with several hundred interviews participants of protestant adult education, asking them: "Why did you choose this institution and not the public adult education center?" The general argument was: There is a special spirit in this institution and courses, and there are special people in the courses.

Typical statements in this tradition are: "Adult education respects body and soul - adult education needs a spiritual dimension - the goal of adult education is a fair and human order of the world - adult education trusts in understanding, caring, and help." "Trust", "hope", and a feeling of humility pervade this root - these terms do not show up in the other roots.

Peter Jarvis (1987) identified this religious root: "From Mansbridge to Cody, from Tawney to Freire there is a consistent pattern of religious belief being a motivating factor in their lives" (p. 304), being "perhaps the most potent motivator for many of this exponents of adult education" (p. 309).

I got the idea to identify this root in the Commission of Professors of Adult Education (CPAE) at the AAACE-conferences. I suddenly became aware that a number of professors come from a religious background - having studied theology, having been pastors, growing out, or being intricately connected to religious groups. And it always was a delight to be friend with these guys: They were trustful, caring, helping, relaxed, supportive - giving freedom - thank God.

Of course - like always in education - this root has its danger and problems: Adult educators based in this root could be so overwhelmed by their truth that they become missionaries and moralists - not trusting and giving freedom but controlling and "preaching" down on the learners. And instead of acting in the world, this work withdraws from the world - back into the walls of a church.

2. Social change and individual emancipation

The AAACE-conference in 1990 in Salt Lake City had found a creative way to discuss the actual development of adult education. It had the title: "On Trial - The Education of Adults." Accused was Adult Education because it had forgotten that the adult education movement had its beginning in populist movements and because it had given up its mission to be an instrument of social action. The

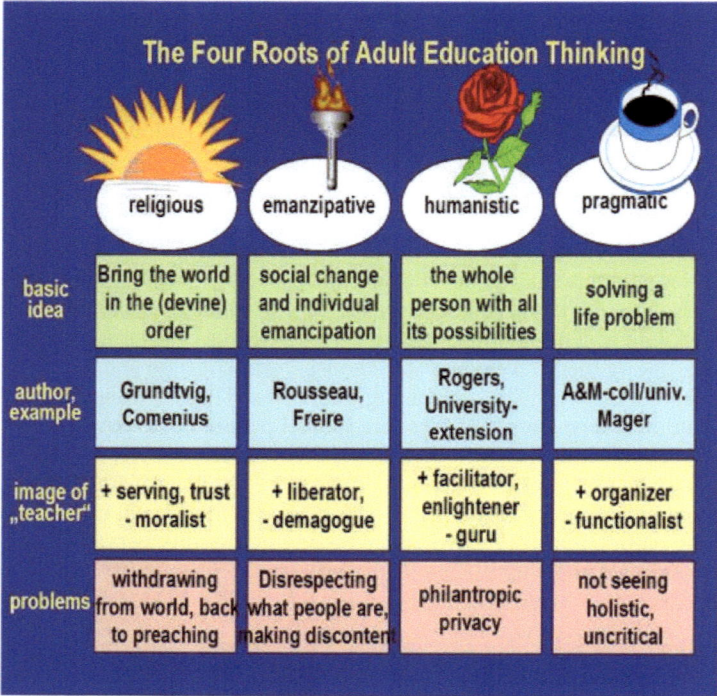

Figure 1: The Four Roots of Adult Education Thinking

real mission of adult education is - in this understanding - to bring through education fundamental social, cultural, political, and economic changes in society. The critic: Adult education has sold its soul to money-givers and commercial interests.

Here the basic idea is: The world, the society is corrupt, it must be changed, perhaps by revolution, perhaps by restoration - but it must be changed! And this change comes from people who have a new awareness, a new understanding, a new ideology - the right one!!! The focus of understanding and action is "the new world". Contemplation, classical education, the arts, and old-fashioned values - that all is a trick to keep us dependent, and oppressed! The new, right awareness leads to action in solidarity: emancipation from whatever, overcoming oppression. Two substreams may be identified: the more moderate "support responsible and emancipative participation in society", and the more critical "adult education as social movement".

Typical statements in this tradition are, for example: "Adult education must empower for action - adult education always has a political dimension action - adult education has to lead to emancipation from old restraints."

The focus of this root is the world, the society, and action. A torch may serve as a symbol: A torch brings light for orientation, but also can set things on fire - sometimes it seems necessary to burn the old world. Authors presenting this root are, for example J.J. Rousseau, Karl Marx, or Paulo Freire ("Pedagogy of the Oppressed"). The communist revolution in Russia in 1917 promised electricity and literacy, Nyerere in the 1980th in Tanzania, Fidel Castro in Cuba wanted to reeducate people with the message: Change the world! Make it better! Fight for it! And by changing the inside through education, people will be empowered to change the outside!

What is the understanding of the role of the adult educator? We can see it positively: The adult educator is a liberator - liberating, emancipating, empowering.. If this position is overdone in a negative way, we have the demagogue, the revolutionist- tended to include pressure, critique, not accepting my positions, letting me feel that I had to change!

The first step of this education is: Make people aware that the way they see the world is wrong! And this is a problem: Starting this educational process, old beliefs must be destroyed and replaced with the new "truth" - truth? This destruction of old believes - for example, a certain type of family, gender roles, politics, government, and economy - hurts the learner. And the question may be asked: Is this new belief a truth - or just another set of beliefs? The be lievers, as in the other roots, of course, will call it "the truth", but if you are not believing?

3. Humanistic or liberal-arts root

Another distinct and authentic root led to adult education: in this understanding, the "real" mission of adult education is to provide a general, "well-rounded" education, unfolding all the cultural, artistic, and other valuable sides of a person. It includes humanistic, non-pragmatic, culture-oriented activities, dealing with literature, languages, drama, art, history, and all sorts of creative themes.

Typical statements of this root are: "Adult education should invite into cultural life - adult education must support all dimensions in a person's development - the goal of adult education is the 'enlightened person'." An educated person in this understanding learns for personal enrichment, and learns for the value of the good, true, beautiful. Germany is known for this tradition - good for "nothing", but able to play piano or speak Latin. The educational philosophy ("Bildung") of Humboldt is a classic example of this root of adult education.

Two sub-streams can be discriminated: a) a more humanistic orientation, such as Carl Rogers' "self-actualization" without specific content, or b) a more Liberal Arts tradition, "subduing" to contents representing the cultural heritage (literature, drama, art, history ...), leading to transformation. The University Extension Movement, since the 19th century, often referred to this idea.

The role of the adult educator, in this case, is the facilitator of learning and the enlightener. There certainly are differences between these two roles, but what connects them: the educational task is to transform a person. So, the focus is on the person and its value.

However, also this friendly orientation has its dangers and limits. The danger of this position is, that the adult educator becomes
- either the guru - more demonstrating his own enlightenment than enlightening the learner,
- or the subject matter specialist - more focused on knowledge and content (Latin, literature, art) than on education.

The focus on cultural values brings the danger of idyllic, idealized, and romantic harmonization far from reality; the bad segments of reality are not perceived. All this can happen in places far from reality - the world is not changed by this transformation in privacy because this knowledge is for its own sake.

4. Pragmatic-performance oriented root

A fourth root of learning as an adult is pragmatic and performance-oriented. All over the world and since the Stone Age, even the Flintstones had to learn for very pragmatic reasons: surviving, making money, solving problems, dealing with illness, famine, the death of the parents. If you want to hunt a bear, you better learn how to hunt a bear. If you want to drive a car, you better learn to drive a car. The A&M faculties came out of this tradition, computer courses, "How-to-repair-your-car", "how to fly a space shuttle". This type of learning challenge can come from "the life", but also can be manmade when competencies are needed for the workplace or hobby. Historically this root may be as old as the first, the religious root.

This may be perhaps the largest part of the adult education field: Human Resource Development, learning in healthcare, agriculture etc. Here usually, the term "Continuing Education" is used. Typical statements in this tradition are, for example: "Adult education must enable participants to solve practical problems - adult and continuing education improve society and economy - to reach a goal it is important that trainers define clear objectives."

Sometimes this orientation is called "utilitarian", "technological", or "instrumental" - often with a more or less critical undertone. As there is no value-loaded background philosophy, no big words are made to illuminate these challenges. It is difficult to name an author or theory representing this root; it is difficult to fill a book to substantiate that orientation. The "how" is more central than the "why" - this seems usually self-evident.

The background philosophy can be formulated very shortly: Learn to be effective! Effective in repairing your car, effective in making money for you and your boss, effective in your community. These words hardly can fill a book.

The role of the adult educator in this tradition is an effective shaper of behavior, an organizer, and a trainer.

"Real" educators miss the mission and vision in this learning - well, when I want to operate an e-mail program I am not interested in missions and visions of adult educators who seem to have all the time in the world when I want just to know how to make that strange @@@@@@ on an American keyboard!

If not handled with care, this tradition becomes uncritical. "The company, government, church, school administration tells us the content, and we teach it well-planned and well-evaluated" - that is uncritical, not reflecting societal needs, personal valuing, and the perspective into the future. It can be under-complex-uneducational: educational activities always transport not only content but also "spirit, world-view, transformation" (Illich: "hidden agenda"). An educator knows and handles this, while a trainer cuts off this "educational" part.

Summing up

The hypothesis of this paper is: Adult education has not one but four basic, in-dependent, genuine roots that lead to adult education: a religious, an emancipa-tive, a humanistic, and a pragmatic root. The problem is: An adult educator who blindly avows himself to one single of these roots, limits the thinking and acting appropriately to a unique educational situation. And will never understand the strengths of other positions - and the weaknesses of the own.

What is it good for to know and identify these roots?

1. It helps to understand the own position better; by this thinking and acting depends not blindly on implicit convictions. Knowing explicitly the strengths and weaknesses of the own position helps to act adequately.
2. It helps to understand and respect (better) where others ground their under-standing of adult education. When you identify someone's roots you can predict how a person will act in a certain situation and foresee arguments/actions to be expected.
3. Even when having your own priority root, it helps to be aware that this orientation is not the only and always right one. It might liberate educational thinking and act appropriately to a unique educational situation and make an adult educator flexible in changing to the strengths of the other roots.

The history of adult education has grown more flowers than one. Professional andragogues and reflected practitioners need them all in the toolbox, thinking head, and valuingheart. The mistake of the Salt Lake City trial was that we were in danger that one root (valuable in itself) tried to claim the whole field (devaluating the other authentic roots). This leads to fights within our profes-sion: Who owns the only true truth? That weakens us all, is historically not correct, and limits our situation-adequate acting.

The wealth of adult education is its richness and diversity. When we accept, understand, and value, that different needs in life formed their own educational roots, then this will give us a variety of thinking and acting tools. And respect and understanding each other.

Theoretical postscript for scholars

The German pedagogue Erich Weniger developed in 1929 a helpful classification system for pedagogical theories. This paper is an example of a pedagogical theory on "level three".

1. Theories on level one are theories of amateurs: Grandmas, university-presidents, political leaders etc. who never read a pedagogical textbook, but anyway passionately believe that their private opinions are the best for educational orientation. These theories are often named "naive" or "implicit" theories.

2. Level two are theories of movements ("self-directed learning", "open learning", "person-centered approach" ...) or institutions ("the Volkshochschule, Frontier College, Co-operative extension"...). These movements and institutions are well documented, discussed, researched. But often this position becomes missionary: my movement, my institution is better than others. Consequently, it will be defended, not reflected – level two.

3. Theories of level three are "theories of theorists". Movements, institutions, and their theories are compared and analyzed. On this level no direct advice for acting is given, but options and conditions that must be reflected for the given concrete situation. Based on these reflections the adult educator then can make decisions for the praxis.

This classification system is a tool helpful identifying the aspiration level of arguments and statements in a pedagogic/andragogic discussion.

References:

Comenius, Jan Amos (1657). *Große Didaktik: Die vollständige Kunst, alle Menschen alles zu lehren* (10th edition). Hrsg.: Andreas Flitner. Stuttgart: Klett-Cotta, 2008 (Original 1657).

Freire, Paulo (1970). *Pedagogy of the Oppressed*. New York: Continuum. Freire, Paulo (21972). *Pädagogik der Unterdrückten*. Stuttgart: Kreuz Verlag.

Illich, Ivan (1971). *Deschooling Society*. New York NY: Harper and Row.

Jarvis, Peter (ed.) (1987). *Twentieth Century Thinkers in Adult Education*. London: Croom Helm Ltd.

Leirman, Walter (1994). *Four Cultures of Education : Expert, Engineer, Prophet, Communicator*. Frankfurt/New York: Peter Lang.

Rogers, Carl R. (1969). *Freedom to Learn*. Columbus/Ohio: Charles E. Merill Publishing Company,.

Weniger, Erich (1929). *Die Eigenständigkeit der Erziehung in Theorie und Praxis* (3rd ed.). Weinheim: Beltz 1964

Zinn, L. M. (2004). Exploring your philosophical orientation. In M. W . Galbraith(Ed.), *Adult learning methods: A guide for effective instruction* (3rd ed.).Malabar, FL: Krieger Publishing Co.

Zinn, Lorraine. M. (1983). development of a valid and reliable instrument for adult educators to identify a personal philosophy of adult education. *Dissertation Abstracts International*, 44, 1667A-1668A.

In this final chapter of the "Concepts segment," a summary is presented in the form of ten "learning-ideas". These learning-ideas have been introduced in the preceding chapter, and now they are further summarized, compared, and systematized. Special attention is dedicated to the concepts developed by the author: "learning en passant"," lifewide learning", and "compositional learning".

3.5 Learning[10] - who is offering more? (2008)[1]

0. The "discovery"

The discovery of the idea happened in passing by: in front of the convention center in San Antonio, Texas, was a more than 25-meter broad map inserted in the forecourt. I literally stumbled across the lines and only after a few steps got the general idea that it was a map.

I found myself in New York looking towards San Francisco. I am crossing the continent and reading the names of the states. I am "flying" towards San Antonio and I am wondering how long the distance is that I have passed in reality by plane. I see children who hop on one leg from one state to another, singing the names of the different states. This was the moment when I achieved the enlightenment: education in passing by – "learning en passant".

---

[1]   First print: Reischmann, Jost (2008) Learnig to the power oft ten - who is offering more? In: Paritätisches Bildungswerk LV NRW u.a.: Study on the move, for everyone, anytime, anywhere. Wuppertal: Page 22-30.

1. The diversity of learning

1.1 Learning organized by institutions – traditional or "non-traditional"

The learning that comes to mind first is school-like learning, organized and controlled by others. But this learning organized by institutions can nowadays also offer more choices for the learner, as for example in distance learning, summer schools, and media-transported learning.

Learning - external organized

Learning idea 1 – externally-organized, institutionalized, closed learning: The learner needs to go to an institution to complete a given curriculum (traditional learning being present at an educational institution). Driving schools, dance schools, and music schools can thoroughly be included here.

Learning idea 2 – externally-organized, institutionalized, open-approach learning: The learning offer goes to the learner; he or she can choose the place, sequence and time but not as much the content, as in distance learning/distance study "Universities Without Walls". Locations for learning can therefore also be libraries, parishes, do-it-yourself stores, doctor's practices or private houses. But the learner doesn't choose those places himself or herself; they are arranged for him or her. Those learning offers within the externally-organized setting can leave the learner more or less possibilities to decide on the own ways of learning. But the decision whether this is possible or not is not up to the learner but to the teacher or the institution.

Learning idea 3 – externally-organized, institutionalized; content-open learning: Here the learner can also decide on content and emphasis of contents. Within traditional academic studies, for example, this way of learning is implied in writing the thesis where the topic and form are chosen by the student and only formal standards are obligatory. While learning ideas 1 and 2 can conclude with a qualification certificate, this is not intended as much with content-open offers.

Learning idea 4 – existing knowledge and abilities are being certified: While the former learning ideas assumed that the learning process of the learners had to be organized, it is being assumed here that adults have gained knowledge and abilities already in different ways: with not completed academic studies, with adult learning courses, with professional further training, with hobbies or during their free time. This "assessment of prior learning" can either happen by collecting certificates or by demonstrating knowledge and abilities in an exam.

1.2 Self-directed learning – intended and (more or less) supported

I came across a new direction of thinking in the book of the Canadian Allan Tough "The Adult's Learning Project" (1979). In a research project he asked adults: "Have you learned something in this past year?" The answers were mainly "no", except the respondents had participated in school-like activities. Changing the technique of the question just a little bit, Tough gained astonishing results :He asked for defined competencies that have been gained - "Have

you learned how to do wallpaper?", "Have you learned something about dis-
eases?", "Have you learned something about parenting?" - and suddenly the respondents started bubbling. They did not talk about participating in school-like
activities but about knowledge and abilities they had gained. And he came to the
result that adults from all social groups spend almost two hours every day in
"learning projects", of which 80% take place without any professional pedagogical guidance. This is questioning our idea of learning provocatively: Is "real"
learning only connected to diplomas and certification or can we also talk about
learning when you are learning something "just for fun or for use"?

With this, a new direction of thinking was established in two different ways.
While the traditional approach of education concerned future goals to be
achieved and deficiencies to be overcome, now the starting point and the perspective had changed:

End page 22
Start page 23

First, you concern the abilities adults demonstrate today, and then you go
back to the past with the question: Which were the situations in which they
were learned? And this opens a new class of a variety of learning possibilities
and learning sources
which received little
attention so far.
Within the andragogi-
cal discussion, the
change of the per-
spective "from teach-
ing to learning" was
debated. But also an-
other thing had

> Learning idea 5 – intended, autodidactic, self-directed learning:
> With the intention of gaining a certain knowledge or ability,
> learners often use a variety of resources – magazines, friends,
> salesmen, craftsmen, instruction manuals, trial and error, but
> also (partly-)institutionalized learning offered by building
> centers, libraries, educational institutions – completely or partly:
> you stay away when you get what you wanted. The intention is
> not a certificate with an exchange value, but a utility value or
> "just because it is interesting". The learner "composes" his or
> her forms and ways of learning from these resources and
> decides on contents and aims himself or herself.

changed: the perception of "different" learning objectives. Knowing how to
wallpaper, knowing about a diet, knowing how to bake cookies – so far those
learning objectives have hardly been considered as "serious" or "right" learning
objectives. The expansion of this perspective is being documented by the
reporting system of further education in Germany, which documents that
besides attended further education events also informal professional further
education activities since the middle of the 90s increased: reading textbooks
referring to the occupation (52%), self-learning by observing and trying (50%),
short-term events like speeches and half-day seminars (37%), instructions from
co-workers or supervisors (34%).

1.3 Learning "en passant" - not intended or partly intended learning

I went to the Grand Canyon as a tourist to see something but not to learn something. And still, I left with gained knowledge. The museum where I bought a

postcard offered models, videos, and flyers that the tourists took while passing by. Again and again, little groups gathered around a ranger who would explain the things that could be seen or even not seen. And at different spots, information panels provided botanical, geological, or biological information.

Pearl Harbour wasn't far away. It takes me only a few minutes to get there by bus. How else should I spend the rest of my day? At the kiosk of the memorial place of the outbreak of the Pacific war of the USA during World War II, I bought a copy of the Honolulu Star-Bulletin from December 7, 1941, which reports on the bombing by the Japanese which had just taken place. This newspaper "taught" me more impressively than my history book could. It took my breath away watching an old couple throwing a floral wreath into the inner harbor and then searching for the name of their son on the panel with the names of the people who had died on that day. Suddenly war and death are no more abstract items. I had learned something.

"Siehe die Wohnung Gottes bei den Menschen. Den 8. Mai 1868" (translator's note: "The home of God is among mortals"). I read this inscription

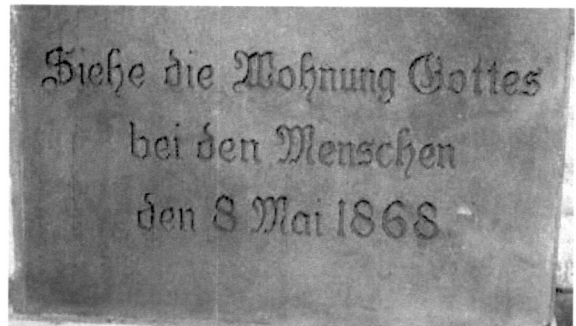

written in familiar squiggled letters on a wall of a church. Unordinary – the church was located in San Antonio, Texas. Why a German inscription? Why this date? Why those squiggled letters that I know from my home church? I enter the church and find a familiar native interior with a Way of the Cross inscribed in German, familiar saints – and a(n English) flyer ("please donate 50 cents"), in which German immigrants report about their hometown, their hardships, and that for the first time a sermon was held in English in this church in 1908 (before that only German was spoken). This learning episode lasted 10 minutes - but I am still thinking of it today.

End page 23
Start page 24

Enough with the examples, but what they show is a different understanding of learning than shown in the five approaches above.

- The contents were different. It was not the historical facts I could have learned better from a "real" history book that I memorized, but the authenticity of a bulletin copy, the image of an old couple who could be grandparents who still mourn for their son. It was not the geological layers of the Grand Canyon that I learned primarily, but the unforgettable inebriation of the eyes that takes one's breath away.

  However, at least for those examples I added some traditional knowledge and abilities using traditional learning sources (experts, lexicons, geological/historical textbooks) or some not-so-traditional ones (newspapers, postcards, or flyers).

- The motivation was different. I didn't go to those places to learn something, at least not in the first way. So besides learning that is explicitly intended, there is also learning that I "pick up along the way" – sometimes even learning that I would rather have avoided ("What do I have to do when I miss my connecting flight?").

- The way of learning is different. There was no class and no autodidactic self-organized learning. And none of those situations lasted a lesson or even seven hours – not even when I add up the time as learning episodes for reading the flyers, discussing them, or looking things up in a lexicon. However, I was using resources that institutions had prepared with the aim of teaching and which seduced me to learn. Because the small "museum" at the edge of

> *Learning idea 6 – partly-intended learning:* There are actions which are not intended for learning but which include or demand learning: you explicitly go for a journey, a concert, a hobby or a citizens' initiative. You accept the learning that happens or is even necessary for this. Later, you still know exactly on which occasion you gained the knowledge and ability, but this part of learning would not have been enough for you to carry out the action. You remember the activity but the part of learning stays implicitly hidden. Often there is no defined learning aim for this kind of partly-intended learning – only afterwards do you realize what you have learned from visiting a concert or a support group.
>
> *Learning idea 7 – not-intended learning:* There are external incidents ("critical personal experiences") which are not planned and not expected, and which lead us to question old things and to develop new perspectives, which "teach" us something whether we want it to or not: an accident, a crisis situation, a map on which you stumble. Those changing incidents can involve a shock or fun and the time to cope with this can take a few moments or several years. The cause situation stays identifiable in the memory.
>
> *Learning idea 8 – not-intended hidden mosaic-stone-learning:* If you consider what a person is able to do – not what he or she needs to be taught – then you discover knowledge, abilities and attitudes of inexplicable origins. They could be complex phenomena (being a parent, taking responsibility) but also simple skills (opening a new bottle cap). Obviously it had been learned at some point (maybe transferable skills, maybe principles or structures) but neither learner nor observer are able to identify the situation in which this has been learned.

the Grand Canyon (maybe it was built to make the people buy souvenirs) with its models and artefacts and the movie theatre at Pearl Harbour (which included a souvenir shop and experts from the local historic society who also offered you supporting membership) which showed in documentaries what had happened there were obviously established by subject-matter experts and mediation experts with the intention to teach – which I gratefully adopted with the feeling of "being taught".

All of those examples show that learning takes place in the whole width of life; some things daily, others along the way, some things in learning situations, others in live situations lifelong and lifewide. And therefore besides the item "lifelong", the item "lifewide" was born.

2. The richness of learning – summarized in the concept of "lifewide learning"

With the concept of "lifewide learning", which I published in German for the first time in 1995, I wanted to point out the variety of the different forms, ways, and occasions of learning. I distinguished between two forms of intended learning (externally-directed institutionalized and self-directed autodidactic) and three forms of not-intended learning (see Fig. 1, page 54 of this book). For the part of the not-intended or only partly-intended learning, I chose the item "learning en passant". Choosing this phrase had to do with the experience of stumbling over the US-American map mentioned at the beginning.

End page 24
Start page 25

What I liked about this phrase was that it expresses activity, advancement, moving oneself to meet things and people and to move on. This association describes better what is meant than all the items that have been used so far for this kind of learning, like non-formal, informal, and not-intended, which only define negatively what is not meant.

Still, we need to be warned against a partial romantic view of lifewide learning. Because not only good things but also wrong and bad stuff is being learned en passant: querulousness of the state, political radicalism, religious fundamentalism, to be caught in their own prejudices. How, why, and wherefore to lie, to betray, to elbow, to resign, to disregard others, and to persist with our own prejudices is what is being learned en passant in biographical life situations. While curriculum-oriented learning, provided by institutional ways, contents and aims are being chosen rationally and responsibly, there is no normative regulation for individual learning. Everyone can choose what he or she likes; there is no one to help during a dry spell, with meanders and kneejerk reactions. This is a general lack of all subject-focused educational approaches. In addition, completeness and uniformity are not the strengths of learning en passant; common and obligatory contents cannot be achieved, many things remain situational, individual, and incidental. If accuracy, completeness, or uniformity/obligingness is intended, learning en passant is not the right way. Complex systematic and highly standardized contents are also not adequate. Only very few people learn a foreign language en passant – a dictionary and a few lessons at an adult education center help to make a different start …

But on the other hand "being an active citizen", "solidarity", and "charity" cannot be learned without a lot of learning en passant. However, the concept of lifewide education is also useful in explaining unrequested learning results because it explains how they contradict the declared and requested learning results that come about. The perception and explanation might help to avoid unrequested results.

"How do people reach what they know, what they are able to do and what they are?" This was the initial question. This question turns out to be generative because it helps to identify and describe different ways of learning, situations of learning and ideas of learning. "Learning en passant" was integrated into the concept of "lifewide education".

3. The next step: "compositional learning"

In the reality of the lives of adult learners, learning often takes place within the interaction of job, free time, family, fun, pressure, and unavoidable experiences, in laughing, crying, and boredom. Especially the biographical approach of andragogy pointed out the integration of the context. If you take a closer look, the examples above also show the interaction of different learning occasions, learning aids, and learning aims: postcards, movies, speeches, trial and error, reading, and doing.

End page 25
Start page 26

Learning idea 9 – compositional learning: Many learning results do not occur from a single learning attempt but from a combination, a "composition" of different learning sources, from intention and coincidence, from self-directed and submitted, from offered and befallen. This "composition" is created by the individual learner according to his or her abilities and needs.

The learning projects described by Allen Tough also prove the use of different learning sources. However our own experience is enough to confirm the composition of different learning sources. If you go for a learning task, often a variety of learning possibilities are being discovered. You suddenly meet "partial experts" who share their experience, you find relevant magazines (articles) at the train station kiosk or your hairdresser, you use instruction manuals and product inserts, you try and get the help of others, you find web pages and support groups – and you find the offer of the regional further education institutions. But it could also be the other way round: You start with a further education class – and afterwards and along the way you start activities that continue the learning.

In an interview within the research of compositional learning, a respondent describes her way of learning photography, which was started through an acquaintance: "I went to a photography class for six Saturdays, then I just started to take pictures straight on.… Luckily I could ask my fiancé. He really helped me a lot. And of course, I had to try it over and over again to improve, to try something new. Then I bought a magazine on photography.… Later there was something about a famous photographer on TV. That is, what I have been trying" (Ellner 2000, p. 39 et seq). Participating in a class, trying, asking a friend, reading magazines, watching TV, trying again: those are all interacting elements of the "composition".

Also "compositional learning" easily leads to romantics: "All humans are lifelong, lifewide, compositional learners". That is true, at least in general, but in reality extend, content, dimension, and quality of this learning are unequal - like in music, compositions can be ingenious or foul. "Compositional learning" is a descriptive category; educational thinking has to reflect, whether it is leading to a better person and world – or not.

4. Learning as "open project"

When leaving the house in the morning, when participating in a theater-work-shop (because of rainy weather), when starting a journey: Do we know how we will come back? Such activities may lead us to learning results or learning-chains without knowing in advance what we might look like afterwards.

This type of learning seems to contradict the necessity of planned and insti-tutionalized offer-ings. It is unique, en-countering, open, "postmodern". Nevertheless, its success depends on a learning-friendly environment:

> Learning idea 10 – learning as an "open project": Learning can also be seen as an "open project" of singular and unpredictable elements, compositions, and results. Not in the forecast but only in the review the sense of learning lines can be discovered. However, the learnings depend on the possibilities encountered "in that way", which decide whether the open learning project fails or leads to essential growth.

Tough (1979) pointed out in his research the necessity of learning resources, Penland (1977) showed the fragility of learning, if the learner takes a wrong path, and our own research (Ellner 2000) shows, how even in this "learning as open project" outside arranged learning can be supportive.

5. Implication for practice:
to see, use, and support lifewide learning

A "didactic of lifewide education" cannot be accomplished here. However, a few proposals shall be given on what these theoretical conceptual considerations could mean for the practice of adult education.

1. *Can you "make" learning en passant?* – Definitely. Not in the way that you drum learning success into the learners – this is also not possible with in-struction-oriented or training-oriented forms of learning. And – already men-tioned – this learning does not have the inescapability and the commitment of institutional curricular learning. But it is possible to arrange situations in which learning en passant and lifewide learning will take place and which support the probability of the success of learning en passant and lifewide learning.

2. *Recognize learning when it takes place*: a parish festival, company outing, or talking in the cafeteria; those are all activities that cause learning as a secondary effect. Learning in an unusual form is often not recognized as learning, and therefore not used and valued. Two examples: The participants of a class are exceeding their break because they are having a lively discussion of a topic from the class. Does the teacher consider this as a disturbance or a chance to learn? It is even more difficult to recognize learning when not only the form but also the content is different from the official curriculum. If participants of a course are being accommodated in a hotel by their employer, what do they learn about the appreciation of their company? The other way round: who has to be accommodated according to the travel expenses rate of the civil service (46 D-Mark per night), and what

End page 26
Start page 27

does he or she learn about the appreciation of their employer? And do we recognize how the bureaucracy mentality is "being taught" en passant?

3. *Learning as connecting and carrying something on*: If learning takes place within the context of life if it connects with existing things and lays the basis for further learning, then this leads to macro-didactic as well as micro-didactic results. The participant-oriented theory has claimed to "pick up the learners from where they are". The questions and problems of the learners are not established this way. Only learning possibilities for existing questions and problems are being offered. More attention needs to be drawn to (informal) learning parallel to the curriculum within and outside courses and also continuing after the completion of a learning sequence.

4. *Complete the existing, and recognize what is lacking*: Some situations of everyday life pose the question: What shall this weird fountain tell us? And now learning something or nothing is a matter of low threshold because learning support is easily available. A flyer which can be taken from the box beside the fountain leads to learning. Other offers can be added. City trails, nature trails, the flyer at the entrance of the church are all learning accesses – whereas those media can be designed more or less to support learning. The learning impulse has already been given; only the learning access has to be completed.

5. *Give impulses, provide learning occasions*: Learning exchanges, counseling offers, hotlines, project and support groups, a calm place to talk,

putting in touch with contact persons – all of these are new tasks for a culture of learning within the perspective of "lifewide education". Therefore there will be new tasks for institutions and teachers of adult education "to provide learning occasions" that go beyond the offer of classes.

The task and aim of this approach to lifewide learning is to support a learning-friendly environment, and therefore to invite people to walk the path of lifelong and lifewide learning. This is not a brand-new idea for educational institutions. Some of this had already been thought and done "en passant". The explicit appreciation can strengthen and support an existing approach.

Under the perspective "lifewide learning" learning is seen as a composition of intention and serendipity, institutionalized outside organized learning, self-directed intentional learning, and nonintentional learning en passant. In this paper ten different perspectives on learning were presented; they open wide horizons of adult learning and education. They challenge theory and practice to think and do the most appropriate. And we are in the middle of this adventure to discover and design this new continent.

End page 27
Start page 30

References:

Cann, Roger J.: Incidental learning. In: *Adult Education* 57.Jg. (1984), H.1, S. 47-49.

Dohmen, Günther (1996): *Das lebenslange Lernen. Leitlinien einer modernen Bildungspolitik.* Bonn: BWFT.

Ellner, Heidi (2000): *"Kompositionelles Lernen" – Untersuchung über eine übersehene Dimension des Lernens Erwachsener.* Diplomarbeit im Studiengang Pädagogik an der Universität Bamberg.

Hiemstra, Roger/Brockett, Ralph G. (1994): Overcoming Resistance to Self-Direction in Adult Learning. *New Directions for Continuing Education*, no. 64. San Francisco: Jossey-Bass.

Penland, P. R. (1977): *Self-Planned Learning in America.* Pittsburgh: University of Pittsburg.

Reischmann, Jost (1980): Hochschul-Diplome ohne Hochschul-Besuch. The New York Regents External Degree. In: *Volkshochschule im Westen* 32. H. 2, S. 84-86.

Reischmann, Jost (1988): *Offenes Lernen von Erwachsenen. Grundlagen und Erprobung im Zeitungskolleg.* Bad Heilbrunn: Klinkhardt.

Reischmann, Jost (1996): Andragogik - Wissenschaft von der Bildung Erwachsener. Alter Name für eine neue Sache. In: Derichs-Kunstmann, Karin / Faulstich, Peter / Tippelt, Rudolf (Hg.): *Qualifizierung des Personals in der Erwachsenenbildung. Beiheft zum Report.* Frankfurt: Deutsches Institut für Erwachsenenbildung. S. 14-20.

Reischmann, Jost (1998): Die Wunderwelt selbstgesteuerten Lernens. In: Hoffmann, Nicole/von Rein, Antje (Hg.): *Selbstorganisiertes Lernen in (berufs-) biographischer Reflexion.* Bad Heilbrunn: Klinkhardt, S. 57-71.

Reischmann, Jost (2009): Formen des Lernens Erwachsener. In: Fuhr, Thomas/ Gonon, Philipp / Hof, Christiane (Hg.): *Handbuch der Erziehungswissenschaft*, Band II/2 Erwachsenenbildung Weiterbildung. Paderborn: Sch.ning, S. 851-862.

Rogers, Carl (1974): *Lernen in Freiheit.* München: Kösel.

Tough, Allen (21979): *The Adult's Learning Projects.* Toronto: The Ontario Institute for Studies in Education.

4. Projects, Examples: Andragogy at Work

In pedagogy and andragogy theory and practice cross-fertilizes each other. This synergy is evident in the development of practical projects, where theoretical assumptions guide the modeling of project designs, and practical work challenges theoretical reflections on the specifics of adult learning. The following examples illustrate this circular relationship between theory and practice and practice and theory.

The first example holds one of the earliest English publications about the project 'Zeitungsolleg'. It is written in the typical optimistic spirit of a project-beginning. The detailed description has the intention that others could copy the project. However, it also shows clearly the (theoretical) claims that are associated with many of the practical decisions made.

Subsequent research and publications yielded more insights[1]. Just one additional result (practice) should be reported, that lead to an innovative understanding (theory) of adult learning: When we asked our readers who used only parts of the offered material, why they used only parts (Poor quality? Boring?) the responses surprised us. Instead of disappointment, they expressed, "We took as much as we wanted". This opened a new understanding of 'partial users' in adult learning: While in schoollike learning 'everything' has to be consumed, adult learners can decide, what and how much is helpful for them at a given time. It seems to be more of a "drop-in" approach than a "drop-out" one. This result might be generalized to other projects.

The concept of 'open learning,' initially somewhat vague, clarified during this project work. Two key insights emerged: 'Openness' is a continuum (from 'more' to 'less'), and it comprises several dimensions, such as 'arrangement', 'learning process', 'content', 'attitude' (Reischmann 1988, p. 115). Once again, it became evident that theory-based practice also fertilizes theory.

4.1 Zeitungskolleg (Courses by Newspaper) (1981)[2]
A new way in open adult education in West Germany

The development of Zeitungskolleg (Courses by Newspaper) by the Deutsches Institut für Fernstudien an der Universität Tübingen, based on the model of 'Courses by Newspaper' of University Extension of the University of California at San Diego, is described. The German experience in providing distance education through newspapers is analyzed.

---

[1] Reischmann, Jost (1988): *Offenes Lernen von Erwachsenen. Grundlagen und Erprobung im Zeitungskolleg.* Bad Heilbrunn: Klinkhardt 1988

[2] First print: Reischmann, Jost (1981): Zeitungskolleg. A New Way in Open Adult Education in West Germany. In: *Distance Education. The Journal of the Australian and South Pacific External Studie*s. Association. Adelaide, Vol. 2, No. 2, pp. 199-211.

What we had

The aim of the German Institute for Distance Studies (DIFF), founded in 1967, is to examine and to realize possibilities for academic study in which the permanent presence of the student is unnecessary. The main tasks of the Institute are the development, testing, and implementation of academic and 'distance courses' in various subjects. ...

End page 199
Start page 200

Therefore, DIFF had considerable experience in the development and implementation of academic printed material, had worked with academic experts on many subjects, had connections with other institutions we served or who served us, had organized programs with a variety of different socio-economic and geographic backgrounds -and we had the firm belief that multi-media and distance learning is becoming more and more important in adult learning.

What we wanted

All of the DIFF programs had a common background: to make academic knowledge available to people who for one reason or another were not able to attend a university. The ongoing discussion about 'de-schooling' the learning process, about universities without walls, about the needs of the adult learner, and the necessity of person-centered learning situations, was a challenge to develop an additional distance educational program that incorporated more recent thinking about adult learning.

So what we wanted at this point was a project that should be:
- flexible in place and time, offering easy access for everybody;
- not aimed at a narrow target group but useful for individually differentiated users;
- meaningful for and close to the problems and phenomena of everyday life;
- satisfying actual needs instead of storing knowledge for future needs;
- different from traditional learning settings, utilizing new media and new learning places; and
- on a serious academic level, not making things easier than they should be.

End page 200
Start page 201

What we learned

In spring 1977 we learned about 'Courses by newspaper' at the University Extension, University of California, San Diego, and its combination of weekly newspaper articles and printed material for college courses, about its topics, authors, and its great acceptance by newspapers and colleges. On the whole, the central ideas of 'Courses by newspaper' made so much sense to us that we started to plan a similar project which we named Zeitungskolleg (newspaper college).

What we tried: the pilot project

In summer 1977 we started to check our resources as well as the interests of possible partners. Professor Günther Dohmen, former Director of DIFF, who had discovered 'Courses by newspaper', and I, Assistant Professor in the Educational Department of the University of Tübingen were convinced by the idea and began to develop Zeitungskolleg. Looking back to the resources available at that time it seems almost incredible that we were able to realize this project in such a short time. Of course, there was no full-time staff. Money, material, and office requirements seemed available in a limited amount - as far as it could be saved from other DIFF projects. It takes at least one year to obtain extra resources for a new project, but we did not want to wait. So I agreed to integrate this additional task into my university activities and a part-time secretary was found. In a few months perhaps some more help might be available.

The next step was then taken: to contact the local newspapers of Tübingen and Reutlingen, a neighboring town, and the director of the Volkshochschulverband of our state. The Volkshochschule is the only adult education organization that exists in every town in Germany. The Volkshochschule is also our partner offering courses for our Funkkolleg.

The newspapers and the Volkshochschule agreed to try a pilot project with us. We had suggested a list of possible topics, but the newspaper editor suggested a topic, which, supported by the Volkshochschule, was formulated as "Landschaft und Geologie" (landscape in the sense of ecology and geology'), a topic which in our part of Germany makes good sense. It was easy for us to accept this topic.

The serious planning of our pilot project then began. At first, we contacted various institutions, professors, and teachers and tried to find out:1) what themes would be interesting for this topic; and 2) who could be

End page 201
Start page 202

authors for the newspaper articles, When we had settled on a reasonable number of themes and authors we went to the dean of the geological institute of our university and asked him to be our academic coordinator: to contact the authors (partly suggested by us, partly by him), to control the academic quality of our material and to advise us in all scientific problems. Here again, we were lucky. Being the vice-president of our university he was very interested in showing a wider public what is done behind the walls of the university. Thus, we got a positive response and were ready to begin.

Later we recognized that our more or less intuitive activity was a real model for all our later preparation of new topics:

At first, we try to find possible topics in talks with specialists.

- We offer these to an expert meeting, consisting of newspaper and Volks-hochschule officials; we discuss the topics and agree on a suitable topic.
- Next, we hold informal talks with experts about interesting aspects of our topic. We also ask them to suggest possible authors and academic coordinators.
- Then we ask a well-known and widely accepted person to become the academic coordinator. We believe it is important that he is not only an expert in the subject area, but also open to interdisciplinary approaches, interested in public presentations, and flexible enough to accept the unconventional concept of Zeitungskolleg,
- We then suggest themes and authors and ask for his comments. When we have agreed on a list he contacts his colleagues and asks them to participate in the project.
- In addition, we ask him to suggest one full-time or two part-time persons in his institute whom we can hire for six to nine months to prepare mainly the printed materials for this project. Usually, we get graduate students preparing for their doctorates.

With this accomplished the more detailed work begins. We have to convince the authors not to write for their colleagues but for newspaper subscribers. And we have to select articles to be reprinted for the supplemental text to be used by those subscribers interested in fuller information on the topic.

End page 202
Start page 203

Finding interested authors, mostly professors of geology, geography, and paleontology at the university, was surprisingly easy. The concern that the traditional German professor would not be interested was absolutely wrong. All our authors agreed to make their work understandable to the common man (and woman). They also accepted our rather newspaper-like formulations of article titles (e.g. 'Landscape in the garbage pail?' 'Water is life', 'Resources for our grandchildren', 'Good things coming from beneath', 'The fighting rivers'.)

They also wrote their articles as clearly as they could, but this was not good enough for newspapers. We had expected this problem (based on the University of California experience), so we hired an experienced journalist from our local newspaper. He wrote primarily about university events for the newspaper and therefore was experienced in translating academic German into a newspaper style. Of course, the authors had to approve his rewriting, and again we received surprisingly positive feedback. Many of the authors liked their rewritten article better than their original manuscripts. For example, one stated, "You made much clearer, even to me, what I wanted to say!' Only one author refused to accept the rewritten article. Finally, we also bought photos and cartoons to illustrate the newspaper articles so they would be more attractive to the average reader.

Looking at the beautifully printed texts produced by 'Courses by newspaper' at the University of California, it was clear that we could not convince any publisher to print a similar book because we had no idea whether anybody would buy it. Instead, we took scissors and glue and made copies of appropriate articles from books and journals. For each newspaper article, one chapter of readings was developed, consisting of academic articles, poems, extracts from schoolbooks, documents, novels, articles from journals and newspapers. They were arranged on the pages as nicely as possible, and after having filled 200 pages with fourteen chapters parallel to the fourteen newspaper articles we made 600 Xerox copies (copyrights of course had been obtained). The quality of the photos was not very good, but we could present an interesting book with considerable information for a reasonable price.

Because we wanted to make our materials available to a wide-spread and diverse audience, and because we wanted to make it available for various purposes - the casual reader as well as the teacher and pupil, the college student as well as the professional, the highly educated as well as the worker - we also prepared a study guide (again using the

End page 203
Start page 204
End page 204
Start page 205

'San Diego Courses by newspaper' model). This booklet has no extra information on the subject but advises on how to use the material. Because we wanted Zeitungskolleg to

Fig 1. Logos of Zeitungskolleg Europe, Children, Mikroprozessors

provide a better understanding of reality we wanted to stimulate people not only to read but also to make immediate contact with the described phenomena. Therefore, a very important aspect of each chapter were the hints on where to go hiking or to the museum, where to find fossils, or which nature clubs to join in a densely populated country. We had fun writing this part because we could test whether our topic and theme were considered close-to-life-subjects. For economical reasons, this study guide (48 pages) was typed by our secretary and then was also Xerox copied.

For course-leaders at the Volkshochschule we developed a twenty-page brochure that contained didactical hints. It was divided into three parts: 1) gives general advice about working with a group of adults, 2) gives a list of films, slides, tapes, experimental sets that can be ordered from libraries or other institutions, and 3) gives three or four examples for each chapter as to what to do in the corresponding group meeting. This brochure is free of charge to anyone.

This original experience showed us that realistic and successful ways had been found that would prove useful for further projects:

* The manuscripts of the newspaper articles are revised by a journalist cooperating with the authors.
* In addition to the articles we usually offer the newspaper one photo per article, two cartoons per article, and a series logo.
* The book of readings is developed mainly by a specialist hired for six to nine months. Suggestions provided by the authors and, of course, the project staff assist this person in his work.
* Each article in the newspaper series is supplemented by one chapter in the book (about six to ten titles).
* The book is a mixture of articles (from poems and documents to extracts of academic schoolbooks) to demonstrate an interdisciplinary approach to motivate as many readers as possible.

Fig. 2. Illustrations for Zeitungskolleg

*   The book design is a group effort. We still use the scissors/glue technique in
      mounting the articles that we want to be reprinted in the original format (this
      is now done by professional offset mounters). The printing quality is also
      more satisfying now.

End page 205
Start page 206

*   The study guide follows the structure of the chapters; each contains the
      following subtitles: central ideas, a summary of the newspaper article, list of
      the articles in the book of readings, hints on how to work with the material,
      questions for self-study, discussion themes, what to do, to try, to visit,
      additional literature (also for youngsters).
*   Accompanying each Zeitungskolleg we produce a little brochure containing
      'hints for working groups'.

End page 206
Start page 207

All this was done between September 1977 (when the topic Landschaft und
Geologie was decided) and February 1978. All printed materials, a poster, and
an information sheet were finished some days before the deadline. It was hard
work, but it was completed on time because all the people involved were
convinced the idea was a good one. And on February 18th, 1978 two
newspapers published the first article to appear in the series.

What we experienced

The first feedback we received was from the newspapers that printed the articles
and sold the text and the study guide (the Volkshochschule sells them also and
they can be ordered by mail). Our materials were so popular that we had to print
another 300 after two weeks, and 300 again three weeks later. We received more
phone calls and letters from people pleased with the series and materials.

Of course, we were then curious. How many subscribers had read our article
and how had they liked them? Luckily, during this first semester, I was
conducting a seminar on research in education. So I gave my students some
practical work. They phoned a representative sample of newspaper subscribers
($N = 214$) of our two newspapers and asked for their opinions aided by a
structured questionnaire. Some of the results:

-     61% of the sample knew Zeitungskolleg.
-     40% had read one or more of the articles:
       5% one article,
       23% two to five articles,
       12% more than five articles.

The age of the readers varied considerably, the average being 48.4 years (s = 14,7; Non-readers 43,1; s = 17,6).

Social classes	Readers	Non-readers
Workers	8%	16%
Lower middle class	32%	23%
Academic level	22%	12%
Others (housewives, retired people, pupils, no answer)	37%	48%

It is obvious (and was to be expected) that the better-educated readers dominate the readership, but still many workers and employees read

End page 207
Start page 208

the articles. In the same direction we asked ,Did you participate in some educational programs within the last five years?' 59% of our readers had done so, but 75% of the non-readers had not.

The following question we only asked those who had read at least one article: 'How would you evaluate Zeitungskolleg in general?' We offered a scale from 1 (= very interesting) to 5 (= not interesting). We received the following results:

1: 29%	2: 50%	3: 20%	4: 1%	5: 0%

76% said that the length of the articles was just right (15%: too long, 9%: too short).

95% said that the articles were understandable even for people who have no special schooling in this subject.

23% said that they were encouraged by this Zeitungskolleg to participate in other related activities.

We also asked a small sample of the purchasers of the supplemental materials (N = 65) how they evaluated it:

40% had read half or more of the book of readings, 40% only a small part, 19% nothing. On a scale from 1 (= very good) to 5 (= very bad) we received these results:

1: 31%	2: 48%	3: 10%	4: 0%	5: 2%

The study guide was used by 54% who evaluated it:

1: 38%	2: 30%	3: 30%	4: 3%	5: 0%

These evaluation data were of course gratifying, but more important was the fact that we could demonstrate that our materials and our program could work.

This convinced the managing board of our institute to approve a fully paid project group to continue with new topics.

From local to nationwide

In July 1978 the first full-time employees for Zeitungskolleg were hired. Today, the staff consists of the project director, an educational specialist for the study materials, an academic journalist, and one full-time (or two half-time) specialist(s) for the specific topics.

End page 208
Start page 209

Also, we have two secretaries and three part-time student helpers. This fall we received funding from the Robert Bosch Foundation to hire a research specialist on a full-time basis. After the decision to continue Zeitungskolleg we were assisted by the Volkswagen Foundation which labeled us an 'unconventional project' and financed the necessary office equipment, a half-time secretary, research resources, and a visit to 'Courses by newspaper', San Diego.

Of course, it was not yet possible to develop a new topic for fall 1978 with a staff hired in July 1978. But the local pilot topic, '"Landscape and geology' had been so successful that we decided to repeat it in a revised version in our state (one of eleven states in West Germany). Thus, we could train the new staff and increase the quality of the materials without starting over again, and we could prepare to cope with a larger number of newspapers and Volkshochschulen.

Naturally, our expanded effort raised new problems (and challenges too). First, we had to contact all daily newspapers in our state. We wrote immediately to all publishers introducing the project, offering the series of fourteen articles and explaining our conditions:

> Newspapers are obliged to print the whole series without changing the text. Our photos and cartoons can be used or not, and the use of local illustrations by the newspaper is encouraged. The newspapers receive the series free of charge. We will provide the Zeitungskolleg to each daily newspaper that wants to print it. We set a deadline before which an article must not be published and the newspapers receive each article at least ten days before this deadline. The article should be published between the first possible day (always a Saturday) and the following Friday; we recommend that it be published on the same day each week,

We enclosed a copy of the fourteen articles of our pilot model with our invitation letter. In response, thirty-four newspapers with a daily combined circulation of 800,000 readers accepted our invitation (approximately 25% of all daily newspapers in our state).

This first state-wide Zeitungskolleg in the fall of 1978 provided a good chance to train our office personnel because we knew that the planned nationwide distribution would require a reliable routine to serve the newspapers, the Volkshochschulen and the people who ordered the supplementary material.

For our state project, we commissioned a publisher to distribute the materials to newspapers, Volkshochschulen, and single buyers. The material is not sold in bookshops because this would have raised the price (which is about $U.S.5.00 for the book and the study guide). We sold about 6,500 sets of material for this topic.

End page 209
Start page 210

In spring 1979 our topic was 'Europa', an important current topic because of the European parliamentary election in June 1979. Again we selected authors and themes on an interdisciplinary basis: they dealt with history, culture, economy, and politics. This series of articles was printed in about 100 newspapers in seven states with a circulation of three million readers. About 150 Volkshochschulen offered courses and about 5,000 books were sold.

We went nationwide with the project in fall of 1979 with the topic 'Attention, children'. The thirteen articles were printed in 148 newspapers with a circulation of 3.2 million (which means 16% of the West German daily newspaper circulation), 7,600 sets of materials were sold and about 120 courses were offered.

The next topic was 'Microprocessors - the electronic revolution'. It discussed in twelve articles the technology as well as the social and economic implications and risks. There were 137 newspapers participating (a circulation of 2.8 million), 120 courses took place, and 5,100 materials sold.

Summing up

The University of California idea of 'Courses by Newspaper' came to us at the right time in the right place and, maybe, to the right people(!). Certainly, we were well prepared. Our theoretical background in open adult education, our experience in media projects, the resources of our institute, and the political situation of our universities fit together. So it became possible within one year after obtaining the basic idea from UC San Diego to plan, implement, and finish a complete pilot project successfully and to go nationwide one year later. This project produced several innovations:
- Zeitungskolleg is interdisciplinary, phenomenon-oriented, and related to the experience, while projects on the academic level are usually subject-oriented.
- Zeitungskolleg is not produced for a narrow target group but should be usable by everybody. The whole program (and each single part) is prepared for a heterogeneous group of participants.
- Zeitungskolleg has no compulsory catalog of aims and objectives. We encourage our participants to pick out what seems helpful and reasonable to them.

End page 210
Start page 211

- Zeitungskolleg has no definition of success, The variety of newspapers, themes, and users creates an open learning situation that would be spoiled by any formal testing. We trust in self-evaluation.
- Zeitungskolleg is not specializing, but integrating. It develops a framework in which further information can be incorporated. So we try to promote the generalist, not the specialist.

'Courses by newspaper' and 'Zeitungskolleg' have certainly enriched the variety of flowers in adult education with a creative and innovative species. After looking backward in this report I now want to look forward. Where in the world will 'Courses by newspaper'/Zeitungskolleg No. 3 be started?

After five years and ten different Zeitungskollegs, this project was terminated following critical remarks from the controlling agency for public money (Landesrechnngshof). Arguments were for example: too expensive, enough other sources for information available, not enough material purchased, and the absence of examinations, so no control over learning effects ... But what remains: In practical terms, it introduced many innovations in presenting new types of learning material and sources On the theoretical side, it contributed to an extended understanding of adult learning.

The starting point of the following contribution stemmed from a practical need: to enhance the andragogical competencies of subject matter specialists in company-training. A model was constructed wherein a professional andragogue coaches the subject matter specialist before, after, and directly within their courses.

However, the interconnectedness between practice, theory, and research quickly became apparent: during the model construction practical decisions challenged the theoretical framework, and concepts and constructs guided ideas and practice. This example also can be read as an example of the circular relationship between practice and theory.

The central innovative idea in this "coaching" approach is, that subject matter competency and andragogic competency are not blended in one person (like in the old teacher image), but can be separated into two persons. It remains a remarkable discovery that andragogues trained in coaching can effectively support subject matter specialists without having much knowledge of the content to be learned.

4.2 Coaching: Facilitating the Training of Subject-Matter Specialists (1998)[1]

Development and Evaluation of an Andragogical Model of Continuing Vocational Education

Practical Problem

Research in Germany shows that subject-matter specialists with little or no andragogical competencies - educational amateurs - offer most of the continuing vocational education and in-service training in companies. Because of the complexity and specifics of the training contents and their company-related expertise, companies need these subject-matter specialists and practitioners as trainers. But the short-time instructional effect as well as the long-time readiness for lifelong and lifewide learning remains limited. Educational training of these subject-matter specialists often is not the answer to this problem: Either it is not available, not effective enough, or can not be justified when a practitioner is teaching only a few hours.

Research Questions

Given this situation, the research question is how to improve the quality of perception, planning, performance, and evaluation of training by training-amateurs in companies. This question not only includes the problem of higher

---

[1]   First print: Reischmann, Jost (1998): Coaching: Facilitating the Training of Subject-Matter Specialists. In: Academy of Human Resource Development: 1998 Conference Proceedings. Baton Rouge, LA: AHRD; ahrd.org, p. 216-221.

effectiveness of the training measures but also of a transformed perception of training as personnel and organizational development within the culture of a company.

On a first level this is a practical developmental task: How can andragogical competency be brought into courses, when subject matter specialists are needed because of the complexity of the subject, but have no andragogical competency at their disposal?

On a second and more conceptual level this means to clarify the role(s) of the person(s) delivering continuing education: How is the transmission of knowledge and skills interwoven with the transformation of values and attitudes?

And finally, the evaluation question has to be asked: Is such a model successful, and where are the limits?

Methodology: Model-Construction

To answer these questions a traditional educational research strategy was used: the construction and experimental implementation of an educational/ andragogical model. Although the construction of a model is widely used in the history of education (i.e. John Dewey, Alexander Neill, Peter Petersen, Paulo Freire) it is often not perceived as a research strategy. The reason may be that we see these models (i.e. project learning, Summerhill-school, Jena-Plan-Schule, dialogic learning) as finished results and oversee the beginning implementations with its uncertainties, failures, corrections, and re-designing of practice and theory. The tentative implementation of an educational model makes it necessary to match theory with a convincing practice, and unexpected practice calls for explanation and theory. So the construction and implementation of a model is a systematic access, yet open for surprising incidents, for new or better knowledge combined with experientially tested practical results. In this function it is a research method.

The advantage of the construction of an educational model as research strategy is that

a) in the process of developing, implementing, and evaluating the model the practicability and usefulness of the developed method is tested,

b) in the necessary interaction between theory and practice the underlying concepts have to be clarified, and that

c) his holistic and qualitative approach supplies the researcher with "observation within context".

Within this experiential setting empirical data (qualitative and quantitative) were collected by participatory observation in about 70 courses, by semi-structured interviews with about 70 subject matter specialists and their coaches, and through a rating scale (CERAS, Reischmann 1996) developed for this project for participants of the courses [see 4.3 in this book].

Theoretical Framework

Like in most situations, a bundle of theories was included:

One theory this development was based on is the person-centered approach of Carl Rogers (Freedom to Learn, 1969): Learning has to be meaningful to the learner, should happen in a non-threatening environment, is supported by doing, is more successful when the learner can influence the learning content and method and take over self-responsibility, and focuses not merely on knowledge, but also emotions. In this theory, we found a concept that was founded more on counseling, more on facilitating learning than instructing.

Allen Tough's work on "The Adult's Learning Projects " (1979) indicates, that most of the learning of adults happens in settings more similar to normal life than to formal schooling and that adults undertake learning projects when real-life problems call for solutions. This corresponded to our observation, that shortly before and while the subject matter specialists were delivering their courses they were very willing to ask for support. Such an individual time schedule could not be answered with formal training offerings but needed individualized and flexible settings.

Malcolm Knowles' concept of "Andragogy" (i.e. 1979, 1984) developed over three decades a theory that focused on the specifics of adult learners: their self-concept, experience, learning-readiness, time perspective, and orientation to learning. Especially helpful is that he takes into account also the learning in and for the workplace. Working with the training demands of subject matter specialists which often are high-ranked specialists in their company makes it indispensable to refer to these specifics.

Several concepts were available that contributed to the perception of the described task: Peer-counseling, team-teaching, mentoring, or supervision. In addition, we found that Joyce/Showers (1981, 1982) described experiences with the coaching process related to teacher-training clearly and promising. Also, modern staff development theories which focus on cooperation, self-directedness, and self-responsibility influenced the theoretical framework of our work.

The Model: Coaching the Subject Matter Specialist

To increase the quality of vocational training a "tandem"-situation was developed: the subject matter specialist is individually "coached" by an adult educator before, during, and after the course.

Interviews in a pre-study with six IBM managers had shown, that "Coaching" is a term widely used for various concepts and contents - every modern strategy seems to be labeled "coaching". So first a distinct concept of coaching was formulated:

With "coaching in continuing education" we label a training situation in which the subject matter specialist is supported by an adult educator in planning and conducting one specific course. The content competency and the andragogical competency are brought into a course by two separate persons. The subject matter specialist remains responsible for the content, while the adult educator helps him/her to design and conduct the course in a way that facilitates learning. This coaching is seen as individualized support for a limited time: coaching lasts between three and eight sessions; after that, the subject matter specialist goes on again on his own. This limitation keeps both aware that the training is and remains within the responsibility of the subject matter specialist, and that the coach's offerings are a time-limited chance.

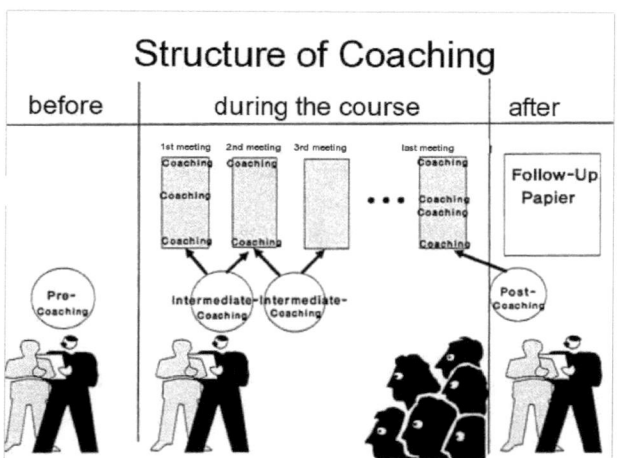

The activities of the adult educator as a coach are: Before and during the course (pre-coaching) he/she helps to design the course and the sessions. After the sessions (post-coaching) he/she gives feedback and helps to plan the next session. This resembles traditional counseling and supervision. Also, the coach is present in the course for observation which supplies the information for feedback. In these activities the coach offers clarification as well as information: Clarification why processes develop(ed) in a certain way, information about methods, and how to handle them. In addition - and this is what is particular about our coaching - the adult educator plays an active and responsible role during the course meetings. The coach takes over pre-planned actions like introducing the participants, giving learning-aids, and introducing special methods such as group work. Hereby the coach serves as a model. He/she also becomes spontaneously active when it seems necessary.

These activities are - first - aimed to increase the educational competency of the subject matter specialist for subsequent courses. The suggestions and feed-back in the pre- and post-coaching are explained and give a situation-specific introduction to adult education methodology and philosophy. Theory becomes directly related to practice. The suggestions and feedback refer to the individual subject matter specialist, his concrete needs, the specific topic, and situation. Answering real-life problems makes this exchange meaningful and related to doing. By demonstrating educational behavior directly the coaching adult educator acts as a model (Bandura) - and not the usual schoolmaster-style: telling others what they must do, while sneaking away from showing competency.

These activities want - second - to increase the success of the course: directly through activities of the coach, indirectly through the teaching of the subject matter specialist improved by the coaching. Coaching intends to encourage:
- better knowledge of the content ("subject matter compe¬tency"),
- better learning in the future ("methodic competency"),
- better cooperating ("social competency").

This complex andragogical activity, including counseling, observation, modeling, and supervision, we call "coaching". The difference between peer-counseling or team-teaching is, that both persons are experts - but in different fields. So there is no reason for competition: both experts do their job, trying to let the other participate in his/her competency, exchanging, sharing, and caring together for the best learning success.

Of course, it is not expected that such short-time coaching makes subject matter specialists into educational experts. Depending on which educational competencies the subject matter specialist started, coaching wants to prepare for the next step by offering genuine andragocical perspectives applied to the subject matter specialist's individual training task.

How to become a "Coach"?

Coaching is executed by professional adult educators. The variety of situations and contents they are confronted with, the necessity to act and react immediately, and the ability to take care of the subject matter specialist as well as the participants make it inevitable that they have at their disposal a wide variety of educational theories and methods. It is necessary that they are able to intervene in a style and mood that does not offend or threaten either the subject matter specialist or the participants. Counseling competence is helpful for this.

For persons who studied adult education (mostly students of our department) and for experienced practitioners (two major car manufacturers) we developed a four-day training. It contains:
- non-directive communication skills,
- group-dynamics,
- learning techniques,
- didactical planning of courses.

About 70 persons going through this training reported after their first practical coaching experience that they were able to apply the basic coaching-ideas and coaching-strategies after this training.

Results and Conclusions

More than 70 coachings by different coaches have been accomplished. Besides the direct experiences, qualitative and quantitative data were collected.

Experiences with the implementation: The first of the implementation experiences is, that institutions and subject matter specialists often hesitated to try this arrangement. They found the idea convincing, but either regretted that „Right now I have no suitable training" or did not want to do it themselves: „I know somebody who would really deserve coaching". There seems to exist a high level of fear of allowing somebody to observe training. But when one or two trainers could be convinced, then based on their experience other trainers asked for coaching.

A specific difficulty was the activity of the coach in the courses. Only half of the subject matter specialists allowed this, the other half limited the attendance of the coach to observation. Teaching and training as a cooperative venture seems unthinkable for many trainers, thus continuing the image of the lonesome fighter.

An unexpected but repeated observation was the divergence between how subject matter specialists described their planned courses and how they acted in real course situations. Counseling and supervision, relying on the description of the actor, seem after this experience often based on unrealistic data.

In a certain type of training, coaching was more or less impossible: in "high-pressure lectures " when the subject matter specialists were oriented solely to presenting their content, and when they wanted to present too much content.

The subject matter specialist neglected even simple arrangements planned in the pre-coaching, for example taking a break. By trying to interfere the coach was made responsible for the fact that not all material could be presented - which made the subject matter specialist nervous as well as the participants. To put it in the words of one of our course leaders: "Through your repetitions and summaries I did not come as far as I wanted. Sometimes I thought: My God, I wish I could go on now!". Here we found clear limitations for coaching and learned to withdraw to pre-coaching and reviews/feedback as interventions.

Besides these limitations, coaching was found to be applied in a wide variety of courses. Various contents (hard technical or soft creative) could be coached as well as different participants (managers or apprentices) or training schemes (full-day or 90-minute units, long-planned or shortly started). It also turned out that our type of coaching was applied not only in companies but in adult education centers, religious institutions, and military education, even in schools and at university (my students coached each other in seminar-presentations). And surprisingly it made sense not only for inexperienced trainers we had designed it for, but also experienced and trained teaching specialists reported positive experiences. Some coaches even reported that they transferred strategies of our „coaching in continuing education" to learning situations that had to do nothing with teaching courses, like helping managers handle staff or customer problems.

Qualitative Evaluation: At the end of each coaching subject matter specialists were asked for written feedback about their perception of the coaching situation (process) and the results they see for their future courses (product). Similarly, the coaches delivered a report. Reports of about 70 coachings are available. Also, participants of these courses were interviewed.

The counseling in the pre-coaching and review situation was positively evaluated. "I absorbed the methodical and didactic suggestions like a dry sponge ... I could have reduced my preparation to half if I had the coaching earlier".

Interviews with the subject matter specialists showed that the presence and activities of the coach during the courses were seen ambivalently. As described only half of the subject matter specialists allowed the coach to become active in the course. When coaches could become active the subject matter specialists often criticized that the additional structuring and repeating by the coach cost extra time. Positive statements were made about the coach's activities (for example: preparing the chairs and tables, activating the participants, introducing participants by name, presenting visual aids, introducing breaks, and helping individually). A surprising number of didactic operations of the coaches were perceived and named in the final interview. It seems, that the subject matter specialists used these times of non-activity - as intended - to observe the educator in a relaxed mood: "I could observe your dialogue with the participants by standing aside".

Intended consequences for future courses were reported by most of the subject matter specialists. That included certain operations - introducing the participants, structuring the presentation, including exercises, taking breaks, using visual aids, reducing and concentrating the content, but also more general attitudes: "to make more personal contact", "to include the participant more in the course", "I conducted the course as a mathematician, not an educator ... That I want to change", "What I learned is to keep an eye on the learners", "there remained a lot of ideas that are helpful in a course - just the knowledge, how many possibilities a trained educator has, that are not available to an engineer". Of course, we do not expect that all these intentions will be practiced in the next course. However, our evaluation shows that our coaching opened the eyes of the subject matter specialists to educational ideas and operations.

We also asked for feedback from the participants. In the "high-speed lectures" we could not get much feedback. Here coaching was often perceived as an intrusion in a closed system: One subject matter specialist reported that participants complained that the coach going to the blackboard was insolent.

But most other courses found the presence of two persons surprisingly normal, although they recognized, that there was no perfect teamwork between the subject matter specialist and the educator.

Quantitative Results: For the quantitative evaluation, four pairs of courses were used in a pre-experimental design (Campbell/Stanley 1967): When a course

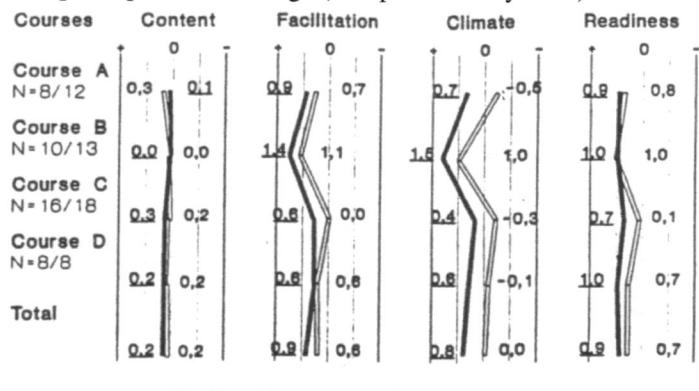

Participants quantitative rating coaching

is repeated (same content, same course leader, other participants), the second course was coached and the first used for control. Using CERAS (Course Evaluation Rating Scale – Reischmann 1996) the dimensions "perceived content success", "Facilitation = experienced learning support", "climate", and "readiness for further learning" were controlled.

The dimension "content success" did not show much difference, while in the three other dimensions the coached courses scored better. An explanation for the similar rating in the dimension "content success" could be that the coaching activity repeatedly activated the participants to control their learning success. This made them aware of gaps and failures, while the courses not coached left them more passive and in the uncontrolled feeling of being successful.

Respecting that the coachings were the first we did with these course leaders and lasted only between three and five half days it is positive that after such a short time already effects could be observed by the participants.

Contribution to new knowledge in HRD

A first contribution to the knowledge of HRD came even before coaching started: The direct observation of a great number of subject matter specialists as trainers nearly unanimously revealed a shocking inability to teach. That everybody who knows something can teach it turned out as a dramatic myth!

An overt contribution is the development of an additional training scheme for the improvement of continuing education in companies combined with a way to qualify subject matter specialists for training. Our experiences so far showed limits as well as possibilities: In several settings - as described not in all - coaching could be arranged and was perceived helpful. The coached subject matter specialist reported, that they felt a lot of support through our coaching and that they intend to change their following courses. Coaching seems to be a way to bring andragogical competency into courses. But we also found limitations: when the subject matter specialists were oriented mainly to presenting their content, and when they wanted to present too much content, then direct coaching was more or less impossible; pre-coaching and reviews remained as possible interventions.

To qualify "coaches" a four-day training for professional adult educators was developed. Trained coaches reported that this enabled them to act as coaches. Even more, they reported that this approach influenced and changed their perception of their work in HRD in an often transformative way.

On a conceptual level the unclear term "coaching" could be clarified and discriminated against other concepts such as counseling, supervision, team-teaching, or mentoring.

The "division of labor" between the subject matter specialist and the adult educator, such decomposing the teacher role that combines didactic and subject-matter knowledge, helped to clarify the role of the adult educator. Even in technical training, it became clear that in all teaching/learning contexts content- and attitude-learning is interwoven.

Through this experimental model, it became obvious that training in a traditional way supports the "lonesome fighter" mentality. Coaching offers - for many learners first time in life - a life example of cooperation between two equal adults.

This developed model of coaching combines theory and practice of HRD. It contributes to solving a practical problem. Even more, it helps to clarify the role and importance of professional adult educators in the context of the culture of a company.

References

Campbell, Donald T./Stanley, Julian C. (1967): Experimental and Quasi-Experimental Designs for Research on Teaching. In: Gage, N. L. (Hg): Handbook on Research on Teaching. Chicago: Rand McNally, 171-246.

Henschke, John A. (1988): A Comparison of Three Transfer of Training Strategies in Inservice Adult Teacher Training. In: Proceedings to the Midwest Research-to-Practice Conference in Adult and Continuing Education, ed. Chere Campbell Cobbins, Madison, Wisconsin, University of Wisconsin, October 1988, 48-53.

Joyce, Bruce/Showers, Beverly (1981): Transfer of training: the contribution of "coaching". Journal of Education. 163, 163-172.

Joyce, Bruce R./Showers, Beverly (1981): Improving Inservice Training. In: Joyce, Bruce R./Brown, Clarc C./Peck, Lucy (Hg): Flexibility in Teaching. New York, London: Longman, 166-173.

Joyce, Bruce/Showers, Beverly (1982): The Coaching of Teaching. In: Educational Leadership, Vol 40, 4-10.

Knowles, Malcolm (1978): The Adult Learner: A Neglected Species. Second Edition. Houston: Gulf Publishing Company.

Knowles, Malcolm and Associates (1984): Andragogy in Action. San Francisco: Jossey-Bass.

Reischmann, Jost (1996): Course Evaluation Rating Scale CERAS. University of Bamberg, Germany. Download at http://typo3.reischmannfam.de/fileadmin/jr/CERAS/CERAS.htm

Rogers, Carl (1969): Freedom to learn. Columbus, Ohio: Charles E. Merrill Publishing Company.

Tough, Allen (1979): The Adult's Learning Projects. Second Edition. Toronto: The Ontario Institute for Studies in Education.

In constructing a quality measuring instrument, as required in the preceding contribution, the initial step is to define what "quality" means. Practice (instrument) needs theory (what and why to measure).

Of course, it may be discussed, whether the operationalization in CERAS is the one and only description of quality. But the advantage is that the content is open for critique and can become improved.

This instrument can still be used today. A noteworthy supplement is the computer program (Windows) available for download (www.reischmannfam.de/ CERAS/index.htm), enabling a rapid and comfortable analysis within minutes (1 minute per questionnaire).

4.3 CERAS: Course Evaluation RAting Scale (2013)[1]

This rating scale was developed as a fast, easy-to-handle, and economic instrument for course feedback (application time 12 minutes) in adult/continuing education. It is applicable in courses that meet at least three times; it is not suitable for lectures or overview-presentations.

The items are taken from four dimensions, by which the quality of a course is defined: Perceived content mastery, learning-readiness, facilitation of learning, and climate.

Perceived Content Mastery, e.g.:	Facilitation of Learning, e.g.:
13 It was worthwhile for me to participate in this course. 21 In this course, I got sufficient knowledge. 33 My practical work benefits a lot from this course	14 The course was presented so that successful learning was easy. 18 The course was lively and interesting. 22 The participants were encouraged to bring their own questions and experiences into the course.
Learning readiness e.g.:	**Climate, e.g.:**
27 The participants were encouraged to bring their own questions and experiences into the course. 31 If this course is repeated, I will certainly recommend it to others. 3 The course has prepared me to work further in this subject on my own.	36 It was hard to say something during the course. 39 This class made us feel like partners. 4 During the course, there was a feeling of mutual support

CERAS was developed to raise the quality of adult/continuing education courses.
- Course leaders can use CERAS for feedback and self-reflection of their work, and/or for exchange with their participants about the best possible collaborative design of the learning situation.

---

1 Based on a paper presented at the Research-to Practice-Conference, September 23, 2013 in St. Louis, Mo.

- Institutions can use CERAS in the framework of their quality-management.
- CERAS can be used as an instrument in research.

CERAS should be applied shortly before the end of a course or a course chapter, to have the chance to talk with the participants about the outcomes, such serving for feedback. One way could be to apply the questionnaire before the last break. Then two participants could be asked to type the questionnaires into the computer. Then they could print out the results for all participants so that in the final phase of the course these results could be discussed with all participants.

Limit: As a rating scale this instrument does not measure on an absolute level, but relative to the expectation of the participants. Higher or lower scoring does not necessarily relate to higher or lower performance but may be caused by the expectations and standards the participants have. Results in various settings show, that these different standards exist. Therefore comparison between courses should use appropriate designs, i.e. pre-post or randomized designs.

The presented English version is a translation of an instrument developed in the German language. The German version has undergone the conventional procedure of statistical validation and has proven to be reliable. The English version needs before use statistical validation (N=200 should be enough).

The items of the questionnaire are not related to specific course contents so it can be applied in many courses independent of the respective course content. One criterion for selecting the items was that these items can be influenced by the course and its leader. Items asking for stable, unchangeable attitudes of the course and the course leader are omitted.

Each item should be evaluated on a Likert-scale with 5 choices:
1.yes: agree completely
2. agree mostly
3. ambivalent
4. disagree mostly
5. no: completely disagree

Download:

All needed files can be found on
http://www.reischmannfam.de/CERAS/index.htm.

The .pdf document "CERAS-questionnaire.pdf" contains the original 39-question version. "CERAS-questinaire-additems.docx" is a WORD-document and allows you to add up to 9 additional questions. We suggest copying the rating scale on the front- and back sides of one page (otherwise you might get single pages that can not be related to the second half).

Structure and substructure of the Course Evaluation RAting Scale (CERAS)

Dimension "Perceived Content Mastery "
Subdimension "subjective success"
13. It was worthwhile for me to participate in this course.
21. In this course, I got sufficient knowledge.
25. I now feel confident about the content covered in the course.

Subdimension "objective success"
1. I have mastered the contents of the course.
9. As a result of this course, I acquired extensive knowledge.
17. I feel that gaps still exist in what I had to learn.
29. If there would be a test at the end of the course, I would certainly get a good grade.
37. I could now teach the course content to others.

Subdimension "practical application"
5. It is still difficult for me to apply what I have learned.
33. My practical work benefits a lot from this course

Dimension "Learning-Readiness"
Subdimension "positive attitude towards adult education"
27. The participants were encouraged to bring their own questions and experiences into the course.
11. It would be fun if this course continued.
19. This course strengthened my self-confidence that I am able to learn successfully.

35. I am completely satisfied with what I got out of this course.

Subdimension "consequences of the experienced learning"
7. Because of the course, I did additional work in the area.
31. If this course is repeated, I will certainly recommend it to others.

Subdimension "learning the learning"
3. The course has prepared me to work further in this subject on my own.
15. During the course, I became familiar with resources (e. g., books) which I can use to help myself if I can't remember something.
23. During this course, I received advice which will make my learning in the future easier.

Dimension "Facilitation of Learning"
Subdimension "general learning support"
14. The course was presented so that successful learning was easy.
10. To learn the entire course content, one had to concentrate very hard.

Subdimension "methodic design"
18. The course was lively and interesting.
38. Every class session was clearly organized.
34. Certain course content should have been explained better.

2. It would have been easier for me to learn if the course was taught more concretely.

Subdimension "relatedness to learner"
6. All participants were encouraged to actively participate.
22. The participants were encouraged made to bring their own questions and experiences into the course.
26. The course leader listened to and addressed facts and arguments submitted by participants.
30. The usefulness of the content was repeatedly and clearly demonstrated using problems provided by the participants.

Dimension "Climate"
Subdimension "emotional feeling of the learning process"
16. In the class group, there is now an honest feeling of unity and team spirit.
24. The climate in the course tended to be impersonal and cold.
32. During the course, there were sufficient occasions to really laugh with one another.

Subdimension "quality of social interaction"
4. During the course, there was a feeling of mutual support.
8. I now know the names of many more of my classmates than at the beginning of the course.
12. We were able to influence what was going on in the course.
20. Within the class sessions, we discussed the course repeatedly (e.g., course conduct, content, evaluation).
28. I got to know the other participants in the course as real persons, not just as classmates.
36. It was hard to say something during the course.
39. This class made us feel like partners.

The following contribution has occasionally left readers confused as to its connection with adult education. After reading the preceding articles in this book, which outline our understanding of andragogy and adult education, this question should be answered easily. However, it also has to be admitted, that in the beginning, we had only an intuitive feeling that this could be a nice practical project. As we went deeper into the practical development, the more we discovered the theoretical value and foundation. So, the sequence of the following article looks wrong: As it is typically, in academic writing, it starts by describing first the theoretical context, then the practical project. In reality, it was more of a circular process – some practice, some thinking, some designing, some reflecting, some experiencing ... In pedagogy/andragogy this might be an often employed way for acquiring new knowledge: practice challenges theory, theory enlightens practice.

4.4 Bamberg donates time: Andragogues develop a city (2005)[1]

Abstract:

In this paper a project of cultural learning in a community in Germany is described: Students of andragogy organized a public exchange of "gifts" without monetary value; the idea was that the donator offered to share two to three hours of the personal life in a joint activity. About 200 people including local respected authorities participated. The event on the marketplace before Christmas became a public festival; the idea was widely welcomed with joy. The regional press reported; many gift-encounters took place. A challenging discussion took place about the relationship between adult education and andragogy.

Theoretical Context

(Adult) Education always is embedded in a socio-historic context, fulfilling the needs of the respective society and individuals. The focus of interest changes with the changing of society. Different functions, orientations, and "roots" of the idea of adult education become visible in this historical process:
- Today the "*transmission perspective*" (Pratt) seems predominant: Adult education is seen as a tool for effective training, often related to company training, needing to be effective, to enable transfer and application.

---

[1] First print in: Commission of International Adult Education (CIAE) of the American Association for Adult and Continuing Education (AAACE): Proceedings of the 2005 CIAE-Pre-Conference. November 6 – 8, 2005, p. 1-5. Pittsburgh, PA

- Looking back not much more than one decade the idea of *social justice and reform, of empowerment and emancipation* (i.e. Freire) was the predominant understanding of adult education.

End page 1
Start page 2

- Some years before "becoming a person" (Rogers), the development of the *"fully functioning", holistic individual* with all his "intellectualia, sensualia, spiritualia" (Comenius) was in the centre.
- *Compensatory education* - giving a second chance to learners who missed a first chance - is another root we can find in the historical look-back.
- In many historical contexts education for *building community*, society, and "parish" can be found, supplying a unifying idea helping individuals to become part of a wider social body with solidarity, care-taking, and identity.

More such basic roots could be named, but this discussion should not take place here. What this listing of roots and dominances should make us aware:

a) Asking for the "only right and legitimate adult education" would be ahistoric: Different orientations, "roots" seem to be predominant for a while, and then are replaced through another new or old orientation. Andragogy (Reischmann 2005b) as the scholarly approach to adult education can identify and describe these orientations, can compare them, and describe their strengths and weaknesses - and can take care that they are not forgotten when new mainstreams become predominant and seem to "take over" the whole understanding of adult education.

b) "Predominance" does not mean that the other orientations disappear. In the variety of fields where the education of adults happens, many parallel streams flow beside and across the mainstream. Even in times when mainstreams become overwhelming, claiming to be the only "right" adult education, andragogy must safeguard the wealth of the historical memory of the subject. This allows it to have a wide(r) variety of understanding and intervention strategies for the various fields of the education of adults.

In the historic and systematic memory of andragogy many formats for the education of adults are stored. Besides the intentional learning in adult education institutions or in autodidactic learning projects adults learn in various partly-intentional or non-intentional situations ("learning en passant"). Andragogy considers all these formats, formal or informal, traditional or non-traditional.

End page 2
Start page 3

This theoretical context became the framework for a practical project in an innovative format. Theory and practice flow together in this project, enriching both. This "flowing together" can be seen as an example of the enriching and necessary relationship between theory and practice in andragogy.

The project "Bamberg donates time"

Bamberg and Christmas is the important context: Bamberg is a little city in Germany - 80.000 inhabitants, old, with rich history, what you can see in each building, the cathedral, and the city hall in the middle of the river. We have an archbishop and city officials that are very visible. The more old-fashioned citizens and the sometimes a bit crazy university people, tourists from Japan and the neighboring cities give a vivid mixture. Christmas is a very special time with illumination, concerts, Christmas market, hot spiced wine, and Bamberg sausages smelling through the narrow streets ...

The Scandinavians know the custom of "Julklap": In school classes, societies, workplaces people give a gift into a basket, and on a certain day all meet and each takes a gift out of the basket - each is giver and taker at the same time. A student of mine came up to me and said: Why don't we organize Julklap for the city? I said: What has that to do with adult education?

I will leave you for a while with this question, while describing, what happened.

A team of about one dozen students of andragogy at Bamberg University planned the project "Bamberg donates time" - a mutual donation circle for the "whole city": Citizens were asked to offer a "gift" to share with somebody else. An important step was to decide what the gifts should be. The specific idea of this project was that these gifts should have no (or little) monetary value; the idea was to share two to three hours of the personal life in an activity the donator offered to share: showing how to prepare a specialty meal, playing together with a model railroad, inviting to harvest cherries in the garden. "Sharing time" and "opening doors and hearts" were the images we used.

Two steps became the key to the success of the planning:

- At first, a number of the leading people in the city were asked for their donation and participation. And without hesitation, the archbishop, the city mayor, the county mayor, the general of the US-base agreed to participate.
- Then the local newspaper was contacted for support. They with great engagement picked up the idea, and invited publicly to join "Bamberg schenkt Zeit" - "Bamberg donates time". They introduced the project with a half-page article, and more: Twice a week they published a list with the people who had offered gifts, and the gifts they wanted to donate. And starting with the town mayor, the archbishop ... (including interviews) was a thrilling start for the newspaper-journalists as well as the newspaper-readers.

Sunday afternoon two weeks before Christmas on the Christmas market below the decorated Christmas tree the exchange of partners and gifts took place in the form of a lottery. More than 200 people – including local and society representatives, hobby specialists, and "normal" families - offered gifts for exchange. The Archbishop offered his gift (an invitation to his house for dinner, afterward a visit to the Bamberg symphonic orchestra, sitting with him in the first row). And then he grabbed in the big sack and pulled out a name. The person was called up, came forward to the podium, and offered him one violin lesson with the promise, that he would afterward be able to play a Christmas carol on the violin. The city mayor invited his "lottery match" to a guided tour through rooms in the city castle which are not open to the public, and was invited to a meal with North German cooking in the home of the donator. The representative of the foreign citizens invited to a Greek festival and was invited to cherry-picking and make marmalade. The county major invited to a hike a local castle and was invited to a canoe tour through the local river; the general major of the US community invited to a military ceremony and was invited to the local basketball team.

End page 3
Start page 4

The radio station interviews the "celebrities" (city mayor, county major, representative of the foreign citizens, bank director, General Major of the US community, representative of the archbishop...) about their gift in the marketplace.

There was a lot of laughter in the two hours of this lottery. People were talking to people, commenting on the matches, Grandpa Rudi with his barrel organ played Christmas tunes, and many of the matching partners could be seen afterwards on the Christmas market enjoying sweets, hot maroons, and mulled wine.

Local and regional media reported. In the next months, the newspaper repeatedly showed pictures of activities caused by "Bamberg donates time". This brought sustainability to the "meeting and sharing" idea of the project. A rough observation revealed that about half of the "matches" met twice, exchanging both gifts, one quarter met once, and one quarter never met. Those who met mostly reported "having fun together", but also more reduced "it was ok". No real negative events were reported.

This small project turned out more successful and joyful than expected. And it might provoke the question: Should others copy this idea for their community/university/society?

But despite the convincing practical idea, the question remains: Is that adult education?

The andragogical background

The question "Is that adult education?" refers back to one's individual understanding of "adult education". This individual understanding is embedded in the socio-historic context, as reflected at the beginning of this paper.

If somebody defines adult education primarily by the existence of teachers, curricula, school buildings, and/or predefined outcomes, then this project confuses and challenges this understanding. And this may be *the first and main value of this project:* It challenges us to recheck our thinking, and it forces us to clarify our understanding. In professional language: It opens the *way out of the hermeneutic circle.* So the first insight is (either banal or surprising): Adult education has beyond the mainstream face many genuine and helpful faces. Combined with the theoretical-historic approach, offered by andragogy, this wider perception helps to overcome the narrowed view of mainstream thinking and to perceive the wider field of "lifewide adult education". This opens alternatives for flexible thinking and innovative practice. In the interaction between action and reflection in a project as described andragogical professionalism can be developed, applied, and proofed.

In addition to this more theoretical value "Bamberg donates time" confirms clearly a number of practical educational effects. A first group of effects can be seen in the *individual learning experience* in the project:
- Most gifts offered learning chances on a content level ("learning star constellations", "seeing the city with the eyes of an architect").
- All gifts brought insights on a person-to-person level (sharing the personal time and "*lifeworld*" of others) and offered chances of "learning en passant" (Reischmann 1996).
- With the question "What would I donate?" many people started thinking in a loving way about others and themselves: learning solidarity.

Above this individual development, a second group of effects can be identified leading to "*building community*": This project offered the chance to think about sharing and meeting and supported a culture of solidarity and interchange of people in the community. What happened was a "city-culture in

End page 4
Start page 5

smiling" with the message: "So we want our city to be!" and "Let us do it together in this city". For this message it was important that prominent citizens participated. (*Organizational learning and development, learning organization, society building*).

And a third group of effects focussed on *andragogical professionalism*: The public should learn the variety of competencies andragogues have, and what andragogues are good for: Not only teaching knowledge but also developing solidarity, living together, and building a culture. And of course, the students that organized the project could collect experiences in professional project management.

Adult Education in this project is understood not as a transmission of knowledge, but as a gift and chance for persons and communities to become better. That makes it a good occasion to rethink what "education" means, and what the task of andragogues is.

When we see and accept the diversity of learning and the diversity of dealing with learning, when we integrate the specific strengths in the "division of labor" in this field - practitioners, scholars, organizers, and learners, then we will more appropriate and more creative help supporting adult learning and adult learners, and help "the world" to become a better place to live in.

When andragogy safeguards the wealth of the historical memory, this opens - like in the described project - a wider understanding (theory) and more adequate intervention strategies (practice). Theory is not only theoretical but can be - as seen in "Bamberg Donates Time" - very practical.

Literature

Comenius, Johann Amos (1991): Pampädia - Allerziehung. In deutscher Übersetzung herausgegeben von Klaus Schaller. Sankt Augustin: Academia Verlag.

Freire, Paulo (21972): Pädagogik der Unterdrückten. Stuttgart: Kreuz Verlag.

Pratt, Daniel P. and Ass. (1998): Five Perspectives on Teaching in Adult and Higher Education. Malabar, Florida: Krieger.

Reischmann, Jost (1995): Die Kehrseite der Professionalisierung in der Erwachsenenbildung: Lernen „en passant" - die vergessene Dimension. In: Grundlagen der Weiterbildung - Zeitschrift, 6. Jg., H. 4, S. 200 - 204.

Reischmann, Jost (1999): Adult Education in Germany. Roots, Status, Mainstreams, Changes. In: Andragogy Today: Interdisciplinary Journal of Adult and Continuing Education. The Adult & Continuing Education of Korea. Vol. 2, No. 3, S. 1-29.

Reischmann, Jost (2004): International and Comparative Adult Education: A German Perspective. In: PAACE Journal of Lifelong Learning. The Pennsylvania Association for Adult and Continuing Education. Vol. 13 (2004), p. 19-38.

Reischmann, Jost (2005a): Bamberg wichtelte Zeit. Andragogen bilden eine Stadt. In: DIE Zeitschrift für Erwachsenenbildung. 12. Jg. (2005), H. 2, S. 8.

Reischmann, Jost (2005b): Andragogy. In: English, Leona (ed): International Encyclopaedia of Adult Education. London: Palgrave Macmillan. S. 58-63.

5. International Comparative Adult Education

In the history and development of adult education, it seems that traveling to and exchanging with foreign countries was attractive to "historic" as well as present persons. I was fortunate to have Günther Dohmen as head of the Institute of Adult Education at Tübingen University, a person deeply engaged in the international field. This provided me with the motivation as well as contacts for my travel into the international arena.

A specific field of this international exchange is international comparative adult education: the comparison between two or more countries. As will be described in 5.2 I became introduced to this field in 1992.

5.1 Comparative Adult Education (2005)[1]

Comparative adult education (CAE) describes a scholarly approach to understanding adult education, in which one or more aspects are compared between two or more countries. "Comparison" methodically identifies similarities and differences between the aspects under study; their significance for theory and practice should be explained.

This general definition needs two additional specifications:
1. Although comparison within a single country (intra-national)

End page 136
Start page 137

   can occur, the term mostly - in North America as well as in Europe - stands for "international comparative adult education", meaning the comparison between two or more countries.
2. Also, many types of international comparative research do not include explicit comparison: "It is generally accepted that most of what is included under the rubric of comparative studies in adult education ... does not include comparison in the strict sense" (Titmus, 1999, p. 36). Perhaps in these cases "comparison" refers to the implicit comparison with one's own country that inevitably happens when analyzing a foreign country.

Why International Comparison?

The first reason is *knowledge and understanding* - to become better informed about adult education in other countries, its historical, societal, and cultural roots, "and thus to develop criteria for assessing contemporary developments and testing possible outcomes!" (Kidd, 1975, p. 7). This understanding reflects

---

[1] First print: Reischmann, Jost (2005): Comparative Adult Education. In: English, Leona (ed): International Encylopedia of Adult Education. London: Palgrave Macmillan. S. 136-141

back to one's own country: Observations made in a foreign context help to better perceive and understand adult education not only in the other but also in one's own country.

A practical reason for international comparison is *"borrowing"*: it is hoped that learning from experiences abroad helps to adapt foreign experiences to one's own practice, avoid repeating mistakes, and "reinvent the wheel". On a theoretical level, it is argued that the international-comparative perspective assists in overcoming *one's own ethnocentric blindness*: international comparison helps "to better understand oneself, and to reveal how one's own cultural biases and personal attributes affect on judgment" (Kidd, 1975, p. 7).

It is expected that learning from each other supports *peace and tolerance*: "One of the foremost challenges of our age is ... to construct a culture of peace based on justice and tolerance within which dialogue, mutual recognition, and negotiation will replace violence, in homes and countries, within nations and between countries" (UNESCO, *Hamburg Declaration on Adult Education,* 1997, chapter 14).

In smaller countries, it is certainly easier to experience international knowledge, understanding, and respect through everyday experiences. For the United States of America, spanning an entire continent and having armed forces, business presence, and cultural influence all over the world, this is more difficult.

The International Interest in Andragogy

In the history of adult education and andragogy, we find a continuous interest in adult education in other countries. In the century between the lives of Grundtvig (Denmark) and Freire (Brazil), a number of names and ideas attained international currency. The Danish "Folkehojskole", the English university extension movement, the Swedish study circle, and the American encounter-group movement became models for adult education in other countries; often the differences between the "borrowed" and the original have not been perceived.

International travel and exchange have, from the early years, offered keypersons in the adult education movement an important way to shape their understanding: Lindeman (USA) traveled to Germany, Mansbridge (Great

End page 137
Start page 138

Britain) to Australia and Canada, and Borinski (Germany) to Scandinavia. Conferences have also contributed to the international exchange: At the first conference of the World Council for Comparative Education in 1960 in Ottawa, Alexander N. Charters, Professor of Adult Education at Syracuse University, New York, and Roby Kidd, Canadian expert and scholar, conferred in a working group on international and comparative adult education. In 1966 the legendary Exeter conference took place in New Hampshire; the "Exeter papers" were published by the Syracuse University Publications in Continuing Education. In 1970 Alexander Charters and Beverly Cassara, Professor at the University of District of Columbia, published the papers from the World Council of Comparative and International Education in Montreal. In Prague, Czechoslovakia, in 1992, Colin Titmus, Great Britain, a leading researcher in this field, chaired a working group at the VIIIth World Council of Comparative Education Societies. The 1993 conference "Rethinking Adult Education for Development" assembled the comparativists in Ljubljana, Slovenia. Hamburg, Germany, hosted the UNESCO CONFINTEAV Conference in 1997, and the International Society for Adult Comparative Education (ISCAE) held its 2002 conference in St. Louis, Missouri, USA, in conjunction with the American Association for Adult and Continuing Education (AAACE) and the International Association of Adult Education.

These examples indicate that in many countries an international interest occurs in adult education. Certainly, cultural differences limit the transfer from one country to another. Comparative research, by helping to understand the differences and similarities among countries and their significance for adult education, clarifies the possibilities and limits of understanding and borrowing.

Types of International Comparative Adult Education

Knowledge about the education of adults in other countries can be gained from various sources, and several types of comparative research can be categorized. A first, "pre-scientific" source is the reports given by international travelers, mostly characterized as "subjective-impressionistic". More systematic descriptions are categorized as "travelers' reports" and less systematic "travelers' tales". Their value is debatable. Because of random observation and subjective description, it is not clear how reliable and how representative the descriptions are. On the other hand, the plea is made that just this subjective focus of eyewitnesses can mean a specific strength.

At the scientific level, six different types of international-comparative research are identified:

- The first is country reports, which try to describe the system of adult education in one country, as proposed, for example, at the 1966 Exeter conference: "to identify and describe the existing adult education programs within each country in order to make the relevant data available to scholars in their own and in other countries for comparative analysis" (Charters & Siddiqui, 1989, p. 3). Country reports were presented mainly during the 1970s, and 1980s; some are rather impressionistic, and others follow a well-developed outline and structure.

- The second is program reports or topic-oriented studies. During

End page 138
Start page 139

  and after the 19805 an increasing number of program reports can be found. Because attempts to describe a whole national system were seldom successful, this type focuses on descriptions of adult education programs, institutions, and organizations in a distinct country. Included in this category (sometimes categorized separately) are the *topic-oriented studies* or *the problem approach*, where not a program, but a certain topic or problem is discussed in the context of a nation. These reports/studies are more "international" and less "comparative". Because only one country or program is presented, no comparable object is available; the readers have to draw the comparative conclusions themselves.
- The third, juxtaposition, collects and presents data from two or more countries, but no explicit comparison is given. Statistical reports represent this type, as well as collections of country reports (for example Jarvis, 1992). Juxtaposition can also be topic- or problem-oriented when a topic is discussed in relation to various countries. For example, Pöggeler's (1990) *The State and Adult Education*, brings together articles discussing the role of the state in different countries.
- The fourth is comparison, in the strict understanding of "international comparative adult education" reports from two or more countries, and offers an explicit comparison making the similarities and differences understandable: "A study in comparative international adult education ... must include one or more aspects of adult education in two or more countries or regions. Comparative study is not the mere placing side by side of data ... such juxtaposition is only the prerequisite for comparison. At the next stage one attempts to identify the similarities and differences between the aspects under study ... The real value of comparative study emerges only from ... the attempt to understand why the differences and similarities occur and what their significance is for adult education in the countries under examination (Charters &: Hilton, 1989, p. 3).
- The fifth, field- and method-reflecting texts, reflects the methods, strategies, and concepts of international comparison, and includes summarizing reports about developments in the international comparative field on a material or meta level. The article at hand is an example of this category.
- Finally, there are the reports from international organizations. A bit outside of this system, but still counted as part of the international tradition, are reports from transnational institutions such as UNESCO, OECD, or the World Bank. Joachim Knoll, Professor (emeritus) at Bochum University, Germany, is one of the key persons supplying such information.

Difficulties and Problems of International Comparative Work

One problem is that the continuity of scholarly work is not guaranteed. Only a small number of scholars work in international comparative adult education as their main field; others enter for only a short period of time. The knowledge developed in

End page 139
Start page 140

comparative adult education is spread over many places, languages, and countries, which makes it difficult for new researchers to start working in this field. To build up continuity it is necessary to bring together the knowledge, experiences, discussions, and standards of the "why" and "how" of international comparison so that researchers can refer to and build upon an internationally shared set of research methods. To serve the continuity in this field through networking, conferences, and publications, the International Society for Comparative Adult Education ISCAE (www.ISCAE.org) was founded.

Often discussed is how comparison can be done between *different cultures*: are researchers knowledgeable enough to understand the aspects under study in a foreign cultural context? This can be a problem, especially for American researchers who typically lack international experience. But the reality of international comparative studies shows that this problem can be reduced when the aim is not "perfect" but "better" understanding, and when the work is carried out in dialogue with foreign partners for communicative validation (Knox, 1993).

A clear handicap is *language*. International communication takes place in English, yet for the majority of the world this is a foreign language. Communicating - and even more, publishing - in this foreign language takes many times more effort than in one's native context. English literature is often not available, and it makes no sense to refer to non-English research literature because the latter does not exist for the international readership. Researchers from non-English countries, when working in the international context, lose most of their scholarly background - theory, methodology, and content - that is based on their native language. On the other hand, native English speakers with no command of a foreign language always depend on more or less reliable translations.

Another problem is the regular *attendance at central international meetings*. To enter this field and to stay in its networks entails traveling and being visible. This is difficult, especially for junior scholars. International comparative projects have *higher costs* and *more problems* than research carried out in one country. When weighing the potential outcome of these investments for one's career, it may be more beneficial to work at the national level.

Despite these problems, those working in international comparative adult education report personal enrichment and reward from experiencing the wider international world.

References and Further Reading

Charters, A. N., & Hilton, R.]. (Eds.).(1989). *Landmarks in international adult education: A comparative analysis*. London: Routledge.

Charters, A. N., & Siddiqui, D. A. (1989). *Comparative adult education: State of the art. With annotated resource guide*. Vancouver: Center for Continuing Education, University of British Columbia.

Jarvis, P. (Ed.).(1992). *Perspectives on adult education and training in Europe*. Malabar, Fl: Krieger.

Kidd, J. R. (1975). Comparative adult education: The first decade. In C. Bennett, J. R. Kidd, & J. Kulich (Eds.), *Comparative studies in adult education: An anthology* (pp. 5-24). Syracuse, NY: Syracuse University.

Knox, A. B. (1993). *Strengthening adult and continuing education: A global perspective*

End page 140
Start page 141

on synergistic leadership. San Francisco: lossey-Bass.

Pöggeler, F. (Ed.) (1990). *The state and adult education*. Frankfurt, Germany: Verlag P. Lang.

Titmus, C. (1999). Comparative adult education: Some reflections on the process. In J. Reischmann, M. Bron, & Z. Jelenc (Eds.), *Comparative adult education 1998: The contribution of ISCAE to an emerging field of study* (pp. 33-50). Ljubljana, Slovenia: Slovenian Institute for Adult Education.

UNESCO Institute for Education (1997). The Hamburg Declaration on *Adult* Learning. Hamburg, Germany: UNESCO, 1997, retrieved Jan. 21, 2004, from www.unesco.org/education/uie/ confintea/documents.htm)

www.ISCAE.org International Society for Comparative Adult Education.

www.hku.hk/cerc/wcces/ World Council of Comparative Education Societies.

I never anticipated becoming a persona in international comparative adult education. For sure, I liked to travel, especially to conferences in the USA. In 1992, I presented a paper critically reviewing important books by two leaders in the international field: Alexander Charters and Alan Knox (see 5.4 in this book). During the subsequent business meeting of the Society for Comparative Adult Education the president, Alexander Charters, surprisingly announced: "I want Jost to be the next president". I was so puzzled that I forgot to say "No".

The invention of the Internet during those days - one of these historic moments - opened up new chances for interaction: a homepage was established (www.ISCAE.org) to disseminate information about this society, and a mailing list facilitated rapid and cheap communication with the members - vital for a society that wanted to grow worldwide. International conferences, meetings, publications, and networks followed these first steps.

5.2 Notes from the meeting of individuals associated with the Society of Adult Education held in Anaheim, California (1992)

Tuesday, November 3, 1992

The following individuals attended a meeting regarding the Society for Comparative Adult Education.

Alan B. Knox	Wisconsin University
Jost Reischmann	University of Tuebingen, Germany
Kevin Freer	Ohio State
Max van der Kamp	University of Gioningen, Netherlands
Denise Reghenzani	Embassy of Australia, Washington D.C.
Marcie Boucouvalas Virginia	Virginia Tech Graduate Center
Mark Tennant	University of Technology, Sydney, Australia
Richard Henstrom	Brigham Young University, Provo, Utah
Alex Charters	Syracuse University

Minutes

1. **Alex Charters** welcomed the group and made comments on the following topics:
   a. Comments on changing the name:
   - the need to make the name shorter
   - It's not a committee
   - there is still some discussion with respect to the recent decision to call it the Society for Comparative Adult Education (SCAE)

- should "International" be in the name? Some felt that "International" should be used somewhere in the title.
b. He commented that the leadership is being expanded.
c. The society is open for change and welcomes comments.
d. Emphasized that this is a comparative group, not necessarily international, but that the composition is international and many of the research projects will be.
e. The membership needs more balance on an international basis.
f. All people named on the list recently sent out (with respect to the officers) were elected,
g. There is a conference proposed for Slovenia for about October 6-9, 1993.

2. Jost Reischmann is the new president and made the following comments:
   a. He acknowledged Alex Charters' contributions and founding of the society and how he has served faithfully for so many years,
   b. Why do researchers have to start at point zero in our area? There needs to be more exchange,
   c. Marcie responded to a question that there are now 65 members.
   d. People meeting people is not happening on an institutional level yet. Institutions are not relating to each other.
   e. There could be a reconsideration of the name of CAES. Suggestions were: "International Comparative Adult Education Society", "International Society for Comparative Adult Education", and "Comparative Adult Education International Society".
   f. There are no items on publications. A new No. 15 may be out next spring.
   g. There was a discussion on a possible conference of this society: roundtables, seminars, and some planning are being reviewed now. Gerald Normie may possibly be used.
   h. Is there a need for a handbook or methodology plan?
   i. The society needs to be limited to international comparison: with a focus on adult education.
   j. The 1995 World Conference in Beijing was mentioned. This society needs to be more involved - more identified with this world conference.

The purpose, further development, and activities of ISCAE will be described in the following 5.3.4.

This extensive contribution encompasses several distinct aspects that can be read separately: it starts (1.) with "travelers tales", offering spontaneous impressions from travels abroad, then (2.) it provides a more in-depth exploration and extension of the reasons and traditions associated with international comparative adult education. In (3.) various types of international/comparative research are systematically outlined. The contribution then (4.) introduces the International Society for Comparative Adult Education, its purpose, and history. Finally (5.) problems of working in the international field are described.

5.3 International and Comparative Adult Education: A German Perspective[1] (2004)

1. Some personal "Travelers Tales" - visiting the USA from Germany

Traveling abroad or meeting foreigners at home often leads to confusion and misunderstanding. What is true for the everyday experience is also true for the world of academia:

- When I bring a dozen or so of my students from my university in Germany to a conference of the American Association for Adult and Continuing Education (AAACE), my colleagues are surprised: The average age of my German adult education students is about 23. The average age of the American adult education students my colleagues bring to the conference seems to be around 40.
- When somebody wants to know if my students are undergraduate or graduate, I do not know how to answer. In the German higher education system there is no equivalent for that distinction. So I explain: After 13 years of school students then matriculate at the university where they study pedagogy and andragogy for the next four to five years; after that, they go out to be valued professionals for the next 40 years.
- "But where are the adult learners?" my American colleagues Trenton Ferro, John Henschke, and others ask me when visiting my university. I am confused: "Why and to what end should adults

End page 19
Start page 20

learn at a university and not with their employer or at adult education institutions?"

- Adult educators from a nearby American army base asked me to accept them as doctoral students - and offered to pay me for the doctoral classes. I am scandalized! That they would offer me - a German professor! - money for a planned academic degree feels to me like taking bribes.

---

[1]   First print: Reischmann, Jost (2004): International and Comparative Adult Education: A German Perspective. In: *PAACE Journal of Lifelong Learning.* The Pennsylvania Association for Adult and Continuing Education. Vol. 13, p. 19-38.

All of these examples have one thing in common: They lead to confusion, questions, and the need for more exchange and clarification. We become aware that we have in our heads concepts of "how things are" (e.g., that, in order to become an adult education professional, you have to be in the second half of life; universities are structured in undergraduate/graduate categories; adults want and have to change their careers by attending universities; education is not a civil right but is a commodity available to those who are able to pay), but these concepts that seem "normal" to us suddenly do not help in the international context. This perplexity leads to one of two choices:

1. To laugh about the strange strangers, stick to our concepts, and hope that those strangers will adapt to the "right" (= my) way. This choice describes the ethnocentric position, leading - if power and money come into play - to colonization.
2. To become aware that our concepts are not the only right concepts in the world and that we are not threatened, but enriched, by understanding foreign concepts. This choice leads to an international and international-comparative understanding.

Without applying "methodological rigor," I shall report some observations and evaluations based on about 25 visits to the USA in the last 25 years - most of them related to adult education conferences and university visits. In general, I regard adult education, in theory as well as in practice, as not particularly more developed in either Germany or the USA. Not much is known in Germany about adult education in the USA, and the same fits the other way around. At most conferences of AAACE I was the only German, and Americans nearly never show up at German conferences because they don't speak German. When I published the book *Adult Education in West Germany in Case Studies* (Reischmann, 1988) [www.reischmannfam.de/lit/1988-AdEdinGermany.pdf], I discovered with great surprise that this was indeed the first book

End page 20
Start page 21

about Germany's adult education written in English. So it is no surprise that we do not know much about the other country.

In the 1980s there was, for some years, an active exchange between AAACE and the German Volkshochschul Association, DVV, using organized travel groups. Many contacts and friendships date back to that time, but the persons who were active at that time are now 20 years older and retiring. Consequently, these contacts soon will be outgrown, and no young people are following in the footsteps of these pioneers. Instead of more contact, there is less.

From the German perspective, this decline can be explained with several reasons. First, there is a content problem: Main topics of American adult education, like Adult Basic Education, ESL, or GED preparation, are marginal in Germany because we do not have these problems. Also different are most of the historical, institutional, and theoretical themes discussed in the USA. Consequently, a German visitor is seldom inspired to attend an American adult education conference on the basis of its content; a similar observation would apply to an American visiting a German conference. This circumstance does not mean that opportunities for learning and insight do not exist, but they are hidden from a first-time visitor. After many years of attendance, it is easier for me to know the people, the institutions, the topics, and the titles that allow me to expect inspiration, seriousness, and innovation. The AAACE/DVV exchange program overcame this obstacle and was a great help for beneficial and mutual exchange because topics, questions, and interests were exchanged in advance and made possible a "guided" experience. The international unit of AAACE offers a similar function with its pre-conference, helping the few foreigners attending not to get lost in the big and confusing main conference. There is also a social problem that foreign visitors often encounter: They are welcomed warmly and publicly in the opening session and everybody shakes hands, but at 8:00 p.m. the foreign visitor suddenly finds himself standing alone in an empty hotel lobby, and all those who welcomed him have disappeared. Spending the night watching television in the hotel room does not develop much international exchange.

Foreigners also face a financial problem. The international airfare is expensive, fancy conference hotels cost a fortune (and the traveler needs the experience to know that the motel across the street costs only one-third of that), and, on top of that, the conference fee of $275 that AAACE charged even for students goes beyond the limits; if this amount continues to be the fee for each of the dozen 24-year-old students who came with me to St. Louis, I will not bring students to the AAACE conference again. A

End page 21
Start page 22

tentative contact we started with a Turkish university a short time ago illustrates the difference: The whole group was offered a free stay in dormitories, and, spontaneously, a Turkish-German organization offered help with the airfare.

This financial problem is especially difficult when visitors come from countries with soft currency. With shame, I remember an AAACE conference shortly after the Iron Curtain broke down. A colleague from Czechoslovakia was an "invited" speaker, was flattered to be one of the handful of foreigners who made it possible to call the conference "international" - and disappeared from the conference after two days because the conference fee and the hotel cost him his income of several months. Conferences in Germany seldom cost more than $100 because "hosting" a conference is seen as a matter of pride for the local university or organization, which supports the conference from its own budget as an investment in its reputation.

If "looking beyond borders" is desired, then foreign visitors to the USA present an opportunity for international learning to their American hosts. What is flowing back from visitors - and I include my students - is often overlooked. Foreign visitors are not only "takers"; they can also be "givers" - when this opportunity is seen and the hosts are themselves willing to learn.

While contacts with American institutions often cause mixed feelings on the part of foreigners, the person-to-person contacts are mostly much warmer than expected. In the example of the Czechoslovakian colleague, several American colleagues spontaneously offered that he could share their room without paying; I guess German colleagues would not be so open-hearted. On this person-to-person level, I never met an "ugly American." I have made many wonderful friendships in the USA, and meeting Americans is a delight in general. In hotels or department stores, at tourist attractions or universities, people were always supportive, friendly, and helpful, especially when they recognized that I was a foreigner. Personal experiences abound - the wonderful family in Utah that hosted my daughter for half a year, the (not forgotten!) "Care packages" families in Germany received after World War II, the chewing-gum we got from the GIs - these and many other good memories will bring me back to the USA at the next chance I get.

Moving to a more systematic argumentation, the "travelers tales" cited above can be read in two different ways. First, there is the content level: The writer is presenting honest impressions, based on personal observations, without methodological rigor, interpreted and generalized against a (not overtly reflective) personal background. Secondly, this segment can

End page 22
Start page 23

be read from a methodological perspective: What type of contribution does this article make to the international discussion? What are the strengths and weaknesses of this type of contribution? This second perspective leads to a more general reflection of the field of "international" and "comparative" adult education.

2. Why "International" and "Comparative" Adult Education?

The main focus of *international* adult education is to educate to become, and behave like a more "international" person, thus leading to more exchange, understanding, and respect, on both a personal and national level.

The more narrow and academic concept of *international comparative* adult education (the difference between these two terms will be described below) is justified basically by two central arguments: On a practical level "borrowing" is expected. We attempt, learning from our experiences abroad, to adapt these experiences successfully for our own international practice; further, we avoid making mistakes and, consequently, do not need to "re-invent the wheel." On a theoretical level, it is expected that the international comparative perspective helps us to overcome ethnocentric blindness; we learn, prompted by observations made in a foreign context, to perceive and understand better the field of adult education and how it operates in our own country. This understanding of the benefits of international work already was pointed out clearly by Roby Kidd in 1975. International comparative adult education helps us

- to become better informed about the educational systems of other countries,
- to become better informed about how people in other cultures have carried out certain social functions by means of education,
- to become better informed about the historical roots of certain activities and thus to develop criteria for assessing contemporary developments and testing possible outcomes,
- to understand better the educational forms and systems operating in one's own country,
- to satisfy an interest in how human beings live and learn,
- to understand oneself better, and
- to reveal how one's own cultural biases and personal attributes affect one's judgment about possible ways of carrying on learning transactions. (Kidd, 1975, p. 7)

End page 23
Start page 24

In the emerging history of andragogy - the "Wissenschaft" or science of the education and learning of adults - we find a continuous interest in adult education in other countries. In the century between Grundtvig (Denmark) and Freire (Brazil), many names and ideas attained international currency. The (English) university extension movement, the (Danish) "Folkehojskole," the (Swedish) study circle, and the (American) encounter group movement have become models for adult education in many other countries; often the differences between the "borrowed" and the original have not been perceived. Research shows a lot of cross-cultural communication; an example is the British-Dutch-German relationship in adult education between 1880 and 1930 (Friedenthal-Haase, Hake, & Marriott, 1991). International travel and exchange has, from the early years in the adult education movement, offered many key educators of adults in various countries an important way to shape their international understanding; Lindeman (USA) traveled to Germany, Mansbridge (Great Britain) to Australia and Canada, and Borinski (Germany) to Scandinavia. Even today the "international guild of adult education" can be found in face-to-face meetings held in Ibadan, Ghana (the International Conference on Comparative Adult Education in 1991); Frascati, Italy; Prague, Czechoslovakia (the World Congress of Comparative Education in 1992); Ljubljana, Slovenia (the "Rethinking Adult Education for Development" Conference in 1993); Hamburg, Germany (the CONFINTEA V Conference of the United Nations Educational, Scientific, and Cultural Organization [UNESCO] in 1997); and St. Louis, MO, USA (the International Society for Adult Comparative Education [ISCAE] conference held in conjunction with AAACE and the International Associates of Adult Education in 2002) - just to name a few. As early as 1919 the World Association for Adult Education (WAAE) was founded with the mission "to bring into co-operation and mutual relationship the adult education movements and institutions of the world, in order that peoples may proceed in greater power through wisdom - the mother of all things - to knowledge."

These highlights indicate that the international argument was and is used in the theory of adult education as well as in the practical work carried out in many countries. The effects of the international argument are sometimes evident and lasting; sometimes they remain rhetorical or marginal. Certainly, cultural differences limit the transfer from one country to another. Comparative research, which helps understand the differences and similarities that exist between and among countries and their significance for adult education, clarifies the possibilities and limits of understanding and borrowing. This research is indispensable in a world where

End page 24
Start page 25

it is necessary to gain an understanding of the various ways adult education is experienced in many countries.

3. Putting Meanings Into Boxes: Definitions

The definition boxes in this field are not really distinct. There are clearly two different aspects when talking about international work in adult education: a more practical, action-oriented perspective and a more academic, reflection-oriented understanding.

International Adult Education (A): Practical, Action Oriented
The more practical, action-oriented understanding of international adult education refers to all activities supporting learning experiences aimed at the connection with other nationalities and cultures - within or outside of one's own country. This perspective includes foreign language courses (which make up about one-third of the offerings in German adult education centers), excursions to museums or exhibitions in neighboring countries (which is easy in Germany where, in less than four or five hours by bus - depending on the starting point - Amsterdam, The Netherlands; Paris, France; Zürich, Switzerland; Salzburg, Austria; or Prague, Czechoslovakia can be reached), including walking around, some shopping, and a local beer. This understanding also includes educational travel tours to foreign countries.

Sometimes this "looking beyond one's own national borders" is a welcomed byproduct (like in vacation traveling); sometimes it is explicitly planned. For example, after World War II states in Europe supported programs that brought juveniles and young adults together in order to build and decorate war cemeteries in the hope of mutual learning for a better understanding and peace for future generations. The Peace Corps followed a similar idea. City sisterships provide another example. Also, UNESCO and the World Bank are big players in this type of international adult education. By taking my students to a conference in a foreign country, I invest these efforts in the hope of "making them more international." This goal is accomplished, on the one hand, by learning techniques (developing language skills by, for example, making phone calls and knowing how to find something to eat and a bathroom) and, on the other, by attending to emotions and values (the reduction of stress and feelings of threat and fostering the perception, valuing, and appreciation of "the different").

Certainly, this approach is both much easier and more necessary in "old Europe," where foreign countries, languages, traditions, and historically-

End page 25
Start page 26

developed hate is, in many places, only minutes or a few hours away; the goal is to overcome the ethnocentricity of national borders. This approach is more difficult on the North American continent, where the United States has just two bordering countries. One of them - Canada - is often not perceived as "foreign"; the other – Mexico - is often perceived as an exotic, developing country and source for a cheap (illegal) workforce not really worth learning from or about. So, in the United States of America, where portions of the population never leave their state, much less their country, gaining international perspectives is much more difficult. Consequently, foreign countries have criticized American political or economic decisions for not having an understanding of the international perspective - and not only in the recent past. "Intercultural adult education" is a term that relates closely to this more practical, action-oriented understanding of international adult education. Intercultural education can happen in one country. Here the aims are activities and reflections that serve the understanding and peaceful cooperation between ethnic groups in a society (including the majority in this learning process).

There exist many international organizations in adult education (field of practice) and andragogy (scientific approach), and national associations also have task forces or divisions that deal with international topics. Some of these organizations see themselves as more involved in this practical, action-oriented aspect of "educating adults in international perspectives." Others - for example, the International Unit of AAACE - reflect a second understanding.

International Adult Education (B): Academic, Reflection Oriented
This more academic, reflection-oriented perspective will be the focus of the remainder of this paper. This perspective emphasizes gaining knowledge and understanding about adult education in other countries and is accomplished with

some methodological rigor. Knowledge about the education of adults in other countries can be gained from various sources:

0. Travelers tales. A first source, rated primarily as "pre-scientific," comprises "travelers tales," the reports we get from international travelers. An early portion of this article was written on this level. Such reports are delivered mainly by traveling writers or vacationers, but also by scholars who attend a conference abroad and have to report to their funding agency - and publish this report simultaneously in a journal. If these descriptions are more systematic, they are labelled "travelers reports"; if less systematic, "travelers tales."

End Page 26
Start page 27

These types of international documents are characterized mostly as "subjective-impressionistic." Their value is considered to be ambivalent; the critical argument is that, because of random observation and subjective description, it is not clear how reliable and how representative the descriptions are. On the other hand, the plea is made that, especially because of the subjective focus of eyewitnesses, this type of report might possess a specific strength. In the framework of a new appreciation of qualitative research, these reports may receive renewed interest.

At the scientific level, six different types of international/international-comparative research are identified.

1. Country reports. A first stage of international adult education was the country report - as proposed, for example, at the 1966 Exeter conference: "to identify and describe the existing adult education programs within each country in order to make the relevant data available to scholars in their own and in other countries for comparative analysis" (Charters & Siddiqui, 1989, p. 3). *Country reports* were presented mainly during the 1970s and 1980s. "Adult Education in the Republic of . . ." is a typical title of this type of report. These studies try to describe the system of adult and continuing education in one particular country. They could be written by an author within the country or by a person from the outside. Some of these reports were, and are, rather impressionistic. Others followed a well-developed outline and structure.

2. Program reports; topic-oriented studies. During and after the 1980s we find an increasing number of *program reports*. These studies describe foreign adult education programs, institutions, and organizations. Examples of this type can be found in the writing of Charters and Hilton (1989b) or the case studies collected by Knox (1989). Included in this type (which, sometimes, are presented in a separate category) are the *topic-oriented studies* or the *problem approach*; a certain topic or problem is discussed in the context of a nation.

Country reports, as well as topic-oriented studies and the problem approach, are mostly more "international" and less "comparative." Because only one country or program is presented, no comparable object is available. Especially when an author presents his own country or program to a foreign readership in various countries, it is difficult for him to compare with another national system. If, for example, a German author describes a German program in an English publication, should he draw parallels to the English, Scottish, US-American, Canadian, or Australian systems?

End page 27
Start page 28

The failure to do so leads mostly to the consequence that the readers have to draw the comparative conclusions themselves.

3. Juxtaposition. A third type of comparative research is *juxtaposition.* Data from two or more countries are presented. These reports show that in country *A* we can observe *a*, while in country *B* we find *b*. A series of statistical reports represent this type, but no explicit comparison—Where are the similarities? What are the differences?—is given. An example of this type of publication is the German international volume, *Handbuch der Erwachsenenbildung (Handbook of Adult Education*, 1978), edited by Franz Pöggeler, or Peter Jarvis's (1992) *Perspectives on Adult Education and Training in Europe.* This juxtaposition also can be topic- or problem-oriented when a topic is presented in a series of contributions from various countries. For example, in Pöggeler's (1990) *The State and Adult Education* a series of articles deal with the role of the state in individual countries.

We move now to the "strict" understanding of "international comparative adult education."

4. Comparison. The *comparison* goes one step further; it reports from two or more countries and offers an explicit comparison that attempts to make the similarities and differences understandable. ISCAE uses here the definition of its "founding father," Alexander N. Charters:

> A study in comparative international adult education . . . must include one or more aspects of adult education in two or more countries or regions. Comparative study is not the mere placing side by side of data; . . . such juxtaposition is only the prerequisite for comparison. At the next stage one attempts to identify the similarities and differences between the aspects under study. . . . The real value of comparative study emerges only from . . . the attempt to understand why the differences and similarities occur and what their significance is for adult education in the countries under examination. (Charters & Hilton, 1989a, p. 3)

This type of research can be found, for example, in the final chapter of Charters and Hilton (1989b).

In a narrow understanding country reports and reports about programs or topics in one country are not part of international comparative education. Also juxtaposition - the side-by-side placing of data and descriptions from two or more countries - is not at the stage of comparison.

End page 28
Start page 29

In this narrow understanding, it is necessary that similarities and differences get worked out explicitly with some methodological rigor. While the more general international aspect of adult education has a long tradition, only a small and limited amount of research into adult education has been done comparatively.

5. Method-reflecting texts. Finally, *field-* and *method-reflections* are seen as a part of international comparative adult education. This category includes reflections about the methods, strategies, and concepts of international comparison, as well as summarizing reports about developments in the international comparative field on a material or meta-level. Research methods, problems, and pitfalls were a central focus of ISCAE's first conference and are documented in Reischmann, Bron, and Jelenc (1999).

6. Reports from international organizations. A bit outside of this system, but still counted as part of the international tradition, are reports from such transnational institutions as UNESCO, the Organization for Economic Co-operation and Development (OECD), and the World Bank.

What is not given a final answer is the question: Where does "international adult education" end and where does "international comparative adult education" begin? One discrimination seems clear: "Comparison" can only be done when at least two objects are available. So an international comparative study has to refer to at least two countries. Charters and Siddiqui (1989) draw clear limits:

> A study that compares two or more aspects of adult education in a single country is merely an instance of intra-national comparative adult education. Similarly, a study that describes one or more dimensions of adult education in two or more countries without comparing them is an example of international adult education, not of comparative adult education. (p. 5)

Following this definition, many presentations and papers and much research should be labeled as more appropriately "international" rather than "comparative." On the other side Collin Titmus (1999), a respected British scholar in international comparative adult education, offers a much less strict understanding: "It is generally accepted that most of what is included under the rubric of comparative studies in adult education . . . does not include comparison in the strict sense" (p. 36). The scientific community will have to come to an agreement about this question.

End page 29
Start page 30

Most researchers in comparative adult education agree that international comparative adult education is at the beginning stage. However, activities, research, conferences, and the existing literature prove that a great deal of clarification already has been done, knowledge is available, and methods are developed. Nevertheless, one central problem seems to be that the continuity of scholarly work is not guaranteed. Only a small number of scholars work in international comparative adult education as their main field; others enter for only a short period of time or work, and the developed knowledge is scattered around in many places, languages, and times. Having a place and institution where the comparative experience could be collected and stored would help to bring more continuity into the field of comparative adult education. This function was the founding idea of ISCAE.

4. ISCAE: International Society for Comparative Adult Education

The name of the society sounds impressive, and the fact that the society has a "President" (Jost Reischmann, University of Bamberg, Germany) [in 2004, for actual dates see http://www.iscae.org/board/board.htm] and a "Secretary" (Marcie Boucouvalas, Virginia Polytechnic Institute and State University, USA) is nearly as impressive as the list of names, functions, and countries of the board members: Michal Bron Jr., University College of South Stockholm, Sweden; Jindra Kulich, University of British Columbia, Canada; Gretchen Bersch, University of Alaska at Anchorage, USA; and Raja Jayagopal, University of Madras, India. The reality, however, is much more modest. Today ISCAE could best be described as a network of about 110 persons in 35 countries [written 2004, in 2024 ISCAE had 358 members from 66 countries]. Members meet at international conferences where they would be participating anyway. There are no statutes and no accounting or membership fees. Copying and mailing of ISCAE communications is divided among three universities from Germany, the USA, and Australia and their respective budgets. Contact becomes much easier through the use of an e-mail list and by accessing ISCAE's homepage (www.iscae.org) on - in this case quite literally - the World Wide Web. Depending on the vocational workload of the volunteers, it sometimes gets quiet for a while around ISCAE.

Many colleagues who are working in the field of international and comparative adult education have been added to the ISCAE mailing list for various reasons and occasions; as a result, they become "members." Perhaps this mailing list is, besides the actual meetings, the most important treasure of ISCAE; it allows immediate access to persons, institu-

150

End page 30
Start page 31
tions, and information in many countries. Need information about adult education in Alaska? No problem! Send an e-mail to Gretchen Bersch, University of Alaska at Anchorage. Making a short visit to Ljubljana, Slovenia? Just call Ana Krajnc or Zoran Jelenc, who will be glad to present their work. One of my students was recovering from examination stress in Australia. I gave her the address of Roger Morris. "Yesterday he invited me to attend his class," she tells me on a postcard. So the terms "network," "worldwide person-to-person contacts," and "international research exchange" may best characterize the work of ISCAE today - as well as the term "beginnings," because we can find in the development and status of ISCAE steps and processes that are typical for the origin of a society.

The Purpose of ISCAE

ISCAE wants to serve the international community by
- supplying a network of contacts to others interested in comparative adult education,
- fostering exchange through conferences, and
- documenting and sharing developments and standards through publications.

ISCAE tries to promote a narrow focus of its specific task: The focus of ISCAE is to develop, support, and share studies that attempt to identify the similarities and differences of one or more aspects of adult education in two or more countries or regions, trying to understand why the differences and similarities occur and what is their significance for adult education in the countries under examination. Also, ISCAE tries to collect, discuss, and share standards of a methodology for international comparison that might help researchers toward a better understanding of comparison and more sound, reliable, and economic ways of making international comparisons. That intention means that ISCAE invites especially those researchers who are interested in doing comparative work, that is, researching one or more aspects of adult education in two or more countries.

There is a central question: Which standards, principles, and methods of research in comparative adult education already exist and what are they? Further, which pitfalls and problems are known that then, perhaps, can be avoided? There is a very practical idea behind this theoretical part: When new researchers enter the field of comparative adult education - perhaps only for a limited time and a single project - they often

End page 31
Start page 32
experience similar problems and difficulties because this field of research has not yet developed an internationally shared set of research methods. Although experience and knowledge have been developed for many years, they have not

been spread over many places and countries. To avoid re-inventing the wheel—again and again—it is necessary that the knowledge, experiences, discussions, and standards of the "why" and "how" of international comparison gained in many places and languages be brought together and made available so that researchers can refer to and build upon them.

The History of ISCAE

Similar to other adult education initiatives, the name of one person symbolizes the beginning: Alexander N. Charters, professor and Vice-President for Continuing Education, now Professor Emeritus, at Syracuse University, New York, gave birth to the idea of this society and developed it over more than three decades. Peter Jarvis, editor of the reputable "International Perspectives on Adult and Continuing Education" series published by Routledge, assigns this value to Charters' activities: "Alexander Charters has been in the forefront of international adult education for many years" (Jarvis, 1989, unpaginated).

Alexander Charters' significant work in international comparative adult education was developed during his tenure at Syracuse. While there Charters helped to establish what now is one of the largest compilations of English-language materials in the field of adult and continuing education. The collection occupies 900 feet of shelf space and contains more than fifty groups of personal papers and organization records - print and non-print material (audio- and videotapes, hundreds of photos) that document the history and development of adult education. For example, the collection includes records of the Adult Education Association from 1924 on, Malcolm Knowles' papers from 1930 on, and even files for ISCAE. To honor the efforts of Alexander Charters and his wife, Margaret, the collection was renamed in October 1998, as the "Alexander N. Charters Library of Resources for Educators of Adults." Many of the milestones of the development of comparative adult education are connected to his name:

1960 - At the first world conference of the World Council for Comparative Education in Ottawa, Alexander N. Charters and Roby Kidd, a reputable Canadian scholar of adult education, organized a working group and presented papers about international and comparative adult education.

End page 32
Start page 33

1966 - The legendary Exeter conference took place in New Hampshire; the "Exeter papers" were published by the Syracuse University Publications in Continuing Education (SUPCE) and are still an important historical document today.

1970 - Alexander Charters organized a series of meetings about comparative adult education at the World Council of Comparative and International

Education in Montreal. He published the papers together with Beverly Cassara, then at the University of District of Columbia.

1992 - Colin Titmus, Great Britain, an expert in international and comparative adult education and author of leading publications in this field, chaired a working group of members of this society at the VIII World Council of Comparative Education Societies in Prague.

Until 1992 the society had used the name, Committee for Study and Research in Comparative Adult Education (CSRCAE). Alexander Charters, more than 70 years old at the time, urged the members to convey the responsibility for the society to younger scholars. At the 1992 annual conference of the American Association of Adult and Continuing Education, held in Anaheim, CA, a new president and secretary were elected, and the society was renamed the "International Society for Comparative Adult Education (ISCAE)".

The first conference initiated and organized by ISCAE took place in 1995 in Bamberg, Germany, attended by 31 members from 14 countries. The central focus of this conference was the discussion of the methods, problems, and pitfalls of international comparative research. The second conference, held in 1998 in Radovljica, Slovenia, was attended by 35 members from 16 countries. The third conference took place in St. Louis, MO, in 2002. The intention is to plan conferences every three to four years, in different countries and on different continents, and to sum up the results and experiences in publications (either printed or - as currently proposed - electronically for a world-wide access).

Rapid technological development has made international communication much easier. In the beginning fax, and nowadays e-mail, have speeded up this exchange significantly. While e-mail could be used for, perhaps, 10% of the exchanges in preparation for the 1995 ISCAE conference, this amount increased to more than 80% for the 1998 conference. The book that documents the results of the first two ISCAE conferences, involving editors in three countries, could be prepared in the allotted time only with

End page 33
Start page 34

the help of e-mail. ISCAE's website and e-mail list provide opportunities for documentation and contact that might, in the future, help researchers worldwide refer to the "state of the art" in international comparative adult education.

However, technology is only one part of the international exchange. ISCAE offers a person at the other end of a telephone call or e-mail message. Furthermore, it offers a chance not only to maintain virtual contact but also to meet face-to-face. The latter is the purpose of the ISCAE conferences and the meetings of ISCAE members at other international conferences. These person-to-person contacts are very rewarding; people working in the international field are mostly easy to accommodate (e.g., as guests in your home), are curious and tolerant (otherwise they would not be in that field), are enriching by their fantasy, offer humility and hospitality, and have an open approach to persons. These characteristics open doors, especially in the international context.

Another attitude can be learned in this international exchange: not to see things too narrowly. Because ISCAE tries to focus on "real" international comparison, reports such as "Adult Education in the Republic of X" should not be presented at ISCAE meetings. Nevertheless, the "tries" and "shoulds" indicate that the reality sometimes is different. Although the "narrow" definition of comparison has been cited in the "Call for Papers," some country and program reports have been presented as well. Should we reject the papers of colleagues who traveled halfway around the world and needed an accepted paper to get funding for attending the conference?

The hope is that ISCAE's conferences and publications will become increasingly the place where the researchers in comparative adult education will be able to focus and concentrate on discussing, documenting, and exchanging their accumulating body of knowledge. The accrued value is both professional and personal: easier access to comparative knowledge; deeper understanding of "how things are" and "how things could be"; and a tolerant, flexible, and open attitude.

5. The Difficulties of International Research and Volunteering in an International Society

It certainly is challenging and rewarding to get a wider view of our world through an international orientation, but there are also handicaps that make this work difficult. Just three of them are named here.

A first handicap is *language*. International communication takes place in English. For the majority of the world, this is a foreign language. Com-

End page 34
Start page 35

municating - even more, publishing - in this foreign language takes a great deal more effort than doing research in one's native context. This handicap is manifested in a variety of settings:

- Native English speakers are always faster during discussions.
- Secretaries are often not trained to write English. So the researcher has to type everything himself: notes, minutes of meetings, letters, manuscripts, questionnaires, and the like.
- When publishing, a native English speaker always has to be found for editing. Trenton Ferro, editor of this article, can verify what that means!
- Institutions, laws, and political or cultural backgrounds are often so different that it is difficult to find an appropriate translation.
- When making citations, the English literature often is not available in foreign libraries.

- It makes no sense to refer to the knowledge and experience of non-English research literature because the latter does not exist for the international readership. Consequently, people from non-English countries, when working in the international context, lose most of their research background - theory, methodology, and content - that is based on their native language.

Another handicap is the difficulty in *maintaining regular attendance at central international meetings*. Person-to-person contacts are absolutely essential in this field. To enter this field and to stay in its network is nearly impossible without traveling and being visible. This visibility requires a considerable investment of time, energy, and money, and this investment has to be made also in times when no comparative project is being carried out and no extra project money is available. In my experience through ISCAE I know that most conference participants attend on their own money, sometimes with some very limited support from their university or foundations. (I always was happy when 30% of my total expenses were paid by the university; usually it was much less). Such expenditure makes it especially difficult for young scholars to come into the field of international comparative adult education or to stay in it after a comparative project is finished.

Of course, international comparative projects have much *higher costs and a lot more problems than research carried out in one country*. A foreign partner has to be found and has to be convinced to join a project. Many details have to be clarified before and during the research process and at the end of the publication; such discussion requires continuous

End page 35
Start page 36

exchange. In most cases, one partner also carries an extra load of translation when the other partner does not speak his language. It is difficult to find foundations willing to support international projects. National foundations often are not interested in paying the costs of the foreign partner. Even when one researcher can travel to two or more countries and thus avoids the handicap of co-authorship, comparative research means a high investment of money, time, and effort. When weighing the potential outcome of these investments for one's career, a scholar often finds it more beneficial to work at the national level. Funding agencies should do more not just to assist international comparative research projects but especially to encourage and finance the possibility of bringing young scholars into this field. Also, ways should be found to support those volunteering in international societies.

6. Prospects

International adult education and international comparative adult education share the fate of many good ideas: Everybody agrees that they are important, but not many are willing to take the load of the international work on their shoulders and purses. Experiences in international and international comparative adult education have been developed with many countries for some 70 years in Europe and 40 years in the USA. The important task is to encourage continued work in this field, building on previous results in order to develop these experiences further.

More international knowledge, respect, and understanding certainly are needed in today's world. In smaller countries, these ideals can be reached more easily through everyday experiences. For the United States of America, a big country spanning an entire continent and having armed forces, business presence, and cultural influence all over the world, this is a much more difficult task. The personal benefits of being a more "international" person include understanding, open-mindedness, tolerance, and humility - and good times with good friends in many places in the world (for example, in a *Biergarten* during the summer in Bamberg, Germany).

From a global perspective, learning from each other is an essential, basic necessity. The UNESCO *Hamburg Declaration on Adult Education* (1997, Chapter 14) put this perspective in words: "One of the foremost challenges of our age is . . . to construct a culture of peace based on justice and tolerance within which dialogue, mutual recognition, and negotiation will replace violence, in homes and countries, within nations and between countries".

End page 36
Start page 37

References

Charters, Alexander N., & Hilton, Ronald J. (1989). Introduction. In A. N. Charters & R. J. Hilton (Eds.), *Landmarks in international adult education: A comparative analysis* (pp. 1-14). London: Routledge.

Charters, Alexander N., & Hilton, Ronald J. (Eds.). (1989). *Landmarks in international adult education: A comparative analysis*. London: Routledge.

Charters, A. N., & Siddiqui, D. A. (1989). *Comparative adult education: State of the art. With annotated resource guide*. Vancouver, British Columbia, Canada: University of British Columbia, Center for Continuing Education.

Friedenthal-Haase, Marthe, Hake, Barry J., & Marriott, Stuart (Eds.). (1991). *British-Dutch-German relationships in adult education, 1880-1930: Studies in the theory and history of cross-cultural communication in adult education*. Leeds, UK: University of Leeds. (Leeds Studies in Continuing Education/Cross-Cultural Studies in the Education of Adults, No. 1)

Jarvis, Peter (1989). Editor's note. In Alexander N. Charters & Ronald Hilton (Eds.), *Landmarks in international adult education: A comparative analysis* (unpaginated foreword). London: Routledge.

Jarvis, P. (Ed.). (1992). *Perspectives on adult education and training in Europe*. Malabar, FL: Krieger.

Kidd, James Robin (1975). Comparative adult education: The first decade. In Cliff Bennett, James Robin Kidd, & Jindra Kulich (Eds.), *Comparative studies in adult education: An anthology* (pp. 5-24). Syracuse, NY: Syracuse University. (Syracuse University Publications in Continuing Education No. 44)

Knox, Alan B. (Ed.). (1989). *World perspective case descriptions on educational programs for adults*. Alexandria, VA: American Association for Adult and Continuing Education. (ERIC Document Reproduction Service No. ED311188)

Pöggeler, Franz (Ed.). (1978). *Handbuch der Erwachsenenbildung*. Stuttgart: Kohlhammer.

Pöggeler, Franz (Ed.). (1990). *The state and adult education*. Frankfurt: Lang.

Reischmann, Jost (1988). *Adult education in West Germany in case studies*. New York: Lang. www.reischmannfam.de/lit/1988-AdEdinGermany.pdf

Reischmann, Jost, Bron jr., Michal, & Jelenc, Zoran (Eds.). (1999). *Comparative adult education 1998: The contribution of ISCAE to an emerging field of study*. Ljubljana, Slovenia: Slovenian Institute for Adult Education.

End page 37
Start page 38

Titmus, Colin (1999). Comparative adult education: Some reflections on the process. In J. Reischmann, M. Bron, & Z. Jelenc (Eds.), *Comparative adult education 1998: The contribution of ISCAE to an emerging field of study* (pp. 33-50). Ljubljana, Slovenia: Slovenian Institute for Adult Education.

UNESCO Institute for Education. (1997). *The Hamburg declaration on adult learning*. Hamburg, Germany: UNESCO. Retrieved November 21, 2003, from http://www.unesco.org/education/uie/confintea/documents.html

This contribution, derived from a presentation from 1992 (refer to section 4.2), documents that at that time substantial publications addressing adult education in various countries, were already available. Furthermore, it serves as an example of critical reflection on both the content and methodology of such studies, hopefully encouraging more contributions to the further development of international comparative adult education.

5.4 World Perspective and Landmarks in Adult Education - a Critical Re-Analysis (1999)[1]

1. Introduction

Publications in international comparative adult education in the last decade offered a new level of comparative work. This new level consists of material as well as methodology. On the material side, case studies and program descriptions became available from more and more countries, and - here we enter the methodological field - which more often followed a structure or outline that makes them suitable for comparative purposes. Authors started making comparisons, well knowing that this is a highly subjective, „soft", interpretative, hermeneutic work, open to all sorts of criticisms.

The following research is based on two sources: On the Alexander Charters/Ronald Hilton's book "Landmarks in International Adult Education" (1989), presenting eight "landmark" programs - "judged - often by both contemporaries and later observers - to have been successful" (p. 5) - from eight countries including an elaborate comparative analysis, and 200 case studies from 32 countries collected by Alan Knox 1986-1988 in his „World Perspective on Adult Education" (1989). Both sources represent the type of "outreach research", bringing authors from different countries together. A precondition for this type of research is a network of cooperating experts in the countries involved. Both sources document the existence of such a network and by this, indicate a level of scholarly exchange available today in international comparative adult education.

End page 195
Start page 196

Charters'/Hilton´s Landmark Book

Charters' and Hilton's „Landmarks in International Adult Education. A Comparative Analysis" (1989) consists of two equally important parts:

---

1   First print: Reischmann, Jost: World Perspective and Landmarks in Adult Education - A Critical Re-Analysis. p. 195-212. In: Reischmann, Jost/ Bron, Michal/ Jelenc, Zoran (ed) (1999): *Comparative Adult Education 1998: the Contribution of ISCAE to an Emerging Field of Study.* Ljubljana, Slovenien: Slovenian Institute for Adult Education.

First, they offer a description of eight adult education programs in eight countries, written by national experts for these programs:

Country	Author	Program
Sweden	Rubenson	Study Circles
Denmark	Himmelstrup	Folk High School
Yugoslavia	Krajnc	Workers Universities
Great Britain	Fieldhouse	Workers Educational Association
Canada	Morrison	Frontier College
France	Lengrand	People and Culture
USA	Long	Co-operative Extension
West Germany	Dohmen	Volkshochschule

This part of the book is a valuable source of information in order to look beyond the local hills which often obscure our view. These program descriptions are helpful for use as textbooks in seminars, even when considering that since the writing of the program descriptions some of the countries went through major changes (i.e. Yugoslavia, West Germany).

Second Charters/Hilton present a "similarities and dissimilarities assessment", starting with a comparative description of the key elements and issues of the landmark programs. The method they employed was a rich and detailed use of quotations out of the program descriptions. This does not only illustrate their findings but also enables the reader to control the conclusions by going back to the database presented in the program descriptions. Here we see an important methodological gain, as this procedure increases the "objectivity" of this type of research. As a result of their comparisons, they offer a summary with "six themes which seemed to the book authors nearly overpowering in their

End page 196
Start page 197

emphasis and reiteration" (p. 194). These six reiterated themes they found emphasized throughout their program descriptions were:

1. Passionate statements, extolling high moral standards; purposes, high minded, and rightly intended: goals are global, needs assessment impressionistic.
2. A nearly inspirational faith in individuals to transform themselves and their society.
3. The faith in the adult education enterprise to successfully transform individuals and societies.
4. The commitment to openness and the lack of concern for system.
5. National trends and national goals were everywhere observed.
6. The centrality of the learners.

Evaluation, Critique, and Questions

This comparative analysis can be seen as a model for future research: it shows - and that seems to be new in comparative adult education - an analysis profoundly grounded on a database also available to the reader. And the six "reiterated themes emphasized throughout the program descriptions" claim to point out typical characteristics of adult education.

But there were also limitations in the database Charters/Hilton used for their observations and interpretations. Their database is limited to nationwide and successful "landmark-programs" and western industrialized countries. To examine whether their findings can be generalized the question occurs: Can these six reiterated and emphasized observations also be found in programs that are neither "landmark" nor "western industrialized countries?" To explore this question a different database - not "landmark", not "western industrialized countries" - was needed.

Alan Knox's Case Studies

Between 1986 and 1988 Alan Knox collected about 200 "case studies" (available through ERIC clearinghouse). They were not expected to be "landmark", and they came from 32 countries:

End page 197
Start page 198

Country, Number of Cases		Country, Number of Cases		Country, Number of Cases	
Argentina	2	Hungary	2	Saudi Arabia	1
Australia	24	India	4	St. Lucia	1
Cameroon	2	Ireland	15	Sweden	6
Canada	11	Israel	2	Switzerland	1
Chile	2	Italy	9	Tanzania	1
China	5	Japan	3	United Kingdom	1
Czechoslovakia	2	Korea, DPR	1	USA	13
Finland	8	Netherlands	20	USSR	2
Germany, West	14	Nigeria	7	Yugoslavia	8
Ghana	2	Norway	1		
Greece	1	Portugal	1		

Alan Knox also asked the authors to follow a certain outline. Both outlines can help further comparative authors to structure their research.

Alexander Charters/Ronald Hilton (1989) Landmarks in Adult Education Protocol for Program Description:	Alan Knox (1986-1988) A World Perspective on Adult Education Sections of Case Descriptions
A. Program needs and identification of needs B. Mission and objectives	A. Setting B. Outcomes 1. Goals of program 2. Benefits to learners

C. Historical precedents/antecedents	C. Process 1. Program planning. 2. Methods of teaching/learning 3. Improvement, evaluation, staff-training 4. Participation, marketing
D. Cultural/societal considerations	D. Inputs for operation of program 1. Participants, 2. Needs, 3. Staff, 4. Content,5. Finances, 6. Facilities, 7. Other
E. Principal players/facilitators	E. Evolution, history
F. Operational considerations	F. Influences that affect(ed) the program
G. Evaluation standards	G. Other
H. Influences and Impact	
I. Program chapter author's perspectives	

End page 198
Start page 199

As there were many parallels with Charters' protocol the Knox studies could be used to prove whether the Charters' analysis could be replicated with the Knox database.

Selected Case Studies

To use a different cultural background for additional analysis, six case studies from non-western, non industrialized countries were selected (the studies will be cited in the following text with the first two letters of the country-name and the page-number given by Knox):

- Tanzania (Aida Isinika): Training for rural development - governmental program.
- Nigeria (Clement N. Anyanwu): Community education in Nigeria - Guinea Worm Eradication Program - Ministry of Health.
- India (E. P. Burns): Hayden Hall: A Comprehensive Community Development Approach with programs in food, health care, basic adult education.
- Cameroon (J. A. Nyemba): Agricultural Extension Programs in Cameroon - governmental program.
- Ghana (Joe K. Ansere): Ghana Modular Programme: Distance study program for teachers.
- Saudi Arabia (Al Rasheed/Al Sunbul): Illiteracy eradication and adult education by a royal nationwide program 1970-1985.

There is not enough space here to report details of these studies: directly Charters/Hilton's six „reiterated themes" are checked in this database a) for confirming and b) contradicting statements. To understand contradictions, what will be looked for are c) possible methodological pitfalls and d) interpretations regarding the extended database.

End page 199
Start page 200

2. Comparison of „Reiterated Themes"

Theme 1: High moral standards with low defined objectives

Also, the additionally researched and aforementioned studies offered passionate statements of lofty intentions: The Saudi-Arabia-study cites Mohammed "Seek knowledge from cradle to grave" (SA 9), the Nigeria-study wants "citizen enlightenment" (NI 5) and claims the "transition from tradition to modernity" (NI 18), and the India-study has "human development as overall goal" (IN 2). This confirms Charters/Hilton's conclusions of high moral standards with low defined objectives.

But there was a second type of statements which was difficult to classify and evaluate with regard to "theme" 1: "helping villagers improve their quality of life" (TA 3), "to promote better living for the whole community" (NI 3), "empowering and helping the villagers ... become more self-confident and self-reliant" (IN 2) - do these statements proclaim "high moral standards" or do they describe concrete objectives? This view is a subjective interpretation and has to do with the connotation of phrases. Certainly, native English speakers will do this interpretation more easily. But the native language of most of the authors (in Charters book six of eight) is not English. So what sounds like a clear statement to a native English speaker possibly has different connotations for the author and possibly for the reader, too. This pitfall of comparative research always has to be taken into consideration when written documents constitute the research database.

A third type of statements clearly was in contradiction to Charters/Hilton's conclusion. In all additionally analyzed studies many clear objectives and utilitarian goals could be found: "the usual materialistic gain should be considered"

End page 200
Start page 201

(SA 4), "focused on increased agricultural production and a higher income level" (TA 4), "improve coffee or cotton production" (CA 4), "improve the primary health" (NI 8), and the Distance Study Teachers Program in Ghana is justified: "teacher continue to contribute to the economy by working and paying taxes while at the same time they are studying" (GH 3).

How can these differences be explained? One explanation is, that rich western countries can afford lofty and humanistic programs, while in situations were people struggle for life, programs have to give basic and concrete help. But that interpretation does not ring true: "Landmark programs" like Co-operative Extension or the German Volkshochschule also give basic and concrete help and are by no means limited to non-utilitarian humanistic topics. So another explanation for this discrepancy has to be offered: It could be, that Charters/Hilton's selection of their sample has produced an artifact: The majority of their landmark programs are multifunctional, offering a variety of courses. But the program descriptions from non-western/non-industrialized countries are mostly monofunctional: either health, or farming, or reading. It is not unlikely that describing a multifunctional program seduces authors to focus more on general aims. Compared to these "passionate statements" counting up the many well-disposed concrete objectives seems trivial to the authors - and are therefore left out. Classical test theory has dealt with the pitfalls and biases produced by the sampling process (Campbell/Stanley 1967); this example shows that criteria developed in the quantitative research tradition can also be useful in qualitative comparative research.

Based on both databases and the methodological reflections an interpretation combining the utilitarian and the high moral arguments shall be offered: The authors of the program descriptions see the concrete measures in their programs overwhelmingly related to an educational philosophy with high moral standards.

End page 201
Start page 202

Theme 2+3: Inspirational faith in learner and adult education enterprise with low evaluation methodology

Charters/Hilton (1989) willingly selected "landmark"-programs. A criterion for their selection was: "Each (program) was judged - often by both contemporaries and later observers - to have been successful ..." (p. 5). They wanted successful programs - and their eight authors offered them program descriptions with statements of successful accomplishments. No wonder they can summarize: "None of these programs were built upon modest aims, and yet none of their authors seemed to expect aught but success" (p. 195). What else could be expected in "landmark-programs"?

So is their finding of "inspirational faith in learners and adult education enterprise with low evaluation methodology" more than a circular definition of a selected sample? To avoid the classical validity-pitfall "selection" - it is not possible to generalize from a selected sample to the unselected population (Campbell/Stanley 1967, p. 176) - the non-landmark-database of Knox was interesting. Several confirming statements can be presented, validating the faith in the adult learner and the adult education enterprise: "enormous benefit for the individual and the society" (SA 7), "villagers learn from each others' experiences" (TA 11), "the influence of the program is in every way spectacular" (NI 22), "enthusiastic participation" (NI 5), "This is a program that is making a real difference in the lives of thousands of people in a neglected corner of the world" (IN 4).

But critical statements also can be found. The author of the Cameroon study states that farmers had a bad experience with extension programs and that a literature review gives no clear statements of increased output. Also, the distance study program (Ghana) reports disappointment, and the Saudi Arabia

End page 202
Start page 203

study reports dropout problems. Here in this non-landmark-database clear limitations of the "inspirational faith" (p. 195) Charters/Hilton stated could be found. But still the positive statements are overwhelming.

To explain this the following interpretation may be offered: When someone is asked to write about a program of one's own choice - as Knox did - it is likely that a program is chosen that is worth reporting: that is a successful program. That does not mean that authors are unable to see failure. And it does not mean that all programs are successful. Certainly, most of the existing programs are successful, because other programs disappear quickly from the market. So this positive image of most program descriptions could be explained by the selection by the authors and the "sustainability" (also derived from classical test theory) of successful programs.

Another observation of Charters/Hilton has to be discussed: In their landmark programs, they found "a curious acceptance of the efficacy of these programs without a restless searching after supportive data upon which to draw conclusions" (p. 172) and "evaluative judgments, in which objectives, objective data, and even ... subjective data are almost unnoted" (p. 173).

Also here the two databases show differences. Partly our additionally analyzed data support Charters/Hilton, in so far as the type of systematic school- like control and measurement is not to be found. But a lot of other control and evaluation statements are made: "production had increased threefold ... shift in leadership style from a directive to a more participatory type ... increased attendance in village meetings ... in general more villagers appeared to be taking initiative and responsibility to solve those problems that are within their control" (TA 7f). "Continuous evaluation has been key to the success of the TRD program" (TA 15). "Out of the twelve wells projected ... nine are now ready and functioning. ... The people ... have learnt to boil and filter (water) ... More importantly, they have grown to disabuse their minds of the age-old belief that the Guinea worm disease is an act of God" (NI 22). And the India

End page 203
Start page 204

study reports a drastic change in the program after several months of evaluation. So evaluation indeed is a topic in our additional case studies, but in a different way than in traditional research-oriented programs.

But three programs explicitly claim further evaluation - always in the context of critical statements: The more critical Cameroon study complains about the missing systematic measurement (CA 5), the only limited successful distance study program for teachers claims a "full-scale evaluation" (GH 9), and the Saudi Arabia study wants more information for evaluation.

In trying to understand these observations - and by this interpreting them - two explanations seem possible: 1. The need for evaluation seems to arise when programs are not successful. This could explain why Charters/Hilton in their by "landmark" definition successful programs observed so little evaluation. 2. Adults decide voluntarily to participate in programs. When they get what they want (= successful program), they stay, otherwise they leave - they vote with their feet. This well-known mechanism in adult education makes evaluation different from what it is in the traditional school system. Perhaps a statement like the following fulfills truly the function of a typical adult education "evaluation": "The appreciation (of this program) is being shown by the people opting to beautify the project sites (wells) with flowers and shade trees" (NI 15). But which evaluator, used to tests, questionnaires, and effect measurement, identifies and accepts such a statement as "evaluation"?

Theme 4: Lack of concern for system

A fourth common theme Charters/Hilton described was the "lack of concern for system" (p. 196). "Program flexibility and autonomy are highly valued and protected" (p. 186). Repeatedly statements were made that what is important is "adapting program methods to changes in participation rather than expecting participants to make adaptations" (p. 196).

End page 204
Start page 205

Here again the database derived from Knox's material supplied verification: "The majority of those teachers did not receive any training" (SA 14), the Tanzania-program has "no prescribed syllabus" (TA 19), and the India case study explicitly claims "non-formal education" (IN 1). Also here - as Charters/Hilton did - many statements about flexibility, openness, innovation were found.

But clearly there were statements contradictory to Charters' interpretation of "impressionistic needs identification", "global, sweeping objectives", "lack of concern of practicability". There could not only routines close to the school-system be found (as described in the Saudi-Arabia, the Ghana, and the Cameroon study). Even more, a well-elaborated and - as this author interprets it - typical adult education "system" could be identified: A lot of effort, planning, and systematic approach is applied at the person-to-person level to make possible shared decisions and responsibility. This system does not plan in the classical bureaucratic way from top to bottom, but provides planning-possibilities at the basis, as is characterized in the Nigeria-study: "a new type of education ... that cannot be brought about at a stroke by administrative order ... (but) by organizing the people in groups to carry out what they have collectively realized to be desirable" (NI 19). The author of the India study described systematic training efforts to increase the local credibility: "important part of the training emphasis is on staff development ... They are credible leaders and powerful change agents within their own community" (IN 4). The Tanzania study described: "all trainers must undergo a training of trainers ... the facilitator helps to guide the process of knowledge exchange and its application" (TA 14). This concern for flexibility on the person-to- person-level could be found for example in the Tanzania-study in the portrayal of the "team who are open, committed, co-operative and creative in helping to solve villagers' problems" (TA 23).

"Facilitator" (TA 14), "grass-root-worker" (IN 4), "networks", and "dialogic principle" are labels that indicate a theoretical and systematic orientation (i.e.

End page 205
Start page 206

Freire, Rogers, Illich). So a warning conclusion here is: Results can depend upon our individual understanding of the researched object. If we understand "system" as a bureaucratic, top-down administration, we indeed do not find much emphasis of such a "system". But if we understand "system" in a different way we discover that many authors describe a high concern for a specific "system": a system, that enables local decisions, often made in interaction with the "participants", preferably named "partners".

Theme 5: National trends and national goals

As a fifth "pervasive theme" Charters/Hilton found, that "national trends and national goals are everywhere observed and frequently lie at the heart of most of these programs" (p. 197).

Of course, the authors of the non-western countries also name historical data or employ national perspectives. But the authors put less stress on this argument - even less when taking into account that five of the six are governmental programs. Much more practical reasons - health, hunger - are named.

Perhaps this difference comes from the sampling method Charters/Hilton used: The authors of the landmark program descriptions were well aware that they presented their country within an international study. The Knox' case studies were mostly smaller in scale; in the different countries a "country coordinator" asked national colleagues to write cases studies, so these authors did not feel obliged to represent their country.

So it could be concluded: Ask authors to describe a nationwide program to be compared with programs in other countries - and national trends and national goals will be mentioned. And ask them to describe just a program - and national trends will be specified much less. If this is true, then the method of producing the database influences the result. Again a parallel with classical

End page 206
Start page 207

test-theory (Campbell/Stanley 1967) can be drawn. There this bias is called "reactivity", which means that the outcome is influenced by the way a researcher stimulates the material.

Knox's material even offers proof for this thesis. Some authors used the opportunity to send old papers presenting national systems. And immediately "national trends and national goals" showed up: The report about the Russian Znanie made statements such as "progressive Russian scientists always regarded the work of educating the masses as their second calling" (SU 14), "Adult Education in Beijing Municipality" claimed: "Since the founding of New China 1949, the Chinese government has attached great importance to the improvement of the cultural and technical qualities of the working people" (6C/2). And the colleague describing "Czechoslovakian Adult Education" declared "education of the citizen as a builder of his socialistic homeland" as the main educational function of adult education (9A/16).

Theme 6: Centrality of the learner

The last "reiterated theme" Charters/Hilton identified was "the centrality of the learners ... they are always the center of respect and affection, often the co-architects of their educational programs and destinies" (p. 197).

The additional data confirmed that observation. Perhaps a further analysis could discriminate between "caring for the learners" (i.e. "Revision of curriculum to meet the needs and desires of adult learners" - SA 16) and "caring with the learners" ("the learner does not have to internalize the new knowledge if it does not suit his/her needs" - TA 13). This respect for the adult learner as an adult person who is able to decide about his/her life - even when such a person has no school career and still believes in the divine ordination of a disease - seems to be a common understanding of adult education experts in many countries.

End page 207
Start page 208

3. Consequences

The thesis outlined at the beginning stated that international comparative adult education in the last decade offered a new level of comparative work. Attempts to verify this new level led to consequences and results in three respects:

Material and content results

As a result of the described research works also "side materials" like mailing lists, bibliographies, and other resources helpful for further research became available (i.e. Knox 1988, Charters, Siddiqui 1989). And the Knox- "World Perspective"-project triggered within two years the publication of four additional reports. This constituted a more intense and more systematic level of comparative research.

On the content level of "reassessing observations" in the enlarged database, the following interpretations of "world-wide commonalities" in adult education are tentatively offered:

- Authors of most of the studies describe adult education programs as an inter-action between high moral standards and concrete needs.
- Most - but not all - authors describe programs positively. That may represent the reality of adult education programs since unsuccessful programs quickly disappear from the market.
- Evaluation seems to be seen by most of the authors not as a formal external activity but as an activity pursued by the learners themselves.
- Many of the authors express explicit concern for systematic support of "grass-root" activities. "Think globally, act locally!" could best describe that position.
- The possible expectation, that non-western programs are third class, "missionary style", or dependent on first-world support can be rejected. The case studies analyzed here are professional programs and descriptions, on the level of current adult education

End page 208
Start page 209

theory and practice. But again the limitations of the sampling process have to be reflected: As shown in 1.3 less than twenty percent of Knox's case studies came from non-western non-industrialized countries - too few to generalize.

These results may not seem very surprising - rather they confirm what could be expected on a national level.

Pitfalls and problems of comparative methodology

More interestingly, this analysis led to a discussion of methodological categories and pitfalls well known in the classical empirical research tradition (without suggesting that the sources used got bogged down in these pitfalls):

Pitfall "language": It is typical for international comparative studies that the authors of the documents, the scholars who analyze these documents, and the readers of these analyses speak different languages. My own experience as country coordinator for West Germany in Knox's case study project (Reischmann 1988a) is that a mere translation of national labels often is not understandable to a readership in different countries; instead of labeling institutions or concepts or regulations, we found it more understandable to describe them briefly, pointing out the specifics we wanted to focus on. Here lies a wide range of possibilities for misunderstanding and misinterpretation, where also the trilingual "Terminology of Adult Education/Continuing Education" of the European Bureau of Adult Education or the UNESCO-"Terminology of Adult Education" is of only limited help.

Pitfall "selection": Because of the complexity of qualitative (verbal) data, the sample used is for the most part fairly limited. By selecting the database, we can find similarities not typical for the unselected population.

Pitfall "sustainability": During the progress of the research work observations disappear because they are no longer available. There may be a systematic

End page 209
Start page 210

reason behind this disappearance, so that important aspects are not represented in our final database.

Pitfall "reactivity": Research activity often influences the field we study, thus making our "results" an artifact of our research activity.

Pitfall "interpretation": The same observation can be interpreted differently by different observers. Especially multi-dimensional qualitative material is susceptible to this pitfall. (Providing the database and the data used for a certain interpretation - as done by Charters/Hilton - offers the chance of verification/falsification)

And finally, there might be a pitfall *"ideologically/politically selected perception"*. After several, especially eastern countries have gone through dramatic political and economical changes in the last decade it might be worthwhile to reanalyze the case studies that were written before the changes and find out, if any typical biases could be identified.

Methodological arguments often hurt researchers who have spent months and months in the dirty and dusty fields of research, while the methodologist spends time in his rocking-chair beside the fireplace. One has to be very careful not to spoil the readiness to do that difficult fieldwork by claiming unrealistic methodological standards. On the other hand: a methodological framework, which researchers can refer to before and while working in the field, makes this work easier and more reliable. New knowledge and shared experiences in methodology of qualitative research (i.e. Miles/Huberman 1984, Merriam 1988, Merriam/Simpson 1995) or in comparative research can perhaps encourage the propensity for research in this field.

Evaluative personal statements

Three final personal and emotive statements may reflect some of my introspections while working with this international material:

End page 210
Start page 211

1. Again and again the descriptions and evaluations of the colleagues were incredibly close to my own experiences. Reading all the case studies and landmark descriptions gave me the feeling of being a member of a big world-wide brother-/sisterhood. But these similarities also gave me a latent feeling of distrust: Can adult education world-wide be so similar? Or does our investigation

of the field produce similarities that make us blind to all other types of adult education?

2. Comparative international research has the image of being creative, subjective, soft, intuitive "artwork" with not much possibility for interpersonal, methodological objectivity. After going through this process of analyzing, comparing, and criticizing based on a rich set of data, and rediscovering the old pitfalls known from the quantitative research tradition I feel we are now approaching a more reliable and systematic methodological basis for comparative research.

3. During that work I found it possible to build on material and methods elaborated by other scholars. For other educational subdisciplines this is standard practice, but it is rather new for international comparative adult education. This means the opening of a scientific community that builds on previous research - and on the growing personal relationship between the researchers engaged in this field. Also, this is part of what I consider to be a new level in international comparative adult education.

References

Campbell, Donald T., Julian C. Stanley (1967). Experimental and Quasi-Experimental Design for Research in Teaching. In N. L. Gage (Ed.): *Handbook on Research on Teaching* (5th edn., pp. 171-246). Chicago: Rand McNally.

Charters, Alexander N., Ronald J. Hilton (Eds.) (1989). *Landmarks in International Adult Education. A Comparative Analysis.* London: Routledge.

Charters, Alexander N., Dilnawaz A. Siddiqui (1989). *Comparative Adult*

End page 211
Start page 212

Education: State of the Art. With Annotated Resource Guide. Vancouver: The University of British Columbia, Centre for Continuing Education.

ECLE (1983, 1986): *Adult Education in Europe.* Methodology I, II, Studies and Documents. No. 14, 15, 23.

European Centre for Leisure and Education. Prague. European Bureau of Adult Education (Second edition, 1980): *The Terminology of Adult Education/Continuing Education* (English, French, German). Amersfoort, the Netherlands.

Knoll, Joachim H. (1980). *Bildung International. Internationale Erwachsenenbildung und Vergleichende Erwachsenenbildungsforschung.* Grafenau: Expert.

Knox, Alan B. (1987). *International Perspectives on Adult Education.* Columbus, Ohio: ERIC Information Series. No. 321.

Knox, Alan B. (ed.) (1989). *World Perspective Case Descriptions on Educational Programs for Adults.* ERIC Document Reproduction Service.

Knox, Alan B. (1993). *Strengthening Adult and Continuing Education. A Global Perspective on Synergistic Leadership.* San Francisco: Jossey-Bass.

Merriam, Sharan B. (1988). *Case Study Research in Education. A Qualitative Approach.* San Francisco: Jossey-Bass.

Merriam, Sharan B., Edwin L. Simpson (1995). *A Guide to Research for Educators and Trainers of Adults.* 2nd edn. Malabar, FL.: Krieger.

Miles, Matthew B., A. Michael Hubermann (1984): *Qualitative Data Analysis. A Sourcebook of New Methods.* Beverly Hills: Sage.

Reischmann, Jost (Ed.) (1988a). *Adult Education in West Germany in Case Studies.* Frankfurt, New York: Peter Lang.

Reischmann, Jost (1988b). Zur Literaturlage der Deutschen Vergleichenden Erwachsenen-pädagogik. In Joachim H. Knoll (Ed.). *Internationales Jahrbuch der Erwachsenen-bildung* (Vol.16, pp. 189-197). Köln: Böhlau.

UNESCO (1979): *Terminology of Adult Education* (English, French, Spanish). Paris.

Often in international comparative studies, it is difficult to refer to older basic texts because they are scattered throughout many places, hidden in old publications, difficult to locate. Therefore it seemed worthwhile to edit a book that makes a selection of such old but 'essential' texts available and documents the long history of the international/comparative perspective. 'Standing on the shoulders of giants' offers the opportunity for a grounded reflection, and supports professional work by making it easier, enhancing their quality, adding enjoyment, and fostering self-confidence.

This was the background-motivation to edit the reader "Essential Readings in International and Comparative Adult Education" (Reischmann 2021). The subsequent text is the summary at the end of this book. It has to be accepted that this text frequently refers to other parts (references) of the book; hopefully, it still remains informative and understandable.

5.5 Essential Readings in Comparative Adult Education. Observations and Perspectives (2021)[1]

At the end of a voluminous book with many texts, the question may arise as to what - in short - might be some main observations and insights, as well as suggestions and perspectives. So, in this closing chapter, some issues are selected from the previous chapters that shed clarifying light on the developments of the field. In addition, some suggestions are offered helpful for future work. (The specified page numbers refer to pages in this book)

1. A clear observation is that a **high number of publications** about international and comparative adult education are available in the English language: This book contains a total of 351 references, added up from all contributions. That seems to be a lot; however, overwhelmingly in these 351 references, authors are named only once or twice. It seems there exists nearly no "standard"-literature which "all" contributors use. The highest entries included UNESCO (12, different documents), Charters/Hilton (10), the two ISCAE-publications (Comparative Adult Education 1998 and 2008) (10), Titmus (10), Knoll (6), Hake (5), Jarvis (5), Knox (5), Merriam (5), Reischmann (5) (not counted were the self-citations in the author's own contribution).

That means: It can be expected that future research work will include references to this specialized literature; but also, more efforts are needed to standardize the shared body of knowledge in the field. "Standing on the shoulders of giants" would not only promote quality, but would also help to unite the field.

2. **Different types of research approaches** are considered to be associated with international and comparative adult education. Bereday names 4 "steps"

---

[1]   First print: Reischmann, Jost (2021): Observations and Perspectives. In: Reischmann, Jost (Ed.) *Essential Readings in International and Comparative Adult Education.* Ziel Verlag, Augsburg. P. 315-319.

(p. 46): Description, Interpretation, Juxtaposition, Comparison. Reischmann reports seven "types of international-comparative research" (pp. 13-14) [see in this book 4.1]: traveler's tales, country reports, program-reports, juxtaposition, comparison, method-reflections, and reports from international organizations. Sometimes these different types are described as historical steps from simple to complex (Reischmann, pp. 13-14; Bereday, pp. 38f), but they also can be seen as platforms of their own value.

For future research, it would be helpful if researchers were to localize their work within these different options. The given literature reflects their strengths of each approach and, by using this knowledge, weaknesses can be avoided or at least mitigated.

3. Two different groups of arguments were found explaining the value of the international aspect: a practical one and an intellectual one.

The **practical** one is usually labeled "borrowing", and there are many examples of transfer from one country to the other. This approach, however, is often criticized, for example, by Kidd in 1975 (p. 75) "In earlier times, comparative

End page 315
Start page 316

education was fostered with the definite purpose of 'borrowing' successful forms and activities from abroad to be adopted in one's own system".

The **intellectual enlightenment-oriented** argument is well documented in Kidd's list (1975) of goals (p. 75) [see in this book 4.3]. Already, however, Sadler, as early as 1900 (p. 21), claimed: "The practical value of studying ...the working of foreign systems of education is that it will result in our being better fitted to study and to understand our own".

While the academics highly valued these enlightenment-oriented goals, the "real world" remained more on the practical side. So, for example, UNESCO's "Hamburg declaration 1997" (p. 239) claimed: "intercultural education should encourage learningbetween and about different cultures in support of peace, human rights and fundamental freedoms, democracy, justice, liberty, coexistence and diversity". Moreover, Chapter 9 of this book has many examples, that suggest when international organizations take over international projects, more "down to earth" goals are expected, for example, when in UNESCO's "Sustainable Development Goals" 17 goals are declared "to transform our world".

This tension between different goals will continue to exist in the future. Both principles have their own good reasons. Comparativists should describe what advantages they expect when they decide for one or the other goal - this would make the perspective of the research better understandable. Furthermore, perhaps also to reflect explicitly whether it is possible to combine them.

4. This book confirms in several contributions a postulation that was mentioned already in the early development of comparative education: that **context**

is one of the most important factors in analyzing educational systems. For example, Sadler in 1900 (!) (p. 21) claimed: "we should not forget that the things outside the schools matter even more than the things inside the schools", and (p. 24): "It is a great mistake to think … that one kind of education suits every nation alike". Similarly, Titmus in 1981 (p. 114 ff): "adult education practices can only be understood as products of the national culture in which they exist". Jarvis in 1992 (p. 129) affirms: "any comparative study of the education of adults requires a comparative study of the societies themselves". Several of the contributors showed how this could be done - and displayed evidence of how this raised the value of their research: Marriot (2.4), Titmus (4.2), Reichart (4.4), Charters/ Hilton (5.1), Seitter (5.3), Egetenmeyer-Neher (5.4), Merriam (5.5), Sun/ Erichsen (5.6).

These examples illustrate that reflections on the respective culture contribute to a better understanding as to why things are as they are. This observation may also be a suggestion for researchers to form a basis support for their research.

5. Research is always performed by humans who have their own cultural backgrounds. This "selective perception" threatens, especially in international projects, the perception of "the other". Bereday (p. 41) claims "never-ceasing watchfulness by the observer to control his own **cultural or personal bias**".

End page 316
Start page 317

Artur (3.5) reflects on her "bi-cultural journey", Reichart (4.4), checking difficulties and obstacles in her presentation about Krygyzstan, shows how this danger can be reduced. Merriam (5.5) as well as Sun & Erichsen (5.6) illuminate the dramatic differences of perspectives on adult learning and education between different cultures. Moreover, Bron (7.1) specifies pitfalls in comparative studies based on cultural misunderstanding.

Therefore, a perspective might be that authors and researchers in international comparative adult education explicitly reflect on their cultural or personal bias. It helps, before starting such a project, to collect information about the history and culture of the other country, try to find other literature or pieces of research, and develop a specific mindset: to be open, listening, and curious. As Sun & Erichsen expressed: "In order to listen and learn from the reality of the East, we believe one's mindset must be altered so openness and appreciativeness will come into play so we can recognize values we may otherwise miss" (p. 232). This request sounds easy, but definitely is not. Nevertheless, here applies a principle true in many life situations: It is better to do it half good than not starting to try!

6. It seems that our "essential readings" in the years up to 2000 were written mainly by **white, western males**. Already the Exeter-papers (p. 51) request in 1966: "conferences on the comparative study of adult education should include representatives from Far East countries as well as South American countries

…". However, when collecting selections for this book (in 2020), we still could not overcome these limitations - even with the best intentions. At least the available publications draw this picture. Merriam confirms a Western bias: "Most of what we know about learning has been studied and written about by scholars in "Western" countries." In Peter Jarvis' "Twentieth Century Thinkers in Adult Education" (London, 1987) all 13 "thinkers" are male. That narrows the views that could be richer if this selection would not apply.

As described in chapter 9 some changes seem to emerge in the new (21st) century. Especially the international and transnational agencies reach out to far more regions of the world. The question remains: Is this an opening for mutual understanding, or again "careless over-applying [of] Western norms and values" (Sun & Erichson, p. 232)? It seems there is still a long way to go …

7. The contributions in this book show a clear development: In the beginning, we find primarily **individuals** that generate the international and comparative knowledge, as Kidd 1975 pictures (p. 73): "comparative adult educationists … working almost in isolation". This scenario changed, as described in chapter 4.1 (Council of Europe, ECCLE, Knoll p. 84ff); chapter 9 indicates that today mostly **institutions or societies** are the promotors of international and comparative adult education.

Working only as "individuals in isolation" seems to have diminished. Networks, societies, and organizations now lead the way of the development. Researchers interested in international and comparative adult education are better

End page 317
Start page 318

advised to get in contact with such entities. Working together, international teams of researchers have an excellent opportunity to offer a more differentiated perception when bringing together their diverse cultural backgrounds.

8. **Language** is often described as one of the handicaps in international work - as already noted in the preface of this book (p.11-12). This issue shows up in several of our "essential texts". Not surprisingly, it is seldomly mentioned in the early publications of English-speaking authors (as an anecdote, see Mansbridge's last chapter p. 95f). It seems this problem became more recognized with the increasing number of non-English researchers. The Exeter-conference (1966) claimed within a long list of needs "the need for an international terminology" (p. 57, p. 59) - not being aware that terminology is only a small part of language (and understanding) problems. Bron (p. 254) describes a "crucial issue …whether questions and answers can be meaningfully translated from one language, and one social reality, into another" - Reichart (p. 141) confirms this problem with the observation that "the simply translated questionnaire from the European manual caused confusion among the survey institutes, the interviewers and the respondent". Moreover, Sun & Erichsen

point out another language limitation (p. 231): "when we introduce the East to the West, there is dearth of available literature for reference.

It is easy but unrealistic to claim that everybody must be bi- or multilingual. Nevertheless, even minor measures would help foster language sensibility: For example, native English speakers should take into account that English is a foreign language for most of their audience in an international venture. As a consequence, they should speak loud, slow, clear, and avoid slang words and insider jokes, as well as acronyms - highly loved by Americans. In oral and written communication, it helps when one or two sentences explain what is meant - not just dropping names. Describing the context also improves understanding. Texts from all languages can roughly be translated with computer programs (i.e., Google translator); this opportunity at least provides a general impression of what a paper covers. Still, it cannot be changed that the literature in the field is English-language dominated, and non-English speakers will have the extra-load of translation. That seems to be the price for international exchange.

9. In the process of selecting the texts for this book we "discovered" two different types of publications, both called "international". One type deals directly with topics in different countries, describing financing, training of adult educators, leadership, literacy, politics in different countries. A high number of studies of this type could be found, most of the type of juxtaposition. Much fewer studies could be found of another type: Here, in addition, the authors explicitly reflected the **specific** problems and possibilities of the **international approach**.

Of course, the first type will be important and produced in the future. However, it could be desirable that more studies of type 2 are presented: This type

End page 318
Start page 319

forces authors to reflect on the strengths and limits of international comparison, thus avoiding the danger of overgeneralizing, of falling into the "descriptiness-pitfall" or "comparing incomparables" (Bron, p. 257f). In addition, these shared reflections enable the reader to better understand the complexity of a comparison.

10. Many observations in this book confirm how **travel** was essential on a personal as well as professional level for the protagonists. The Exeter conference in 1966 (p. 62) claimed: "As soon as possible, adult educators in various countries should meet together to develop cooperative programs of study and research" (- maybe the 26 participants hoped for their own travels in the future?). Marriott (p. 26) describes the many travel exchanges and their results between England and Germany in the difficult time after World War I. Chapter 3 (p. 91ff) gives several examples of travels and their value for adult education.

Here the perspective and suggestion to new researchers in international and comparative adult education are clear: Travelling and reliable attendance at international conferences are essential to growing into this field. Of course, this means a high investment in time and money. Besides having better access to information, it has an additional benefit: meeting and making friendship with stimulating persons.

11. A final observation that should be mentioned: Often the authors refer to the people in the "international arena" as people offering **friendship and inspiration**: Charters/Hilton (p. 163) describes as a benefit of international meetings "to celebrate the great good fortune of international collegiality". Arthur (p. 105) appraises "...shared learning enhanced knowledge, and mutual understanding - perhaps particular strengths of comparative adult education.

This "byproduct" of meeting with "the Internationals" not only personally enriches but also builds informal networks that led to publications about foreign adult education as collected in the anthologies of Jarvis (4.3), Charters/Hilton (5.1), Pöggeler (p. 107), and Merriam (5.5). This enrichment may outweigh some of the inconveniences of international work.

There are many reasons to engage in international and comparative adult education. "Standing on the shoulders" of those, who offered essential knowledge about content, methods, and reflections can help strengthen the quality of comparison and make access into this field more enjoyable and easier. We trust that the reader of this book will find in the many multi-faceted contributions more individual insights and perspectives than could be mentioned in this short chapter. The central perspective is to facilitate entering and working in international and comparative adult education.

Following the editing process of "Essential Readings in International and Comparative Adult Education", encompassing 319 pages and 32 contributors spanning 120 years (Reischmann 2021, see 5.5), it seemed to me that this might be too much load for newcomers. Consequently, I tried to concentrate in a short paper on those pieces of advice, that seemed to me most manifest. The result is the following short document comprising seven reflections, intended to be a pragmatic starting point for writing and controlling research in international and comparative adult education.

5.6 International Comparative Adult Education: Seven reflections I expect to read in each study (2024)[1]

Checklist for beginning

Research never is perfect. We should expect in all studies, however, that researchers not only present their findings, but also their reflections on limitations as well as bias, and offer open questions for further research.

While these guidelines are applicable to research in all subjects and disciplines, Comparative Adult Education has its specific pitfalls of which researchers should be aware and on which they should reflect. Examples include personal blindness, political correctness, unavailable data, and misunderstanding of language, just to mention a few. Including such reflections in the research report/presentation/publication will provide a more objective, reliable, valid, honest, and self-critical contribution to knowledge in the field. The hope is that knowing the pitfalls will make international and comparative work sounder and more enjoyable, and avoid - or at least mitigate - weaknesses.

In the following discussion, I will present a selection of seven reflections I suggest be discussed in international comparative studies. This selection is based on 30 years of experience and observations in the International Society for Comparative Adult Education (ISCAE, www.ISCAE.org) and its publications (http://www.iscae.org/publications.htm, especially Reischmann, 2021). Frequently in this paper old sources will be used to demonstrate that there is a long history of reflections on the method of comparison. These reflections presented here can be used as a sort of checklist before, during, or after an international-comparative project.

1. Why compare?

A first consideration should be to reflect, on what is expected from the comparison – the "why". Is it just for curiosity ("Isn't it interesting that .."), is it

---

[1]   First print: Reischmann, Jost (2024): International comparative adult education: Seven reflections I expect to read in each study. In: *Convergence*, April 2024.

to learn and adopt something from abroad ("borrowing"), or is the goal to understand the other and one's own system better?

Already in1974 Roby Kidd offered a list of "common goals" of comparative studies, going beyond "borrowing" and "imitating":
"The most common goals for comparative studies in adult education are:
- to become better informed about the educational system of other countries;
- to become better informed about the ways in which people in other cultures have carried out certain social functions by means of education;
- to become better informed about the historical roots of certain activities and thus to develop criteria for assessing contemporary developments and testing possible outcomes;
- to better understand the educational forms and systems operating in one's own country;
- to satisfy an interest in how other human beings live and learn;
- to better understand oneself;
- to reveal how one's own cultural biases and personal attributes affect one's judgment about possible ways of carrying on learning transactions." (Kidd 1975, 75)

Researchers that reflect on these different "whys" will develop a deeper understanding of their work – and will discover more and richer aspects during that work, thus enriching the results and academic outcomes.

2. Start with description, move to analysis!

A first basic classification discriminates between "descriptive" and "analytical" studies: As a first step, the researcher always will describe with more or less methodological rigor aspects of adult education. In the "old days" of international comparison such was in the focus of interest; to make the descriptions more comparable, already the historic "Exeter Papers" (Liveright & Haygood 1968) developed a description framework studies should follow. Again in the new days especially the "big data" studies, with dozens of countries included, mostly remain on the description level.

These descriptive studies look comprehensive and impressive. For sure, researchers should at first supply a sound factographic basis. But (future) authors should be warned that an overload of data can lead into the "Descriptiveness-pitfall" (Bron 2008, 257), that is, describing instead of analyzing. The value of an international (one-country) study, however, is to make it understandable to others why, in a given national context, "the social, cultural, economic and political forces [that are] operating on the phenomena" (Titmus 1999, 37) are how they are. Moreover, in a comparative study (two or more countries): "That its author(s) look(s) explicitly for similarities and differences. ... A comparison ought to include explanations and reflections on why the similarities occur" (Bron 2008, 257).

Before starting an international comparative study it may be helpful to clarify how much description is wanted and how much analysis is possible, and to be aware that this decision can change during the research process.

3. Identify your type of international research!

When going more into the details of comparative research it might be confusing that - as Titmus stated as early as 1999 - "most what is included under the rubric of comparative studies ... does not include comparison in the strict sense" (36) and may be labeled "pre-comparative". This openness, however, allows the researcher to use different types of research in international (comparative) studies - each with its strengths and weaknesses (www.ISCAE.org).

To reflect on the strengths and weaknesses of the different types, researchers should at the outset identify the type of their attempt (Reischmann 2000, 13f).

- A first kind, mostly evaluated as 'pre-scientific', comprises 'traveler's tales', the reports we get from international travelers. If these descriptions are more systematic, they are labeled 'traveler's reports'. These types of international documents are mostly characterized as 'subjective-impressionistic'. Their value is evaluated as ambivalent: Critically it is argued that, because of the random observation and the subjective description, it is not clear how reliable and how representative the descriptions are. On the other hand, the plea is made that especially in this subjective focus of eye-witnesses there might be strength in this type of report.

At the scientific level, five types of international-comparative research are identified:

1. *Country-reports*: 'Adult Education in the Republic of ...' is a typical title of this type of report. These papers describe the system of adult and continuing education in one particular country. They could be written by an author of this country or by a person from outside. Some of these reports were, and are, rather impressionistic. Others followed a well-developed outline and structure.

2. *Program reports* describe foreign adult education programs, institutions, and organizations. Examples of this type can be found in the publications of Charters/Hilton (1989) or the case studies collected by Knox (1987). Included in this type (sometimes presented in a separate category) are the topic-oriented studies or the problem approach: a certain topic or problem is discussed in the context of a nation. Country reports as well as topic-oriented studies and the problem approach focus more on 'international' and less on 'comparative'. Because when only one country or program is presented, nothing to compare is available; the readers must draw comparative conclusions themselves.

3. A third type is *juxtaposition*. Data from two or more countries are presented: In country A we can observe a, in country B we find b. A series of statistical reports represent this type, but often no explicit comparisons are given (e.g., where are the similarities, and what are the differences?).

4. The "real *comparison*" goes one step further: "A study in comparative international adult education ... must include one or more aspects of adult education in two or more countries or regions. Comparative study is not the mere placing side by side of data... . Such juxtaposition is only the prerequisite for comparison. At the next stage, one attempts to identify the similarities and differences between the aspects under study ... The real value of comparative study emerges only from ... the attempt to understand why the differences and similarities occur and what their significance is for adult education in the countries under examination ..." (Charters/Hilton 1989, 3).

5. Finally *field- and method-reflections* are seen as part of international comparative adult education: reflections about the methods, strategies, and concepts of international comparison, and summarizing reports about developments in the international comparative field – as it is done in this article.

6. A bit outside of this system, but still counted as part of the international tradition, are *reports from the adult educational work of international and transnational organizations* such as UNESCO, the Organization for Economic Co-operation and Development (OECD), and the World Bank.

It is helpful for interpretation and understanding for the author as well as the reader to identify and discuss the reason why the respective type was selected, and what the strengths and weaknesses are.

4. Reflect language as a possible pitfall!

The most common handicap in international comparative work is language: international communication takes place in English. Even this language, however, has its specific traps. Mansbridge, one of the pioneers of adult education in Britain and a restless traveler, reported an awkward situation: At a lecture in the USA he greeted the attending ladies with a word ("homely"), that in British English expresses appreciation, but in American English it means "super ugly"! (Mansbridge 1940, 95f).

It may comfort the new researcher that this problem even happens to high-ranked professionals. Already in one of the early publications (initiated and financed by the Council of Europe with 32 international experts from 12 West-European countries), Besnard & Liétard (1986, 4) noted in their editorial note: "the translation of the present text from French into English was made in ECLE [European Center for Leisure and Education, Prague]. Since there is uncertainty in adult education terminology world-wide, and important differences exist especially between French and English terminology, the translation was not easy".

A first simple piece of advice is that native English speakers should take into account that English is a foreign language for most of their audience in an international context, and, accordingly, to avoid acronyms. In oral and written communication, it helps when one or two sentences explain what is meant - not just dropping names. Describing the context improves understanding.

To reduce the danger of misunderstanding it is helpful to have a network of colleagues in different countries. So the advice is: International societies such as ISCAE (www.ISCAE.org), ICAE (http://icae.global/), and ESREA (https://esrea.org/) are a great help to install such networks and exchanges. As a member of such societies, other researchers become available for correction and inspiration. This exchange can be on an informal person-to-person contact, by Internet, or through participation in international conferences.

Another piece of advice is: to be critical of questionnaires and similar language-dependent instruments. The translation can lead to non-equivalent meanings for the different language groups. Bron (2008, 254) describes it as a "crucial issue … whether questions and answers can be meaningfully translated from one language, and one social reality, into another". Reichart (2017, 141) confirms this problem with the observation that "the simply translated questionnaire from the European manual [to the Kyrgyzstan context, JR] caused confusion among the survey institutes, the interviewers and the respondent" – even in such "simple" categories as "Household type" or "Marital status". Another language limitation Sun & Erichsen point out (2012, 231): "when we introduce the East to the West, there is dearth of available literature for reference."

Quite drastically, Guo & Beckett (2007, 117) call this language-problem to attention: "the increasing dominance of English language worldwide is contributing to neocolonialism by empowering the already powerful and leaving the disadvantages further behind … putting them in danger to losing their first languages, cultures, and identities, and contributing to the devaluation of local knowledge and culture."

On the other hand, what is the alternative? Without English, there would be no 'worldwide' exchange possible. It seems we have to live with that handicap and to reflect on it when it comes up in a research project. This reflection on language issues even can be seen as a result of an international comparative research project: to make aware how different and rich and unique countries and their cultures are.

5. How does culture define the object under observation?

Education is deeply rooted in the culture of a country. Sadler as early as 1900 (!) claimed: "we should not forget that the things outside the schools matter even more than the things inside the schools" (1900, 21). Institutions, laws, and political or cultural backgrounds are often so different that it is difficult to find an appropriate translation and comparison. Merriam (2007), as well as Sun & Erichsen (2012), illuminate the dramatic differences in perspectives on adult learning and education among different cultures. Moreover, Bron (2012) specifies pitfalls in comparative studies based on a cultural misunderstanding ("comparing the incomparable").

Many aspects of culture influence the theory and practice of adult education: history, economy, religion, family tradition, the role of men and women, values - to name just some. Some of them might be more important in a specific research project, others less. Researchers should keep in mind that – as Jarvis (1992) states – "any comparative study of the education of adults requires a comparative study of the societies themselves" (1992, 128). This general claim of the words "culture" and "society" might threaten beginners in comparative research. Some authors use instead the term "context". In both ways: A researcher who reflects on these is already in the stage of "analytical comparison" - trying to understand the topic under observation.

These cultural reflections can take place at the beginning of a research project. Often, however, they come during the research process: Things happen, and information can not be understood immediately. "You never know what happens - that is a shared experience when working in international comparative adult education" (Reischmann 2021, 283). Such an occurrence is typical for international comparative research. These "discoveries" a researcher should document in the report – it is a result of the study, and will help future researchers in their work.

It helps, before starting such a project, to collect information about the history and culture of the other country, try to find other literature or pieces of research, and develop a specific mindset: to be open, listening, and curious. As Sun & Erichsen expressed, "In order to listen and learn from the reality of the East, we believe one's mindset must be altered so openness and appreciativeness will come into play so we can recognize values we may otherwise miss" (2012, 232). This request sounds easy but definitely is not. Nevertheless, here applies a principle true in many life situations: It is better to do it half good than not starting to try!

Comparative research should not only look for similarities but also for differences. They might better enlighten the understanding of the cultural context, and add new perspectives to the improvement of comparative research. Lee (1999) points out at the end of a thorough comparison of values in Korea and Australia, that "characteristics which are significant in one culture and not in the other represents more important cross-cultural data than those characteristics that are relatively significant to both" (178).

6. What bias has the researcher?

"All forms of comparative work involve comparison by somebody" (Titmus 1999, 37). Research is always performed by humans who have their own cultural backgrounds. This "selective perception" threatens, especially in international projects, the perception of "the other". Bereday (1961!, 41) claims "never-ceasing watchfulness by the observer to control his own cultural or personal bias".

Therefore, authors and researchers in international comparative adult education are advised to explicitly reflect on their personal cultural or personal background: the nearness to certain institutions, who pay for the research, feeling of a "mission" (open or hidden?), adult education as a social movement or "learning for earning"? Basically, are researchers blinded by what they see as "normal"? This reflection on the personal bias will have two results: First, it will bring about a deeper insight into the phenomenon under observation and, as well, it - hopefully - changes the personality of the researcher to develop a more open and understanding mindset, as already mentioned above (at 4.).

7. Read about the method of comparison!

This advice may sound unnecessary in the academic field: "When doing comparison, read about the method of comparison!" It is well grounded, though: The experience in many conferences and publications showed that the literature-lists included many titles about the content of the study, but (nearly) no literature refers to the method and discussion about the value, technique, and pitfalls of international comparison. Often it seems the authors started comparison without knowledge of the long tradition of publications about comparison ("Just doing comparison!"). This repeats mistakes, avoids a deeper quality, and makes these studies less informative than they could be. Moreover, it leaves the author with a foggy feeling: to work with an individual approach instead of assuring him to stand based on known and shared standards.

"Standing on the shoulders" of those, who offered knowledge about content, methods, and reflections helps to strengthen the quality of comparison and make access into this field more enjoyable and easier. Easy access to the literature on standards of international comparative adult education is offered in the publications of the International Society for Comparative Adult Education (www.ISCAE.org/publications).

8. Three promises

Of course, this list of suggestions could be much longer - but it seems a good beginning to apply the presented pieces of advice and suggestions. When going through the seven considerations of this article as a sort of checklist for international comparison in adult education three results can be promised:

First: The quality of the research will be better, more reflected, deeper grounded - more objective, reliable, and valid, contributing to the advancement of the field.

Second: At the same time, researchers will feel safer in their arguments, based on the knowledge of shared standards and experiences.

A third result can be promised: The people in the "international arena" are "easy-to-have"-people, who offer friendship and inspiration: Charters/Hilton (1989, 163) describe as a benefit of international meetings "to celebrate the great good fortune of international collegiality". This growing into an international network enriches the researcher personally and professionally.

Try it!

References

(When old texts are reprinted in Reischmann 2021, the pages given in the text refer to the reprint)

Bereday, George Z. F. *Comparative Method in Education*. New York: Holt, Rinehart and Winston, 1964. Reprint in Jost Reischmann (ed.) 2021, 38-49.

Besnard, Pierre, & Liétard, Bernard. *Adult education in Europe. Methodological framework for comparative studies II*. Prague: European Centre for Leisure and Education. No 23, 1986.

Bron Jr, Michał. "Pitfalls in Comparative Studies". In: *Comparative adult education 2008*. Experiences and Examples, edited by Jost Reischmann, Michał Bron Jr. Frankfurt: Peter Lang Publisher, 2008, 65-80. Reprint in Jost Reischmann (ed.) 2021, 254-269.

Charters, Alexander N., Ronald J. Hilton (ed.). *Landmarks in International Adult Education. A Comparative Analysis*. Routledge: London, 1989. Reprint in Jost Reischmann (ed.) 2021, 146-163.

Guo, Yan, & Beckett, Gulbahar H. "The hegemony of English as a global language: Reclaiming local knowledge and culture in China." *Convergence*, XL(1-2) (2007): 117-131.

Jarvis, Peter (ed). Perspectives on Adult Education and Training in Europe. Malabar: Krieger Publishing Company, 1992. Reprint in Jost Reischmann (ed.) 2021, 121-130.

Kidd, James Robbins. "Comparative Adult Education: The First Decade." In: *Comparative studies in adult education*, edited by Cliff Bennett, J. Roby Kidd, Jindra Kulich. Occasional papers – Syracuse University, Publications in Adult Education; no. 44. 1975. Reprint in Jost Reischmann (ed.), 2021, 71-83

Knox, Alan B. *International Perspectives on Adult Education*. Columbus, Ohio: ERIC clearinghouse on adult, career and vocational education, 1987

Lee, Kwan-Chun. Methodical issues in cross-cultural study of adults value system. In: *Comparative Adult Education 1988*, edited by Jost Reischmann, Michal Bron JR, Zoran Jelenc. Ljubljana, 1999, 169-181.

Liveright, Alexander Albert & Haygood, Noreen (Eds.). *The Exeter Papers. Report of the First International Conference on the Comparative Study of Adult Education*. Center for the Study of Liberal Education for Adults at Boston University. Brookline, Mass., 1968. https://files.eric.ed.gov/fulltext/ ED020487.pdf

Mansbridge, Albert. The trodden road. London: Dent and Sons, 1940. Reprint in Jost Reischmann (ed.) 2021, 93-96.

Merriam, Sharan B., & Associates. *Non-Western Perspectives on Learning and Knowing*. Kruger, Malabar, 2007. Reprint in Jost Reischmann (ed.) 2021, 204-221.

Reichart, Elisabeth. "Participation in Adult Education in Kyrgyzstan – Exploring an uncharted territory with familiar methods (?)". In: *Proceedings ISCAE/COMPALL conference (2017)*, University of Würzburg, Germany, 2017, 219-232. Reprint in Jost Reischmann (ed.) 2021, 131-144.

Reischmann, Jost. *The Meaning of 'International Comparative'. Problems and Perspectives*. www.ISCAE.org, 2000. Reprint in Jost Reischmann (ed.) 2021, 13-17.

Reischmann, Jost (ed.). *Essential Readings in International and Comparative Adult Education*. Ziel Verlag, Augsburg, Germany, 2021.

Sadler, Michael. *How far can we learn anything of practical value from the study of foreign systems of education?* Guilford: Surrey Advertiser Office, 1900. Reprinted in Jost Reischmann (ed.) 2021, 21-24.

Sun, Qi / Erichsen Elizabeth. "Bridging Adult Education between East and West: Critical Reflection and Examination of Western Perspectives on Eastern Reality". *Proceedings of the ISCAE-conference in Las Vegas, 2012*, 213-237. Reprint in Jost Reischmann (ed.) 2021, 222-234.

Titmus, Colin. "Comparative Adult Education: Some reflections on the Process". In *Comparative Adult Education 1988*, edited by Jost Reischmann, Michal Bron JR, Zoran Jelenc. Ljubljana, 1999, 33-50.

www.ISCAE.org – homepage of the International Society for Comparative Adult Education.

6. Jost Reischmann: List of English Publications (2024)[1]

Reischmann, Jost (1981): Zeitungskolleg. A New Way in Open Adult Education in West Germany. In: Distance Education. The Journal of the Australian and South Pacific External Studies Association. Adelaide, Vol. 2 No. 2, pp. 199-211.

Reischmann, Jost (1982): Zeitungskolleg - a Mass Media and Distant Learning Project for Open Learning. In: European Bureau of Adult Education (ed): The Development of Information, Guidance and Counselling Services. Amersfoort (Niederlande). S. 61-78.

Reischmann, Jost (1983): "Courses by Newspaper" and "Zeitungskolleg" - Models of Open Adult Learning in the U. S. A. and Germany. In: Konferenzbericht der 1982 National Adult Education Conference in San Antonio/Texas. ERIC Clearinghouse on Adult, Career, and Vocational Education. Colum¬bus, Ohio.

Reischmann, Jost (1986): Learning "en passant": The Forgot-ten Dimension. Paper presented at the Confe-rence of the American Association of Adult and Continuing Education. Hollywood/Fl., 23. 10. 1986. ERIC Clearinghouse on Adult, Career, and Vocational Education. Columbus/Ohio.

Reischmann, Jost (1988) (ed.): Adult Educa-tion in West Ger¬many in Case Studies. Frankfurt Basel New York: Lang. http://www.reischmannfam.de/lit/1988-AdEdinGermany.pdf. ISBN 3-631-40391-7.

Reischmann, Jost (1989): Adult Education World-Wide - Revisited. In: Quigley, Allan B. (ed): Commission of Professors of Adult Education. Proceedings of the 1989 Annual Conference. October 1 to 3, Penn State: Monroeville. p.184-201.

Reischmann, Jost (1990): Facilitating Adult's Learning by Coa¬ching.

Development and evaluation of an andra¬gogical model of continuing vocational education within industrial companies. In: Pieters, Jules M./Breuer, Klaus/ Simons, P. Robert Jan (ed): Learning Environments: Contributions from Dutch and German Research. Heidelberg: Springer, p. 19-30.

Reischmann, Jost (1991): Coaching the Adult Education Teacher. In: Henstrom, R. H. (ed.): Global Awareness in Adult and Continuing Education. An AAACE Preconference Workshop on Internatio¬nal Adult and Continuing Education, Montreal. S.42-51.

Reischmann, Jost (1993): Questionnaire „Outstanding Experts in Adult Education" - Author's Answers. In: Jelenc, Zoran (ed.): Outstanding Experts on Adult Education. Ljubljana: Andragoski center Republike Slovenije, pp. 165-168.

Reischmann, Jost, Henschke, John (1994): Pedagogy and Andragogy: Relation between the Education of Children and the Education of Adults. Report from Workgroup II. p. 50-52. And: Reischmann, Jost: Expertise on the Research Project "Outstanding Experts ...", p. 192. In: Rethinking Adult Education for Development II. Conference Proceedings. Slovene Adult Education Centre, Ljubljana.

Reischmann, Jost (1995): CERAS - Course Evaluation Rating Scale. Bamberg, Lehrstuhl Andragogik.

Reischmann, Jost (1998): Coaching: Facili-tating the Training of Subject-Matter Specialists. In: Academy of Human Resource Development: Confe¬rence Proceedings. Baton Rouge, LA: AHRD; office@ahrd.org, p. 216-221.

Reischmann, Jost (2000): „How can ‚Com-petency' be learnt"? Andragogical

---

1   The full list of publications by Jost Reischmann, including the German publications, can be found at http://www.reischmannfam.de/lit/Jr-lit-einspaltig.htm

Teaching – A Mixture of Knowledge and Ability. In: Gartenschlaeger, Uwe/Hinzen, Heribert (Ed.): Prospects and Trends in Adult Education. Bonn: Institute for International Cooperation of the German Adult Education Association. p. 124-133.

Reischmann, Jost/ Bron, Michal/ Jelenc, Zoran (ed) (1999): Comparative Adult Education 1998: the Contribution of ISCAE to an Emerging Field of Study. Ljubljana, Slovenien: Slovenian Institute for Adult Education. Cotaining:
- International and Comparative Adult Education. p. 11-15.
- World Perspective and Landmarks in Adult Education - A Critical Re-Analysis. p. 195-212.
- ISCAE - International Society for Comparative Adult Education. p. 275-288.

Reischmann, Jost (1999): Adult Education in Germany. Roots, Status, Mainstreams. In: Andragogy Today: Interdisciplinary Journal of Adult and Continuing Education. The Adult & Continuing Education of Korea. Vol. 2, No. 3, p. 1-29.

Reischmann, Jost (2000): Andragogy: Discipline or Belief-system? In: Searching for New Paradigms in Adult Education. International Conference 2000 of the ACE of Korea and KEDI. The Adult and Continuing Education of Korea and Korean Educational Development Institute. Seoul, Korea. p. 49-57.

Reischmann, Jost (2004): International and Comparative Adult Education: A German Perspective. In: PAACE Journal of Lifelong Learning. The Pennsylvania Association for Adult and Continuing Education. Vol. 13, p. 19-38.

Reischmann, Jost (2004): Andragogy. History, Meaning, Context, Function. Download at http://www.andragogy.net. Version Sept. 9, 2004.

Reischmann, Jost (2005): Andragogy. In: English, Leona (ed): International Encyclopaedia of Adult Education. London: Palgrave Macmillan. p. 58-63.

Reischmann, Jost (2005): Comparative Adult Education In: English, Leona (ed): International Encyclopaedia of Adult Education. London: Palgrave Macmillan. P. 136-141.

Reischmann, Jost (2005): Bamberg donates time. Andragogs develop a city. In: Henschke, John (ed): Proceedings of the International Taskforce of AAACE. Pittsburgh, PA. p. 1-5.

Reischmann, Jost (ed) (2006): "On Becoming an Adult Educator - historical and contemporary aspects". Papers presented at the 11th Standing International Conference on the History of Adult Education in Bamberg, Germany, Sept. 27 to Oct. 1, 2006. Internet publication, http://andragogy.net/ conference2006.htm.

Reischmann, Jost (2006): Introduction - and Results. In: "On Becoming an Adult Educator - historical and contemporary aspects". Papers presented at the 11th International Conference on the History of Adult Education in Bamberg, Germany, Sept. 27 to Oct. 1, 2006. p. 3-6.

Reischmann, Jost (2007): Becoming a professor in andragogy - lived history. In: Keith B. Armstrong, Lee W. Nabb and Anthony P. Czech (ed.): North American Adult Educators: Archive of Quintessential Autobiographies for the 21st Century. Discovery Association Publishing House. Chicago, Il. p. 241-248.

Sandmann, Lorilee R./Reischmann, Jost/ Kim, Young Sek (2007): Emerging Adult Educators' Experiences in an International Online Forum. In: Convergence XL (1-2) 2007, pp. 25-40.

Reischmann, Jost (2008): Learning to the power of 10 – who is offering more? In: Study on the move, for everyone, anytime, anywhere! Paritätischer Wohlfahrts¬verband Wuppertal, Projekt EASY. p. 22-34.

Reischmann, Jost & Bron, Michal Jr (2008) (Eds.): Comparative Adult Education 2008. Experiences and Examples. A Publication of the International Society for Comparative Adult Education ISCAE. Frankfurt, New York: Peter Lang Publishers.

Reischmann, Jost & Bron, Michal Jr (2008): Introduction. In: Reischmann, Jost & Bron, Michal Jr (Eds.): Comparative Adult Education 2008. Experiences and Examples. A Publication of the International Society for Comparative Adult Education ISCAE. Frankfurt, New York: Peter Lang Publishers. p. 9-18.

Reischmann, Jost (2008): Comparative Adult Education: Arguments, Typology, Difficulties. In: Reischmann, Jost & Bron, Michal Jr (Eds.): Comparative Adult Education 2008. Experiences and Examples. A Publication of the International Society for Comparative Adult Education ISCAE. Frankfurt, New York: Peter Lang Publishers. p. 19-32.

Reischmann, Jost (2008): Andragogy. In: McCulloch, Gary / Crook, David (ed.): International Encyclopedia of Education. New York: Routledge. p. 23-24.

Reischmann, Jost (2010): Adult Educators as HRD Trainer, Moderator and Coach. Experiences of a Chair for Andragogy in Bamberg. In: Medic, Snezana/Ebner, Regina/Popovic, Katarina (ed): Adult Education: The Response to Global Crisis. Strengths and Challenges of the Profession. Belgrade: Department of Pedagogy and Andragogy, University of Belgrade, Serbia. p. 81-90.

Reischmann, Jost (2014): Lifelong and Lifewide Learning - a Perspective. In: Suwithida Charungkaittikul (ed): Lifelong Education and Lifelong Learning in Thailand. Bangkok. p. 286-309.

Reischmann, Jost (2015): Andragogy: Because „Adult Education" is not beneficial to the academic identity! In: International Perspectives in Adult Education - IPE 71. Bonn: DVV-International, p. 87-97.

Knox, Alan/Reischmann, Jost (2015): Remembering Dusan Savicevic. In: Andragoške studije. Časopis za proučavanje obrazovanja i učenja

odraslih. (Univerzitet u Beogradu, Filozofski fakultet).

Reischmann, Jost (2015): Andragogy. International History, Meaning, Context, And Function. In: Malcolm S. Knowles, Edwood F. Holton III, and Richard A Swanson. London and New York: Routledge. p. 312-320.

Reischmann, Jost (2017): Lifewide Learning - Challenges for Andragogy. In: Journal of Adult Learning, Knowledge and Innovation (Budapest) 1(1), pp. 43 - 50. DOI: 10.1556/2059.01.2017.2

Reischmann, Jost (2017): What are Andragogues good for? Workplaces, Competencies, Study Contents, Identity. Andragoške studije, ISSN 0354-5415. Institut za pedagogiju i andragogiju; Belgrade. 1, jun 2017, p. 9-24. doi:10.5937/andstud1701009R.

Popovic, Katarina/Reischmann, Jost (2017): Andragogik, Andragogy, and Administering Graduate Programs. In: Martin, Larry G./Conceicao, Simone C.O./Knox, Alan B. (ed): Mapping the field of adult & continuing education. Vol. Three. Stylus Publishing: Sterling. p. 343-346.

Reischmann, Jost/Henschke, John/Holford, John/Popovic, Katarina/Sork, Tom (2020/2021): Giants of International and Comparative Adult Education. In: Proceedings of the Adult Education in Global Times Conference. University of British Columbia, Vancouver. p. 604-611.

Reischmann, Jost (Ed.) (2021): Essential Readings in International and Comparative Adult Education. Ziel Verlag, Augsburg. ISBN 978-3-96557-093-1.

Reischmann, Jost (2024): International comparative adult education: Seven reflections I expect to read in each study. In: Convergence May 2024

Reischmann, Jost (2024): Andragogy. Contributions to an Emerging Discipline. Norderstedt, Germany: BoD. ISBN 978-3-75833-061-2.

More interest in internationality in adult education?

Experience the many sides of the international arena of adult education, spanning 120 years, 32 contributors, and 319 pages in:

Reischmann, Jost (Ed.) (2021): Essential Readings in International and Comparative Adult Education. Ziel Verlag, Augsburg, Germany.

Experienced researchers, as well as newcomers in international comparative studies, often face challenges when attempting to build upon foundational texts because they are hidden in old publications and difficult to locate. This book makes a selection of such old but 'essential' texts available, thereby providing access to the multitude of ideas and standards developed throughout the long history of the international/comparative perspective. 'Standing on the shoulder of giants' offers the opportunity for a grounded reflection, and supports professional work by making it easier, enhancing their quality, adding enjoyment, and fostering self-confidence.

Book: ISBN 978-3-96557-093-1
e-Book: ISBN 978-3-96557-094-8

International Review of Education (2022): "Jost Reischmann presents an impressive collection that has the potential to become a "must-have" for people who deal with adult education in an international context. ... . This book is highly recommended to readers who are interested in the history of the field of adult education and/or who wish to get an overview of the key contemporary issues in the field and want to do international research. This volume constitutes a truly essential contribution ... The present and the next generations of researchers should build on this valuable book "

More information and order form:
https://ziel-verlag.de/grundlagendweiterbildung/essential-readings.php
Table of contents:
www.reischmannfam.de/TableContents.pdf
Sample pages:
www.reischmannfam.de/samplepages.pdf